Contents

TO MY MOTHER AND FATHER, WITH LOVE.

Introduction

In 1656 Margaret Cavendish published her fifth book, *Nature's Pictures*, which contained her autobiography. She was met by a storm of abuse and ridicule – a reception which had already been anticipated by the authoress:

> Some censuring readers will scornfully say, why hath this lady writ her own life? Since none cares to know whose daughter she was, or whose wife she is? I answer that it is true, that 'tis to no purpose to the Readers . . . but it is to the Authoress, because I write it for my own sake not theirs . . . to tell the truth, lest after ages should mistake.

The question Margaret raised is still being asked. Why did she write? Margaret identified her need to do so variously as a disease, an addiction, a child substitute and a pastime for her idle hours. Her critical intelligence focused on the obscurity of women's lives. When she wrote that 'Women live like bats or owls, labour like beasts, and die like worms' she voiced the feelings of thousands of inarticulate, anonymous women. She was determined to be different. 'I would rather die in the adventure of noble achievements,' she wrote to her husband, 'than live in obscure and sluggish security, since by the one I may live in a glorious fame, and by the one I am buried in oblivion.' It was to avoid the latter that she deliberately exposed herself to public view in print in a way no woman had ever done before. Margaret published eleven books and two collections of plays. She was the first woman in England to write specifically for publication, and certainly the first to consider herself primarily as a writer.

Public reaction to Margaret and to her books was hostile. Pepys described her as mad, conceited and ridiculous; Evelyn as 'very singular'; Dorothy Osborne, daughter of the Governor of Guernsey, wrote from the seclusion of her father's house in Bedfordshire that her friends were at fault 'to let her go abroad'; Margaret was later characterised as a raree show and all the inhabitants of a Bedlam hospital rolled into one. Her personality was a paradox. In private she was warm, intelligent and painfully shy, but she appeared in public extravagantly dressed in dashing costumes of her own design. Sometimes her menservants, ladies in waiting and coach were dressed to match. Her public persona was a theatrical mask she created to hide behind. She was solitary, gifted and misunderstood. Virginia Woolf wrote of her in *A Room of One's Own*:

> What a vision of loneliness and riot the thought of Margaret Cavendish brings to mind! As if some giant cucumber had spread itself over all the roses and carnations in the garden and choked them to death. What could bind, tame, or civilise for human use that wild, generous, untutored intelligence? It poured itself out, higgledy-piggledy, in torrents of rhyme and prose, poetry and philosophy which stands congealed in quartos and folios that nobody ever reads.

My first contact with Margaret was an extract in an American anthology of women's writing. Words and phrases leaped off the page as she described conflicts and emotions with which, as a woman writer struggling to find my own voice, I could instantly identify across three hundred years of intervening history. Finding nothing still in print, and her works locked away among the rare books in libraries and museums, I began the search which ended with this biography.

The anonymity of women's lives at this period, and the number of records lost or destroyed in the Civil War, make a biographer's task difficult. Apart from Margaret's own published work, very little has survived. Her life, conducted 'privately in my closet' with no witnesses but her waiting maids, has to be reconstructed by reference to external events and to her husband's life, whose public character 'in the Field' and with 'many thousand Eye-witnesses' has been recorded by contemporary historians and compilers of court records. Margaret's biography of her husband is maddeningly casual about dates – something for which she apologised in the preface. Her slim autobiographical memoir, written at the age of thirty before her major achievements, is more an exploration of her own psyche than a chronological account of her 'birth and breeding', and lacks detail. She portrays herself as modest, virtuous, fearful, serious and rather proud, and it is difficult to know how reliable a portrait this is.

Her opinions and the minutiae of her daily life as related in my own biography have been taken from the deeply personal prefaces and epistles that she wrote to her other works. These are apologetic, quirky, sometimes contradictory and often moving, as she constantly explored her own motivation and her limitations as a woman, and defended her right to express herself in print.

I have made extensive use of her plays and letters, in which she has obviously drawn on the events and experiences of her own life.

Introduction

Mistress Bashful in *The Presence* is called 'fitter for a nunnery than a court' – the exact phrase that Margaret uses to describe herself in her autobiography. Circumstantial details of her own romance fit her account of Lord Loyalty's courtship of Mistress Bashful, and their dialogue echoes letters and poems exchanged between Margaret and her husband before their marriage. In other plays Lady Sanspareille and Mlle Ambition make speeches containing sentiments and phrases that also occur in Margaret's prefatory epistles. I have also modernised all spellings throughout – Margaret varied even the spelling of her name – because they can present an unnecessary barrier to understanding.

It is difficult to make a modern reader aware of the magnitude of Margaret's achievements. In the three hundred years before her there had been only isolated volumes written by women: the life of Margery Kempe and the devotions of Mother Julian of Norwich in the fifteenth century; and Mary Sidney, Countess of Pembroke's *Psalms* and the Countess of Richmond's *Mirror of Gold for the Sinful Soul* in the sixteenth. In the seventeenth century works by women became more common. Lady Joan Weston published poems in Latin in 1602, Lady Elizabeth Falkland's *Tragedy of Mariam* appeared in 1613, Mary Wrothe's *Urania* in 1621 and Mary Fage's *Fame's Roule* in 1637. An American woman, Ann Bradstreet, published her poems in London in 1651. There were also occasional anonymous pamphlets and tracts under pseudonyms like Jane Anger and Esther Sowernam. Diaries, letters and memoirs were written by Margaret's contemporaries as private documents and often remained unpublished until the eighteenth and nineteenth centuries. Katherine Philips, Aphra Behn and the feminist pamphleteers Bathsua Makin and Mary Astell, more familiar than Margaret to the modern reader, all published their work after her and were influenced by what she had done.

Work published by women before the eighteenth century is very hard to find, not because there were fewer gifted women, but because their lives were obscure, their achievements trivialised, and there was no tradition of women's writing for them to draw on. They were uneducated, trapped in a round of child-bearing and drudgery, or if lucky enough to be born into a wealthy family, treated as marketable property and doomed to a life of social frivolity in support of their husbands' pretensions. But it was here that the first feminist ideas began to take shape.

Though it is impossible to call the seventeenth-century debates on women's position and capabilities in England a feminist movement, a

3

lively exchange of identifiably feminist and anti-feminist arguments certainly took place, but it was cautious and sometimes contradictory. The word 'feminist' has acquired so many modern associations that its use in connection with earlier times can be misleading. Yet there was a basic belief in the equal value of men and women, a questioning of women's obscure and inferior role in society, and attempts to refute traditional and customary conceptions of women's nature and capacities which make it difficult to know what other word could be used. Margaret was the first English woman to look seriously at her sex in this way. A radical thinker, like the French feminist Poulain de la Barre, she could see no logical reason why a woman should not take her place in the world of men. She was excluded only by 'use and custom', as she and many of her fellow women writers referred to the reasons for the status of women. Weaker physically, but not intellectually and certainly not morally (as Margaret's biting satires show), women were kept in their homes, in Margaret's words, 'like birds in cages' only through lack of education, prejudice, tradition and their own apathy.

Margaret's influence on contemporary women is difficult to chart. But if it had not been for her desire to 'tell the truth' about herself, we might not have had the remarkable autobiographies of Lucy Hutchinson, Anne Fanshawe and Alice Thornton. None of them wrote for publication – only for their families, present and future generations. Their autobiographies are frank, moving accounts of the lives of ordinary women caught up in the Civil War. Both Lucy and Anne also wrote lives of their husbands in direct imitation of Margaret, and the combined volumes tell the complete story of their marriages: how Lucy forged a letter to Parliament to save her husband's life; how Anne stood outside her husband's prison window in the pouring rain until the water 'ran in at the neck and out again at her heels'; how child after child was born and died.

Two other figures in the seventeenth century contributed to the increasing number of literate and articulate women. Anna van Schurman was the most learned woman in Europe. Born in Utrecht in 1607, she was encouraged by her father to develop her precocious intellect. By the time she was thirty she knew Latin, Hebrew, Syrian and Chaldee, and had published an Ethiopian Grammar which astounded Dutch scholars. She was on intimate terms with Descartes, and was described by Balzac in the nineteenth century as *'cette merveilleuse fille'*. In 1641 in Leyden she published a book in Latin, eventually translated into English under the title *The Learned Maid*, which argued the case for women's education.

Introduction

One of Anna's most devoted disciples in England was Bathsua Makin, a rector's daughter and sister of the mathematician John Pell. At the age of thirty Bathsua was appointed tutor to the daughter of Charles I, to whom she taught the rudiments of Latin, Greek, Hebrew, French and Italian. She also ran a school in Tottenham, and in 1673 published *An Essay to Revive the Ancient Education of Gentlewomen* in which she set out to answer the objections of the male sex and cited a number of historical precedents to make her case.

Margaret was almost completely uneducated: her mind, she admitted, was clothed only in the few tattered rags of knowledge that she had spun herself. Consequently her work was full of errors. An education along the lines proposed by Anna van Schurman and Bathsua Makin would have saved her from much criticism and allowed her to focus her genius on specific areas rather than dissipate it in a search for a style and a medium in which to express herself.

Like many other women writing in the seventeenth and eighteenth centuries, Margaret achieved notoriety rather than fame. But their achievements created a precedent for women with literary ambitions. Bathsua Makin had to go back to classical and biblical sources to find paradigms to support her arguments; by the end of the eighteenth century women had only to look over their shoulders. It was the beginning of a firm tradition of women's writing.

Chapter One

Women Breeding Up Women
1623 – 42

The Barbarous custom to breed Women low, is grown general amongst us, and hath prevailed so far, that it is verily believed . . . that Women are not endued with such reason as Men; nor capable of improvement by Education, as they are. It is looked on as a monstrous thing to pretend the contrary. A Learned Woman is thought to be a Comet, that bodes mischief whenever it happens.

To offer to the World the liberal Education of Women is to deface the Image of God in Man, it will make Women so high and men so low, like Fire in the House-tops it will set the whole world in a Flame.

Bathsua Makin, *An Essay to Revive the
Ancient Education of Gentlewomen*

Margaret Lucas came into the world without fanfare, as befitted the eighth child and fifth daughter of Thomas Lucas, gentleman, of St John's near Colchester in Essex. The exact year of her birth is not certain. The records were lost or destroyed during the Civil War, but the date most often given is 1623.

Margaret's mother, Elizabeth, the major influence in her early life, was a strong-minded, capable woman, 'of an heroic spirit, suffering patiently where there is no remedy'. Although she was kind and generous to her children, with others she had an oppressive dignity and was 'of such a grave behaviour that it would strike a kind of awe to the beholders and command respect from the rudest', as Margaret described her in her autobiographical essay 'A True Relation . . .' from *Nature's Pictures*. Elizabeth's dignity and patience had been forged by necessity. More than twenty years earlier Thomas Lucas had killed a man in a duel and been banished by Queen Elizabeth to France, leaving the young Elizabeth Leighton unmarried and pregnant. The dead man had been something of a favourite at court, and the intransigent Queen refused to grant Thomas a pardon. Elizabeth Leighton had to bring up her child alone until, on the accession of James I five years later, Thomas was permitted to return and marry her. However he was too late to legitimate their eldest son, so the infant Thomas was barred from inheriting his father's estates.

7

Having paid the penalty for his early impetuosity, Thomas Lucas seems to have settled peacefully into a country life. Another son, John, arrived within a year of the marriage, and then six more children at regular intervals: two daughters, Mary and Elizabeth, a son, Charles (who was to inherit his father's reckless temperament), two more daughters, Anne and Catherine, and finally, after a gap of almost six years, Margaret.

Thomas Lucas died shortly afterwards, before Margaret was out of leading strings, leaving the management of his estates and the upbringing of his eight children to his wife. They were generously provided for – he left portions of £10,000 to each of his daughters. As his eldest legitimate son was still under twenty-one wardship was necessary, and at that time women did not have the right to be legal guardians of their children. It was important that such a valuable estate should not fall into the wrong hands, and Elizabeth Lucas acted swiftly. On the death of their father the property and disposition in marriage of minors reverted to the Crown. Within hours of her husband's death Elizabeth was writing to the King to ask that wardship be granted to Peter Killigrew, the son of an influential family with connections at court, and begging the King's permission for his marriage to her eldest daughter, Mary.

In practice it was Elizabeth Lucas who administered the estate. Even after his majority John Lucas indulged his taste for scholarship and allowed his mother to continue the task, which she carried out with great efficiency. Margaret had nothing but admiration for her mother's capabilities, as she revealed in 'A True Relation'. 'She was very skilful in leases and setting of lands, and though she would often complain that her family was too great for her weak management, and often pressed my brother to take it upon him, yet I did observe she took a pleasure and some little pride in the governing thereof.' Elizabeth Lucas provided Margaret's first example of the capability of women in the handling of affairs normally reserved for men.

It was a tranquil, affluent childhood. Margaret wrote in her autobiography that, though Thomas Lucas was not a peer of the realm, 'yet there were few peers who had much greater estates or lived more noble therewith'. The Lucas family had been at Colchester since the beginning of the sixteenth century, before the Dissolution of the Monasteries. In 1548 they purchased the site of St John's Abbey and built a substantial house beside the great flint and stone ruins. Its inner and outer courts were constructed – like the family church which still stands – from the materials of the

8

fallen abbey, and it occupied a pleasant position on a rise looking across to the ancient walls and spires of Colchester, less than a mile away.

Colchester was a thriving city with a rich history. Seat of Cymbeline, the king of Ancient Britain celebrated by Shakespeare, it had been an important Roman settlement. Though razed to the ground by Boadicea, the city was rebuilt and became a prosperous centre for the clothmaking trade – a curious mixture of Roman ruin, Norman fortification and Tudor enterprise. It was a city filled with Anabaptists and members of other dissenting religious sects, whose ranks had been swollen by an influx of five hundred Flemish weavers in 1573.

The Lucases were a large, lively family – but not particularly sociable or ambitious; they rarely mixed with strangers, keeping themselves very much to themselves. According to Margaret their insularity was extraordinary. 'I did observe,' she wrote in 'A True Relation', 'that my sisters had no familiar conversation or intimate acquaintance with the families to which each other were linked to by marriage.' This inward-looking, anti-social attitude left its mark on the youngest member of the family. Throughout her life Margaret was painfully shy in the company of strangers, as she admitted in her autobiography, and though she struggled to conquer this affliction her attempts resulted only in awkwardness and public humiliation.

> This natural defect in me, if it be a defect, is rather a fear than a bashfulness, but whatsoever it is, I find it troublesome, for it hath many times obstructed the passage of my speech, and perturbed my natural actions, forcing a constrainedness or unusual motions, but, since it is rather a fear of others than a bashful distrust of myself, I despair of a perfect cure.

'Mistress Bashful' appears in various guises in many of Margaret's plays – though she is dumb and stupid in the presence of others, her heroine's prodigious intelligence is always recognised in the end. Later in life Margaret wrote wistfully of eloquence. It was the gift she would most like to have possessed, she wrote in *Sociable Letters*, for 'natural orators . . . are nature's musicians, moving the passions to harmony, making concords out of discords, playing on the soul with delight'.

Although as a child she chose to spend much of her time alone, there were other children of a similar age in the household. Her elder brother Sir John Lucas, his wife and son lived under the same roof. Her eldest, illegitimate, brother Thomas lived not far away at Fordeham Hall, and her married sisters and their offspring were regular visitors during the summer months. Margaret's upbringing within this extended family was typical of that of other girls of the period, and, as she herself observed, different from that given to her brothers.

Margaret described her mother in her autobiography as a wise, gentle parent, preferring reason to the lash. Discipline was firm but not harsh. Each of the children had their own servants to wait upon them, but such was Elizabeth Lucas' pride that no familiarity between child, however small, and servant was permitted. 'Likewise she never suffered the vulgar serving men to be in the nursery among the nursemaids, lest their rude love making might do unseemly actions, or speak unhandsome words in the presence of her children.'

There were several tutors in the household – the Lucas boys were all educated at home – but Margaret's education was scanty. The shaping of her mind, and those of her sisters, was left to an 'ancient decayed gentlewoman', a forerunner of those 'poor relation' governesses of the nineteenth century. Instruction began with the hornbook, a device shaped like a bat, made of horn and inscribed with the letters of the alphabet and the Lord's Prayer. Once learned, these were laboriously worked out in linen as a sampler. From the hornbook the children progressed to Aesop's *Fables*, Robin Hood, *Don Quixote* and, of course, the Bible. Not infrequently the governess dozed off beside the fire, allowing her charges to slip away. 'We were not kept strictly thereto,' wrote Margaret in 'A True Relation', 'for my mother cared not so much for our dancing and fiddling, singing and prating of several languages as that we should be bred virtuously, modestly, civilly, honourably and on honest principles.' The emphasis was on feminine virtues rather than accomplishments.

Margaret preferred to read rather than to ply her needle. Two other seventeenth-century ladies also expressed an aversion to traditional feminine activities. Anne Winchelsea preferred to delineate the 'inimitable rose' in poetry rather than in 'fading silks', and in her life of her husband Lucy Hutchinson declared herself 'averse from all but my book'; as for her needle she 'absolutely hated it'. Like many other women of her generation, Margaret was forced to turn to her elder brother for information and explanation. Later in life she boasted about her lack of education, for it made her achievements more remarkable, but it is clear that she also regretted it. In her play *Wit's Cabal* she has Mlle Ambition say:

I would my parents had kept me up as birds in darkness when they are taught to sing artificial tunes, . . . so would I have had Tutors to have read to me several authors, as the best poets, the best historians, the best philosophers, grammarians, mathematicians and the like. Thus perchance I might have spoken eloquently upon every subject.

Margaret was the victim of a change in attitude to the education of women in the first part of the century. At best it was considered a waste of time, at worst a vice. A learned woman, wrote Bathsua Makin in *An Essay to Revive the Ancient Education of Gentlewomen*, was thought to be 'a Comet that bodes mischief whenever it happens'. It was only one of many shifts in the status of women in seventeenth-century society. There is little doubt that women a hundred years earlier had lived a fuller, more independent life, though there is some dispute as to the extent of it. A brief flowering of the Renaissance in England had bred such scholars as Lady Jane Grey, Queen Elizabeth I, Mary Sidney and the daughters of Sir Thomas More. William Wotton in his *Reflections on Ancient and Modern Learning* of 1694 wrote that 'there are no accounts in History of so many great Women in any one Age, as are to be found between the years fifteen and sixteen hundred'. After the accession of King James it became unfashionable, if not downright dangerous, to teach a girl Latin or Greek – the 'mother tongues' of learning – and anti-feminist pamphlets proliferated.

Very few girls had the opportunity to go to school. There were a few fashionable academies – notably Robert Perwick's at Hackney, whose inmates were much ogled by fashionable gallants. Both Pepys and Evelyn write of expeditions to Hackney church and Ladies' Hall in Deptford to view the 'pretty young ladies'. These schools trained girls in fashionable accomplishments rather than the mathematics, Latin and Greek advocated by the more advanced educators like Bathsua Makin, Mary Astell and Elizabeth Elstob. Charity schools for the poorer classes of women quickly degenerated into training grounds for domestic service, or, later, sweated labour in the textile industry.

The educated women of the century were usually those who had been educated at home by enlightened parents like Elizabeth, Viscountess Falkland, Lucy Hutchinson and Elizabeth Elstob. Others, like Katherine Boyle (sister of the scientist Robert Boyle), were self-educated, or, like Anne Conway, educated despite their parents' objections. The poet Katherine Philips was almost alone among women writers of this period in having attended a ladies' academy; they were not generally held in regard. Margaret, so vigorous a pleader for female education, had a snobbish distrust of 'board schools'. There were other drawbacks, too, in that there were no outlets for the education acquired in them. The inmates of the fashionable academies of Tottenham and Hackney were destined only to adorn the drawing rooms of wealthy men, 'since all heroic actions, public employments, powerful governments and eloquent pleadings are denied our sex in this age', as she wrote in 'A True Relation'.

Economic trends as well as lack of education, and perhaps also an excess of women over men, were responsible for women's slide into subjection, and the Dissolution of the Monasteries in the sixteenth century had removed the religious foundations which had provided girls with the opportunity of scholarship and the exercise of executive talents. The trend towards wage-earning rather than family self-sufficiency, the enclosure of the waste lands on which women could raise food to supplement their husband's incomes, and the gradual takeover by men of the traditionally female tasks of healing and midwifery, brewing and milling, eroded the responsibility of their role in society. The equal partnership of man and wife degenerated into an economic dependency, and as women's sphere of influence contracted, inevitably the value placed on them by society decreased. At the other end of the social scale an increase in wealth made it possible, even obligatory, for the wives of rich men to live in ornamental idleness, completely dependent on their husbands, and, as Margaret wrote in *Divers Orations*, 'unprofitable creatures, did they not bear children'.

The idea of women's inferiority was based on theological and philosophical arguments. Theologians stated that as man was made in the image of God, woman was therefore imperfect. Plato had put forward the theory that woman was an animal – possessed of mortal life but not of reason. The position of women in society had reached its nadir when Cornelius Agrippa described their condition in 1594:

For now a woman (as if she were only the pastime of men's idle hours) is from her cradle kept at home; and as incapable of any nobler employment suffered only to knit, spin, or practise the little curiosities of the needle. And when she arrives at riper years, is delivered to the tyranny of a jealous pated Husband, or cloistered up in a Nunnery; all public offices are denied them; no Jurisdiction they can exercise; nor make any contract that is valid without their husbands' license . . . By which unworthy, partial means, they are forced to give place to men, and like wretched captives overcome in War submit to their insulting Conquerors.

Once women had become stupid through lack of education, it was only a short step to say that they were not worth educating because they were stupid. As women were gradually excluded from sources of knowledge, they brought themselves into disrepute and acquired through ignorance a reputation for incompetence. Ignorance became the norm; wit or learning an aberration. Women were valued only within a domestic context. By the end of the seventeenth century, as Gisborne wrote in *Duties of Women*, 'She who was completely versed in the sciences of pickling and preserving, and in the mysteries of cross-stitch and embroidery, she who was thoroughly mistress of the family receipt book and of her needle, was deemed in point of solid attainments to have reached the measure of female perfection.' In *Philosophical and Physical Opinions* Margaret, as an adult woman familiar with European customs and ideas, lamented this situation. 'We are become so stupid that beasts are but a degree below us . . . men think it impossible we should have either learning, or understanding, wit or judgement, and we out of a custom of dejectedness think so too.'

The situation was clear. If the only sphere of female influence was the home, the only career that of wife and mother, what point was there in educating women for anything else? And if they had no education, they had no way of extending their activities beyond the home. The vicious circle was complete. The educationalists of the eighteenth century argued that education would make women better wives and mothers, avoiding any mention of the wider implications.

In continental Europe things were changing faster than in England. France had a tradition of women's writing, beginning with the twelfth-century Marie de France and the troubadours of the Langue d'Oc like the Countess de Dia. Christine de Pisan had brought out her *Livre de la Cité de Dames* in 1404, and in 1622 Marie de Gournay published *Egalité des Hommes et des Femmes*. Feminist ideas flourished and were vigorously debated. In Holland, where Margaret later spent some years in exile, the wife who could read and write and worked alongside her husband was a commonplace, though an object of ridicule to visiting Englishmen.

Anna van Schurman of Utrecht was famous throughout Europe for her learning. In 1641 she wrote *The Learned Maid* in support of education for women within the private sphere of their lives.

The neglect of Margaret's education was a disaster, for her inclinations were apparent even at an early age. She was a dreamer, whose favourite pastime was to walk in the garden engrossed in her own thoughts, and her heroes were Shakespeare, Ovid and Julius Caesar. Before she was twelve she had filled sixteen of her 'baby books' with what she called 'fancies'. They were, she confessed in *Sociable Letters*, as confused as the chaos. She was later castigated for errors of grammar and spelling and for complete disregard of gender, errors which a classically based education would have eliminated. She also suffered from the fact that she was ignorant of Latin and Greek and therefore excluded from the sources of knowledge. A thorough grounding in logic would have enabled her to develop her arguments in a more reasoned manner.

As she grew older, other traits of character began to emerge. In 'A True Relation' Margaret confessed that 'I never took delight in closets or cabinets of toys but in the vanity of fine clothes and such toys as only were to adorn my person . . . I took a great delight in attiring, fine dressing and fashions – especially such fashions as I did invent myself.' She admitted a 'delight in singularity' which was in later life to become legendary eccentricity.

Though not a beauty, Margaret had a distinctive personal style. Even her detractors had to admit that she was a comely woman. An undated portrait by Sir Peter Lely shows a young woman with fine eyes, brown hair curled into ringlets, and a gentle rounded figure, perhaps inclined to plumpness. Her dress reveals rather more of shoulder and breast than might be expected of one who shunned the attentions of men and claimed to be a stranger to 'amorous love'. The main defect of her character was the lack of a sense of humour: her expression on the canvas is always serious. 'My disposition is more inclined to be melancholy than merry . . . and I am apt to weep rather than laugh,' she admitted in 'A True Relation'. She was not without wit, but inclined to take everything rather too seriously, condemning dancing, for instance, as a pastime unsuited to the dignity of a married lady.

It was becoming fashionable for the wealthy to spend the winter in London and the summer in the country, to escape the plague and smallpox that visited the capital in hot weather. When she was in London Margaret usually stayed with her elder sister Catherine, now married to Sir Edmund Pye. Margaret had been devoted to

Catherine from early childhood, following her like a shadow wherever she went. Her 'supernatural affection' was a great trial to the older girl; she referred to it years later in a rare missive addressed to Catherine from Holland and published in *Sociable Letters*:

> I remember I have sometimes waked you out of your sleep, when you did sleep quietly, fearing you had been dead. Neither could I let you pray in quiet, for I have often knocked at your closet door when I thought you were longer at your prayers than usual, or at least I did think the time longer . . . such a love as when I lived with you it could not choose but be somewhat troublesome.

Elizabeth Lucas remained at St John's during the winter months, and she hoped that under Catherine's auspices her youngest daughter would develop a little more confidence in social intercourse, but her children were almost as unsociable in London as they had been at St John's and rarely went out into society. Their pastimes were simple – visits to Hyde Park to take the air, the hiring of a barge and musicians for a water picnic at Chelsea Reach, Hampton Court or Windsor, a walk in the fashionable Spring Gardens near St James's Palace. Occasionally they visited the theatre, and it is possible that Margaret could have seen one of the plays written by her future husband William Cavendish, then Earl of Newcastle. One of his most popular plays, *The Country Captain*, was staged in London in 1639.

Towards the end of the 1630s growing unrest began to throw a shadow over this comfortable, privileged existence. Even Margaret, politically immature and sheltered by her family from hard reality, could not escape knowledge of the worsening situation. The involvement of her brothers Sir Thomas and Sir Charles, both of whom were soldiers who fought for the King in Holland and Scotland, ensured her close concern; and the family's proximity to Colchester forced them to follow the train of events with mounting apprehension.

The town had become a focal point for the religious Dissenters – called Sectarians – of Essex. In June 1637 a leading Dissenter, John Bastwick, who had practised medicine in Colchester from the time of Margaret's birth, was found guilty of heresy and sentenced by the infamous High Commission, an ecclesiastical court whose duty it was to enforce the Act of Uniformity against all Sectarians, to imprisonment and to have his ears sliced off in the pillory. His trial inflamed the Puritans of Colchester, who were fervently opposed to Archbishop Laud's High Church policies and their imposition. Seditious pamphlets and tracts proliferated. One, written by John Bastwick while in prison, describes Laud's progress through the streets of London, and its sentiment is typical:

> But see the prelate of Canterbury, and see what pomp, grandeur and magnificence he goeth in . . . having also a great number of gentlemen and other servants waiting on him . . . crying, 'Room, room, My Lord's Grace is coming', tumbling down and thrusting aside the little children a-playing there, flinging and tossing the poor coster-mongers and sauce-wives, puddings, baskets and all into the Thames to show the greatness of his state . . . you would think it were the King himself if you saw not the priest.

The Lucas household was unable to isolate itself from these infections. When Elizabeth Lucas forbade her children to 'have any familiarity with the vulgar servants, or conversation knowing that youth is apt to take infection by ill examples', as Margaret described in *Nature's Pictures*, she was acting wisely. The household was not uniformly Royalist in its sentiments, and it was a servant who eventually betrayed them to the Parliamentary Militia.

The regularity of life at St John's was pleasantly disrupted in 1637 by the visit of Marie de Medici, Queen Regent of France. After resisting for years his mother-in-law's attempts to obtain asylum in Britain after her son, Louis XIII, had exiled her under Cardinal Richelieu's influence, Charles I had finally given in. So this turbulent troublemaker, now enormously fat and ravaged by age, landed at Harwich in Essex accompanied by a household of six hundred persons. She travelled to London by easy stages, and the Lucas house was chosen to accommodate her *en route* for Chelmsford. Entertaining so great a personage, even for one or two nights, put a considerable strain on domestic arrangements. At a time when the average agricultural worker earned the equivalent of 2p a day, King Charles reckoned the cost of accommodating Marie de Medici at more than £100 a day, and set aside fifty apartments for her use.

Despite growing hostility towards her Catholic daughter, Henrietta Maria, crowds gathered all along the route to cheer the French Queen, and even in Sectarian Colchester she met an enthusiastic reception. Privately, people found Marie de Medici's manner haughty and complained that she lacked courtesy. This was Margaret's first glimpse of court life, and though she cannot have made much of it – her retiring disposition and her inability to speak French precluded an active part in the festivities – something stimulated her imagination as she watched. It was to develop five years later into a determination to leave the over-protective family circle and join the court of Queen Henrietta Maria at Oxford.

Between 1637 and 1641 the economic and political situation worsened. Charles had been governing without Parliament for eleven years, since its dismissal in 1629, and raising money by means of unpopular taxes. He had given whole-hearted support to Archbishop Laud's suppression of Puritan elements within the Church. The first signs of revolt were in Scotland, where the Presbyterians were opposed to Laud's imposition of High Church practices and curtailment of their freedom to worship as they pleased. Their aims were embodied in the Covenant, and in 1639 they took up arms to defend it. There was also trouble in Ireland, and Charles was increasingly falling under the influence of the ruthless and unpopular Earl of Strafford. The constitutional crisis caused a loss of trading confidence. Colchester, normally prosperous, was badly affected by the ensuing recession: the clothing trade declined and there was widespread destitution. As a result, the restless merchants and clothmakers joined the Sectarians in their demands for reform. When Charles was forced to summon the Long Parliament in 1640 in order to finance his Scottish campaign, hopes of redress were aroused, and people's attitudes hardened when these hopes were dashed. Public unrest increased, and on 28 November John Bastwick was released from jail, greeted by a triumphant mob and hailed as a religious martyr. Throughout the country, men were meeting by lantern light in fields and woods, drawn by drums and bells to listen to seditious sermons from local leaders of the Sectarian movement. Archbishop Laud, whose regal progress through London had aroused such hatred, was finally impeached and the Earl of Strafford executed, but despite these drastic measures public opinion was not appeased.

The Lucas family, although they 'would in their discourse express the general actions of the world, judging condemning, approving commending, as they thought good', as Margaret wrote in *Nature's Pictures*, remained loyal to King and Church. Margaret, staunchly Anglican, later wrote of Archbishop Laud's magnanimity. Violence escalated around them. Not far away, at Chelmsford, a young clothier tore the surplice from the minister's back and a mob beat down and defaced the church windows. A curate had his clothes torn from his back and his prayer book kicked around the church during a baptism service. In London, mobs demonstrating peacefully outside Parliament clashed with groups of professional soldiers

petitioning Parliament for their pay. The terms Cavalier and Round-
head, applied to supporters of King and Parliament, passed into the
English vocabulary for the first time.

London was full of soldiers, restless, dissatisfied and still unpaid
following the Scottish campaign, who bore a grudge against Parliament as a result. They were described as insolent, hard-living and
dissolute. Margaret's brother Sir Charles was one of their number.
He was idealised by his younger sister, who thought he had a
'practick genius to the warlike arts as natural poets have to poetry',
but his true character seems to have left much to be desired.
According to the Earl of Clarendon in his *History of the Rebellion*
'he was very brave in his person . . . but at all other times and places
of a nature not to be lived with, of an ill understanding, of a rough
and proud nature'. Like most of the other young Cavaliers in
London – younger sons with court connections and a restless sword
arm, hardened by brutal campaigning in Holland – he supported
the King, and his courage and military skill earned him a place in
history.

There was still no formal division of society. As Lenin observed
of another civil war, it was 'merely a chain of events, and the coming
together of many disparate aims'. In June 1641 the violence that
had long been seething beneath the surface of Colchester burst out.
A rioting mob attacked Margaret's home, broke down enclosures
and scattered cattle. The motives behind this outburst were not
entirely political. Despite Margaret's high opinion of her mother's
management and her brothers' benevolence, they were unpopular
locally. The reasons were diverse. Most landowners at this time
were enclosing waste land previously cultivated by the peasants and,
in East Anglia, draining the fens. Changes in the law also meant
that copyholds of inheritance, which brought in very little revenue,
could be converted to leaseholds with large entry fines and an
oppressive yearly rent. By unscrupulous operation of this new
law, tenants found themselves rudely thrust out of properties
that their families had enjoyed for generations, and considerable
animosity was felt towards landlords who took advantage of the
system. There were also complaints from tax-payers that John
Lucas, as High Sheriff of Essex, was too zealous in his collection
of the infamous ship money imposed to finance the King's military
activities.

Whatever provoked it, this outbreak of vandalism signalled the
end of the Lucases' comfortable way of life. Outside the well-ordered
parkland the towns and counties were preparing to take sides. Men

of standing began to lay in arms and assemble personal guards to protect themselves against armed bands of Sectarians. They in turn armed themselves against the Papists whom they feared were about to sweep in from Ireland. Thousands of petitioners poured into London from all over England. Parliament was besieged by women whose families had been ruined by the recession, begging for bread. All stage plays and other forms of entertainment in the capital were suspended.

Parliament issued a Militia Ordnance, which ensured that lieutenants sympathetic to Parliament were put in charge of the County Militias, and in June the King issued a medieval Commission of Array – a device empowering his supporters to raise men and arms for him. Colchester, predictably, sided with Parliament; the Lucas brothers responded for the King. A clash became inevitable, and in Margaret's words from 'A True Relation', 'this unnatural war came like a whirlwind, which felled down their houses'.

There had been rioting throughout Essex during the month of August. Shaken by the events of the previous year, the Lucases were not spending the summer at St John's as they usually did. It is not clear whether Margaret was at home or staying with her sister Catherine. Sir John, his wife, Elizabeth Lucas and her daughter Anne were at home when on 20 August 1642 a 'treacherous servant' informed the magistrates of Colchester that Sir John had assembled a body of twelve horses and men and was to leave on Monday to join the King at York. A watch was set on the house, and some time after midnight there was movement at the back gate. A shot was fired to warn the town, drums sounded and a beacon lit. Trained Parliamentary bands were assembled and a large number of people – some accounts put the number as high as five thousand – gathered in the darkness around the house.

The mayor, fearing that there might be loss of life, 'made proclamation in several places where the tumults were, at one o'clock in the night and several times since, charging the people to depart', as reported in the Royalist newssheet *Mercurius Rusticus* on 22 August. His pleas were ignored, and when daylight came the mob forced its way into the house, looting and plundering. They broke into Lady Lucas' bedroom demanding to know where arms were hidden, seizing her, her husband and his mother Elizabeth, and handling them so roughly that, as Margaret wrote in 'A True Relation', 'they would have pulled God out of Heaven'. Sir John and his men were marched off under close guard and the women carried through the streets to the common jail for their own safety. One man in the crowd, paying off an old score, aimed a blow at Elizabeth with a sword which, had it not been deflected, would have killed her.

Rumours spread through the countryside that there were more than a hundred Cavaliers inside the Lucas house. People flocked there from all over the county, and when they found the house empty they vented their rage upon the building. They battered down the doors and walls, smashed the windows and stripped the house of all its fine furniture and possessions in an orgy of hatred that the mayor was powerless to prevent. Then, not content with the ruin of the house and park, the mob broke into the family church of St Giles and smashed open the vaults.

This savage event marked the end of Margaret's childhood. She was to spend the next eighteen years wandering in England and Europe, living in lodgings and constantly in need of money. She never saw her home again.

Chapter Two

The Discreet Virgin
1642 – 4

Lady Sanspareille: *Would you have me go and live at the Court, madam, . . . and to do as Courtiers do?*
Mother: *Yes, Marry would I.*
Lady Sanspareille: *Alas Madam I am unpractised in their arts, and shall be lost in their subtle and strange ways.*
Mother: *Therefore I would have you go to learn them, that you may be as expert as the best of them, for I would have you shoot such sharp darts through your eyes as may wound the hardest and obduratest hearts.*

> Margaret Cavendish, *Youth's Glory
> and Death's Banquet*, from *Plays*

Elizabeth Lucas and her family were released from Colchester jail on 25 August 1642, three days after an account of their ordeal appeared in the newssheets. Sir John Lucas was taken to London and released on bail almost immediately. The bulk of the family's furniture, tapestries and pictures was lost, despite vigorous attempts by Elizabeth to recover them (in many cases she knew who had taken them). Ruined in monetary terms, but not overborne by their misfortunes, the family gradually began to reassemble in Oxford. King Charles I, driven from London, had set up his court there and Oxford was now the nerve centre of his struggle with Parliament.

The city was crowded with Royalist supporters and refugees who, like the Lucas family, had lost everything but what they had prudently concealed or could carry away with them. Competition for lodgings was fierce. Many an English gentleman was rudely thrust from as good a house as any in England, Anne Fanshawe complained in her memoirs, 'to a baker's house in an obscure street, from rooms well furnished to lie in a very bad bed in a garret, to one dish of meat and that not the best ordered'. Money too was in short supply, and any that could be spared went to the King to support his army. Plate salvaged from country houses or generously contributed by churches and Oxford colleges was melted down to mint money for the war. The Lucases appeared to fare better than most financially – Elizabeth Lucas, with her genius for management, contrived to maintain Margaret in a 'condition to lend rather than to borrow', as she recalled in 'A True Relation'.

The city was full of soldiers, and fortifications were rapidly being thrown up around its outer limits. Troops drilled endlessly in the open meadows, and the streets clattered with hooves by night and day as troops of horse came and went on errands of war. Bands of bedraggled prisoners and wagons loaded with the wounded became a familiar sight. 'We had the perpetual discourse of losing and gaining of towns and men', wrote the disenchanted Anne Fanshawe, 'and at the windows the sad spectacle of war.' War was not the only hazard. With so many people packed together in a confined space the spread of disease was difficult to check. Plague, smallpox, typhus and cholera were to be rife.

Rumour and counter-rumour spread as rapidly as the plague. It was often difficult to determine the truth, as both sides waged a war of propaganda. Hot from the presses at Oxford, the Royalist newssheet *Mercurius Aulicus* bragged 'let the rebels please themselves with their forgeries', and proceeded to answer Parliamentary allegations boldly. In answer to a well substantiated charge that the King's soldiers had hardly any powder for their muskets, the reply was that 'their muskets do the work upon you without powder'. To an allegation that the King's foot soldiers were badly armed and using instead of swords 'certain weapons made like hatchets', the provocative response was that 'they use such only to meet with your woodmongers' brigade'.

Sir Charles Lucas was soon made a lieutenant general of horse in the King's northern army and his name appeared frequently in the newssheets. All three brothers were now in arms. On his release from custody Sir John had broken the terms of his bail and joined his brother Thomas, already commanding a troop with the King's forces. Only the women were left at Oxford, anxiously awaiting the outcome, Margaret recalled in 'A True Relation', 'shiftless in misery'.

On 14 July 1643 Queen Henrietta Maria, who had been to France to raise money for her husband's cause, was reported in the newssheet *Mercurius Aulicus* as having 'made a most triumphant and magnificent entry' into the city. People crowded on to the streets to see her, and the soldiers, with their muskets charged, had to line the streets to hold them back to let her carriage pass. Every wall, window and other vantage point was thronged with spectators. Henrietta had narrowly escaped death by drowning when her ship was caught up in a storm and driven northwards. William

Cavendish, Earl of Newcastle, was detailed to escort her from her landing point to York. But almost immediately they were attacked by rebels and the Queen had to hide in a ditch with her little dog. After 'borrowing' £3000 from Newcastle and appropriating 1500 of his best soldiers as an escort she was able to proceed southwards. Tales of her indomitable courage under fire had preceded her to Oxford, and she posed a romantic figure to the crowds thronging the streets. Her stature was diminutive, and her delicacy was enhanced by loss of weight through worry for her pliable husband and the safety of her children. The small, pathetic figure seated beside the King in the magnificent procession aroused the sympathy of those who watched and tugged in particular at the loyalties of Margaret Lucas.

Oxford aroused all sorts of latent dissatisfactions in Margaret. She read the accounts of her brothers' courageous exploits in the newssheets and watched the soldiers daily come and go. Very conscious of the restrictions placed upon her because of her sex, her mind was filled with romantic fancies and tales of historical heroines such as Joan of Arc and she 'burned to do some heroic act'. Margaret was ambitious, and confessed in 'A True Relation', 'I fear my ambition inclines to vainglory, . . . yet 'tis neither for beauty, wit, titles, wealth or power, but as they are steps to raise me to Fame's Tower which is to live by Remembrance in after ages.' Frustrated by her womanhood, shy and insignificant, there was little she could do to further her ambitions, until, hearing that the Queen had fewer ladies in waiting than she was used to, Margaret was seized with a great desire to be one of her maids of honour. 'Whereupon I wooed and won my mother to let me go.'

Her decision provoked a family disagreement. Elizabeth Lucas was shrewd enough to realise the advantages that might accrue to a daughter placed at court. It was an opportunity for Margaret to acquire a little more sophistication and polish, and probably a husband. Despite the fact that Margaret was now twenty, the rest of the family vociferously opposed the idea, she wrote in 'A True Relation', 'by reason I had never been from home, nor seldom out of their sight, for though they knew I would not behave myself to their, or my own, dishonour, yet they thought I might to my disadvantage – being inexperienced in the ways of the world'. Their arguments were well founded, but Margaret was determined to have her own way. Being of a stubborn disposition, some time in the autumn of 1643, with her mother's approval, she was finally taken to the Queen's lodgings at Merton College and put in the charge of the 'mother of the maids' – a lady appointed to chaperone the Queen's ladies in waiting. Margaret was then escorted up the narrow panelled staircase with its massive carved oak bannister rail and into the Queen's receiving room to take her oath.

In her play *The Presence*, printed in 1668, Margaret described in detail the introduction of Mistress Bashful (who bears many of the characteristics of Margaret herself) to court. Discouraged by her shyness and her solemn manner, the other maids were reluctant to share a room with the new arrival. In addition she stipulated that she could not share a room with anyone who sat up late or kept much company. The Queen's entourage included Anne Fanshawe, who loved practical jokes and, as she herself admitted, was 'what graver people call a hoyting girl' (a hoyden), and 'The Incomparable' Isabella Thynne, feted by the Cavalier poet Edmund Waller and given to scantily clad progresses through the College gardens preceded by a lute player. Margaret satirised them as Wagtail, Wanton and Quick-wit, and her own stiff reserve cannot have gone down well with this lively group of spirits – but, like Mistress Bashful, she hoped to prove her own worth in time.

There could be no greater contrast than that between the quiet solitude of St John's and the fast-moving, cosmopolitan court at Oxford. Negro servants, playwrights, dogs, poets and dwarves jostled elbows in the corridors and quadrangles with captains and generals, earls, marquises and men at arms. Large numbers of professional soldiers, hard-swearing, drinking and womanising when they were not fighting, lowered the tone of a normally decorous court. The atmosphere of reckless amorality was heightened by the uncertainties of war. There was every reason for an inexperienced maid to keep her eyes to the ground and the key turned in her bedroom door. Days were spent running errands for the Queen, standing for hours in crowded rooms holding gloves, fans and shawls, helping her to dress and undress, and accompanying her on her walks in the College grounds. When not required by the Queen, her ladies played cards, flirted with the men and frittered away the time in idle gossip.

Margaret quickly saw through the gilded outer trappings of court life. 'Courtiers have little time to pray,' she wrote cynically in *The Presence*, 'for what with dressing, trimming, waiting, ushering, watching, courting and the like, all our time is spent . . . as for the soul it is not well known what it is.' Her sharp eyes missed nothing. The beautiful manners, the courtly mode of platonic love, the professions of gallantry hid wanton excesses and ugly intrigue.

'Courtiers will run in debt, court mistresses, flatter, cozen, dissemble, profess, protest and then betray,' she wrote. Treachery was common in a struggle whose outcome was by no means certain. Ambition and self-preservation were the primary motives of many and some, like the Earl of Holland, dispassionately weighed the odds and transferred their allegiance to the Parliamentary side. Animosity was obvious between the King's nephew Prince Rupert and the King's other advisers, and there were a number of Parliamentary agents among the King's own men, including – so Parliament claimed – a colonel of his Council of War. Oxford was rife with spies. William Lilly observed in his memoirs that they 'would put their papers in at the hole of a glass window, while they made water in the street'; by the following morning, that paper would be in the hands of a Parliamentary commander. The Earl of Newcastle was approached, but was not nicknamed the 'Lord of Loyalty' for nothing.

Henrietta's retinue was a curious, unsympathetic mixture. It included such diverse characters as Father Cyprien de Gamache, her French confessor, the poet William Davenant (Newcastle's protégé and reputed to be Shakespeare's natural son) and a blond dwarf called Jeffry Hudson who had been presented to the Queen in a pie. Most important of all was Henry Jermyn, whose broad shoulders and sleepy eyes concealed a ruthless strength and cunning brain. Originally master of the horse, by 1643 he had considerable influence over the Queen as one of her closest advisers on political and military matters.

Margaret fared badly among this motley crowd, she confessed in 'A True Relation'. She was a very junior member of the court, in terms of both social status and experience, and was too shy, too serious,

> fitter for a nunnery than a court. I was so bashful when I was out of my mother's, brother's and sister's sight, whose presence used to give me confidence, that when I was gone from them I was like one that had no foundation to stand or guide to direct me. Besides, I had heard that the world was apt to lay aspersions even on the innocent, for which I durst neither look up with my eyes nor speak, nor be any way sociable, insomuch as I was thought a natural fool.

Odd glimpses of the mental anguish induced by her deficiencies are given in her plays. In a Scene from Love's Adventures Lady Bashful is surprised by unexpected visitors and struck mute as a statue. She is forced to endure much ribaldry, and one of the visitors remarks that 'she must marry, she must marry, for there is no cure like a husband, for husbands beget confidence and their wives are brought abed with impudence'. When they have gone the humiliated Lady Bashful exclaims, 'Oh what torment I have been in; hell is not like it.'

The Queen was not an easy person to serve. Although capable of immense charm she was also capricious, stubborn and neurotic, worn down by constant child-bearing and the political stress and strain of the previous two years. Margaret's fantasy of tribulation nobly borne had little relation to the nervous headaches and swiftly altering moods that proved to be the reality. So desperately unhappy did she become that she begged her mother to take her away. Elizabeth Lucas refused, and pointed out that it would be a disgrace for her to come home so soon after being placed at court. So Margaret remained there, homesick, lonely, thrust in upon her own resources but defiant. She longed above all for some future luminous event which might give her the opportunity for self-expression she so ardently desired. 'I had rather be a meteor, singly, alone,' she wrote passionately in her play *The Presence*, 'than a star in a crowd', choosing to identify with the comet, a common symbol, but used by both Bathsua Makin and Margaret to represent the isolation of the learned woman.

The dullness of court routine did nothing to alleviate Margaret's unhappiness. Privacy was at a premium. The Queen occupied the Warden's Lodgings at Merton – one rectangular receiving room with a large window looking out on to what is now the Fellows' Quadrangle, and another smaller room leading off it, which was used as the Queen's bedchamber. These apartments are not large, and, crowded with furniture, courtiers, secretaries, maids in waiting, supplicants and animals, could not have been particularly comfortable.

Members of the Queen's household attended services at Trinity and at St Mary's, scene of the Protestant Archbishop Cranmer's trial and execution in 1556 by the Catholic Queen Mary. The Queen's ladies giggled indiscreetly during the services and made eyes at the soldiers across the church. Margaret was not mature enough to hide her disapproval and lacked the humour to temper it with a smile. 'Being dull, fearful and bashful,' she recalled in 'A True Relation', 'I neither heeded what was said or practised, but just what belonged to my loyal duty and my own honest reputation.' Her companions despised her for a prude. Anne Fanshawe and

Isabella Thynne enlivened their dull days by teasing the President of the College, an old misogynist called Dr Ralph Kettel. Driven to the limits of his endurance by their pranks, he rounded on Anne and is reported by John Aubrey in *Brief Lives* to have said: 'Madam, your husband and father I bred up here, and I knew your grandfather; I know you to be a gentlewoman. I will not say you are a whore, but get you gone for a very woman.' A 'very woman' was, as implied by its coupling with 'whore', the exact opposite of a lady.

One of the diversions of the court was the practice of a kind of platonism. In 1634 James Howell commented on the new craze in *Familiar Letters*, describing it as 'a Love abstracted from Corporeal gross Impressions and sensual Appetite', and consisting in 'Contemplation and Ideas of the Mind, not in any carnal Fruition'. Margaret made scathing attacks on the cult in her plays. All the ladies in the court, she wrote in *The Presence*, 'are becoming Dreaming Lovers to imitate the Princess', who is 'in love with an Idea she met with in a Dream'.

Henrietta Maria, a great lover of theatricals, organised masques and other open-air entertainments in the College gardens. Oxford was reputed to be more festive than London, where all such entertainments were banned. The King, lodging nearby at Christchurch, was a frequent visitor to his wife, using a private way through Corpus Christi to reach her apartments. They were often to be seen together walking in the garden, deep in conversation, followed at a discreet distance by their respective attendants.

Behind all this frivolity the war dragged on. One name which cropped up frequently in the despatches was that of William Cavendish, Earl of Newcastle. He was one of the richest men in England, a great favourite with the Queen and, as governor of the young Prince Charles, responsible for overseeing the Prince's upbringing and education. By the force of his own personality he had raised a huge force in the north, which he was deploying with varying degrees of success. An expert on horsemanship, a playwright, a lover of pretty women and good living, he was not a natural soldier, but his loyalty to the King was total and he threw himself into the fray with determination. Newcastle used his personal charisma to gain support for the King, but his professional skill (or the lack of it) attracted a lot of criticism. It was ironic that while he fought with inadequate resources to keep the Scots at bay in a bitter northern winter, he was pilloried behind his back by enemies languishing in comfort at Oxford. They were quick to censure his mistakes and jealous of his successes. Lady Cornwallis accused Newcastle of lying abed, writing courting letters to the Queen and allowing General King to do all the work. Even Henrietta Maria in a moment of exasperation complained that Newcastle was 'fantastic and inconstant'. But he knew how to make himself agreeable, and she was forced to reassure him that the court did not 'design to do or to believe anything' to his prejudice. 'And if you accuse me of scolding you,' she wrote to him in a letter, 'remember what I told you when I was at York that I only scold my friends, and not those whom I do not care about.'

Margaret's brother, Sir Charles Lucas, was with Newcastle, commanding a troop of horse with considerable panache. Though a few people, like the Earl of Holland, were privately beginning to sense the inevitability of defeat, Royalist fortunes were still high. The summer of 1643 at Oxford stood out brightly in people's memories, contrasting sharply with the disastrous events of the following year. There was a kind of reckless gaiety at the court.

As the days shortened and the paths became slippery with fallen leaves, the optimism of the summer months grew more difficult to sustain. The arrival of the Scottish army in the north of England created a dangerous imbalance. The Earl of Newcastle wrote desperately for reinforcements, declaring that the enemy 'will soon ruin us, being at York, unless there is some speedy course taken to give us relief'. The help he so urgently required was not forthcoming; as Henrietta Maria explained in a bleak letter, hopes of support from her relatives in France had been dashed. As if to add to the gloom which had settled over Oxford, there were outbreaks of plague and typhus; and the Queen's favourite dwarf, Jeffry Hudson, murdered a man who had insulted him and had to flee to the continent. The Queen herself was assailed by the all too familiar symptoms of pregnancy. Weighed down by affairs of state and concern for her indecisive spouse, her health, both mental and physical, deteriorated throughout the winter. Oxford was no longer safe. Parliamentary forces were already massing in Buckinghamshire, with the ultimate aim of taking the city. One by one Royalist strongholds around Oxford began to fall, and alternative places of refuge were urgently discussed as the Queen's pregnancy advanced.

One brief event illuminated the gloom when Prince Rupert captured Newark in March 1644, and for a short space of time bells pealed and bonfires were lit to celebrate. Spirits were also raised by another saga of courage and loyalty which was followed in beleaguered Oxford throughout the spring, acquiring all the characteristics of a soap opera. The Royalist press recorded on 17 April that the Countess of

Derby continued to hold Latham House against the Parliamentary forces, although she had been besieged for more than twelve weeks. Her dashing exploits and refusal to surrender gave renewed courage to those who feared shortly to be in a similar plight. Such was her resistance, and the number of soldiers occupied by the siege, that a current joke had it that the kingdom had been ruined by three women – Eve, the Queen and the Countess of Derby.

The Countess and Lady Brilliana Harley, who died defending her home against Parliamentary forces, were among the many spirited women of the Civil War whose example constantly negated the notion of woman as a weak, fearful creature. Such women provided paradigms for Margaret's stories and plays. Gisborne, author of eighteenth-century conduct books, when discussing in *Duties of Women* the different estates of man and woman ordained by the Almighty was driven to write that though men had a large native stock of resolution,

> In towns which have long sustained the horrors of a siege, the descending bomb has been found in numberless instances, scarcely to excite more alarm in the female part of the families of private citizens than among their brothers and husbands, [and] in bearing the vicissitudes of fortune, in exchanging wealth for penury, splendour for disgrace, women seem as far as experience has decided the question to have shown themselves little inferior to men.

Henrietta Maria's health continued to deteriorate, and she was tormented by pain and anxiety. Early in April she slipped and fell, and for two or three days a miscarriage was feared. Finally it was decided that she should travel to the west country, which was still in the King's hands, take the waters in Bath and then proceed to Exeter for her confinement. Margaret had never travelled further than London before, or been away from her family. Even at Oxford the rigours of court life had been offset by regular visits to her sisters lodged nearby. It required considerable courage to remain with the Queen and part from her mother and her beloved sister Catherine Pye in such uncertain circumstances.

On 17 April 1644 a sad cavalcade of coaches, baggage waggons and horses left Oxford for the west, the Queen accompanied as far as Abingdon by her husband and two of her sons. Among the maids of honour at the rear of that doleful procession Margaret Lucas waved goodbye to some members of her family for the last time. For the rest, it was to be eight years before they were reunited.

The journey to Bath was long and difficult, on bad roads, with the constant fear of capture. At times the Queen was so ill that she could hardly bear to be moved, yet rather than risk falling into Parliamentary hands she pressed on. The newssheets reported that she was travelling at night to evade detection. In Exeter the household was joined by the Queen's French midwife and her physician Sir Theodore Mayerne, who had reluctantly (in view of his own great age and infirmity) undertaken the journey after a desperate plea from the King. The Queen now believed herself to be dying, but her physicians agreed that her symptoms were in part hysterical. On 16 June, to everyone's relief, the Queen was safely delivered of a daughter, though her symptoms were not alleviated by the birth, as everyone had hoped. She continued to complain of constriction of the heart, loss of sight in one eye and paralysis of one arm.

While the Queen was being brought to bed in Exeter, a new danger threatened the royal party. The Earl of Essex was gathering his forces outside the city. There was no longer anywhere in England where the Queen's safety could be assured, so it was reluctantly decided that she must abandon her newborn child and leave for France. Placing the infant in the care of a senior lady in waiting, Lady Dalkeith, Henrietta Maria journeyed secretly to Falmouth in a litter. Margaret and the other ladies followed, taking great pains to avoid the Parliamentary bands roaming the countryside. Anne Fanshawe managed to escape on one occasion by forging herself a pass, and Lady Dalkeith eventually eluded the Parliamentary forces by disguising herself and the little princess as peasants.

News began to arrive concerning a massive defeat at Marston Moor, where Newcastle and Prince Rupert had been routed by Cromwell and Fairfax, with heavy casualties. It was a bitter blow for the Queen's hopes, but a more personal misfortune for Margaret. Sir Charles Lucas was reported to be a prisoner of the Parliamentary commander. Twelve days later, before the accuracy of the conflicting reports could be assessed, Queen Henrietta Maria, accompanied by Margaret and her other ladies, boarded a Dutch ship in Falmouth harbour and set sail for France. The dismal exodus was watched by a small group of sympathisers from the shore and carefully set down for publication in the newssheets. *Mercurius Pragmaticus* of 19 October reported:

The first ship that put to sea was a Flemish man of war, after whom warped out by degrees, nine more, who had most of them the advantage of oars to increase their speed. In the midst of them there was discovered a galley with sixteen oars in which peradventure her Majesty was embarked.

At the time it was regarded as a temporary expedient by those on board, but it would be many years before the Restoration of Charles II made it possible for them to make their homes in England again.

Chapter Three

Lady Travelia
1644 – 5

A ship of Youth into th' World's Sea was sent
Balanced with self-conceit and Pride it went . . .
But when 19 degrees it had but past
Its sight the Land of Happiness had lost . . .
Fears like unto the Northern Winds blew high,
And Stars of Hope were clouded in the Sky,
Down went the Sun of all Prosperity,
And reel'd in th' troubled Seas of Misery.
On Sorrow's Billows high this Ship was tost
The Card of Mirth and Mask of Joy was lost.

Margaret Cavendish, *Poems and*
Fancies

The battle of Marston Moor on 2 July 1644 was the subject of discussion and recrimination long after the death of the protagonists. It was the need to explain and justify Newcastle's actions on that day which persuaded Margaret to write her husband's biography twenty years later and, in doing so, pen her finest literary achievement. Newcastle was not a natural soldier. Clarendon wrote in his *History of the Rebellion* that 'he liked the pomp and absolute authority of a general well – but the substantial part and fatigue of general he did not in any degree understand . . . but referred all matters of that nature to the discretion of his lieutenant, General King'. He led his troops in battle with great courage, but when the action was over 'he retired to his delightful company, music or his softer pleasures, insomuch as he sometimes denied admission to the chiefest officers of the army . . . from whence many inconveniences fell out'.

His character was complex. Philip Warwick, one of the King's secretaries, observed in his memoirs that he 'had a tincture of a romantic spirit and had the misfortune to have somewhat of the poet in him'. This is borne out by an anecdote related by Margaret in his biography. In his youth, having money to spend, he bought a singing boy, a horse and a dog, in contrast to a young relative who prudently invested his money in land. He was a considerable patron of the arts, supporting Ben Jonson and William Davenant, but was never a scholar like his brother Charles.

In 1618 he had married Elizabeth Basset, an heiress, on the death of her first husband. She was nineteen, dark and rather fragile-looking, with the alabaster looks that sometimes betoken a frail constitution. She was often ill, almost permanently breeding, and died suddenly in April 1643 while Newcastle was campaigning in the north. Their letters to each other show a deep and loving relationship.

Whatever Newcastle's shortcomings as a soldier, his loyalty to the King was unquestionable, and he raised a local force of several thousands to put at the King's disposal. His own sons fought under him and he was joined by some of the most distinguished commanders of the Civil War, including George Goring and Charles Lucas. The Scottish campaign proved Newcastle's downfall. Harried by the Scots, outnumbered and outmanoeuvred, he fell back and was besieged at York. Urgent letters to the King and Queen brought no relief. They were being hard pressed on other fronts and Newcastle was forced to wait until Prince Rupert arrived to lift the siege. Exactly what followed is still the subject of conjecture.

Rupert, with characteristic impetuosity, wished to engage the enemy immediately, before they had time to regroup, despite their numerical superiority of almost two to one. When Newcastle and General King opposed him, to support his strategy Rupert used a letter from King Charles whose wording was so ambiguous that several interpretations were possible. Newcastle could see the unwisdom of Rupert's plan. He was familiar with the area and knew the characters of his men. The siege of York was newly raised and the soldiers were tired, hungry and wanting their beer and women. He was also severely ruffled by the Prince's curt manner. Rupert felt that he had more important things to achieve than to bandy pleasantries with an elderly Cavalier. Significantly James King, Baron Eythin, a dour Scot but an experienced general, was also convinced of the folly of Rupert's plan. But neither man could make the impatient Prince change his mind. Indeed, the plan was just daring enough that, had it been put into action immediately and with enthusiasm, it might have succeeded.

Newcastle eventually bowed to Rupert's superior authority with bad grace. He gathered together what he could of his weary troopers – though not without some talk of mutiny – and set off after the Prince, leaving General King to round up the stragglers and bring them on with all haste. This he failed to do. It was General King's delay in entering the field, as much as Cromwell's skill, that turned the day against the Royalists. Newcastle's contempt for him was obvious. They departed into exile in separate boats, and he is scarcely mentioned in Margaret's biography, Newcastle having forbidden her to mention anything to the prejudice of any persons, however true it might be.

So, on 2 July 1644, a warm, damp summer evening, forty-six thousand men faced each other at Long Marston on the edge of the moors. Cromwell and Fairfax had the advantage of the higher ground, and in the clear light of the summer's evening the Parliamentary commanders watched Rupert disposing his troops. They observed the disorderly arrival of Newcastle's weary men; the signs of a battle had postponed the smoke of supper fires, and the men were lying on the ground at ease. They decided to engage immediately.

Newcastle, learning that Prince Rupert did not intend to fight that night, had retired to his coach to rest and eat. He had hardly lit his pipe when the first shots rang out, signalling the beginning of the bombardment. Caught unawares with General King's men only beginning to arrive, and hopelessly outnumbered, the Royalist troops had little chance of victory. There were some heroic moments, but by the time darkness fell more than four thousand men lay dead on the field and five or six thousand had been wounded. Newcastle's 'Lambs' – his own men, recruited, trained and clothed by him in the undyed cloth which gave them their nickname – were slaughtered almost to a man and their officers taken prisoner.

They did not give up easily, and even after the day was lost, William Lilly wrote in his memoirs, would take no quarter. 'By mere valour, for one whole hour, kept the troop of horse from entering amongst them at near push of pike.' Even those who lay on the ground gored the troopers' horses with swords or broken pieces of pike as they rode over them. They fought it out 'till there was not 30 of them living'. One of Cromwell's officers said that 'he never in all the fights he was in, met with such resolute brave fellows'.

Newcastle was the last to leave the field, following the Prince and General King to York where bitter exchanges took place between the three men. By 4 July, despite Rupert's entreaties, Newcastle had made up his mind to leave England, at least for the time being. His pride had taken a humiliating blow, and he would not endure 'the laughter of the court'. He no longer had an army to command,

and at fifty-three had neither the heart nor the will to raise another. As Clarendon put it,

> he was so utterly tired with a condition and employment so contrary to his humour that he did not consider the means or the way that would let him out of it . . . but in a transport of passion and despair at Prince Rupert's losing on a single irresponsible cast the army he had so carefully built up . . . without further consideration he transported himself out of the kingdom.

Margaret stated in her biography that Newcastle had seen quite clearly that the cause was now lost. Others blamed him for losing the cause. John Constable wrote from Holland, 'I must tell you if the Marquis of Newcastle had stayed in England, neither I nor any else had thought of coming over, but his going lost an army, and all those who depended on him.'

Newcastle went first to Scarborough, where he stayed at the castle as a guest of Sir Hugh Cholmley and his wife. The Cholmleys themselves were shortly to flee, although Lady Cholmley stayed behind for a time in order to secure their home and distinguished herself in the defence of the town. They made Newcastle and his dismal party welcome until they set sail for Hamburg on 7 July. Newcastle was accompanied by his two sons, their tutor, Dr Benoist, his brother, Sir Charles Cavendish, his steward, Mr Loving, his master of the horse and general staff. According to his steward, they had only £90 between them.

While Newcastle settled himself in Hamburg, Margaret was aboard the Queen's ship. Such a public departure from England was unlikely to go unchallenged, and the Parliamentary fleet was waiting off the coast of Devon to waylay the small convoy. In its midst were the three crack ships of the fleet, the *Vice Admiral*, the *Warwick* and the *Paramour*, commanded by the intrepid Captain Batty who had earlier harassed the Queen off the coast of Yorkshire. They gave immediate pursuit, and at times came so close that their cannon shot made contact with the rigging. Below decks the Queen's ladies screamed and wept that all was lost. Henrietta Maria compounded the panic by giving orders that the ship's magazine was to be fired if they were captured. She declared that she would rather die than fall into Parliamentary hands – a sentiment not shared by her ladies, who like Margaret did not wish their lives to be 'unprofitably lost'. Soon they were all so weak with seasickness that the Queen was attended only by her Catholic chaplain.

The journey gave Margaret a horror of sea travel which lasted all her life. Of the whole experience, she declared that she had lived in such fear that she wished only to forget. In her autobiography she portrayed herself as a 'Natural Coward', as fearful as a hare where her own life was in danger. The circumstances of her life tend to qualify this assessment of herself; the risks that she outfaced during their headlong flight from Oxford to Exeter and thence to France, the fact that she undertook three more sea voyages, and her subsequent courage in the face of adverse public criticism all argue considerable resolution.

As the ships neared Jersey in a freshening breeze, the sails of friendly vessels sent out from Dieppe to meet them appeared on the horizon and the Parliamentary fleet prudently retired. The wind continued to freshen, and before the convoy could rendezvous with the approaching ships they were scattered by one of the capricious Channel storms and blown westwards along the coast of France. The Queen's battered vessel, its insignia gone, was mistaken for a pirate ship by the fishermen of Brittany until the Queen herself appeared on deck and declared her identity.

Exhausted by terror and physical discomfort, the Queen and her ladies were allowed ashore at Brest and escorted up the cliff path to the village to be accommodated by the local gentry. It was Margaret's first experience of a foreign country. French, the Queen's first language, became the primary means of communication, and Margaret's lack of education meant that she was more isolated than ever within the court. She claimed to have a 'natural stupidity' for the learning of any other language but her own, being better able to 'understand the sense, than remember the words'. However, the French phrases which occur in her work occasionally are evidence that she eventually acquired some knowledge of the language.

The Channel storms were replaced by hot, sultry days spent travelling south and east as fast as the Queen's health would permit. Relief at their escape gave way to numbness. No one knew what the immediate future held, little news filtered through from England, and it was impossible to assess the state of the kingdom accurately. Rumour and speculation kept the party in a constant state of anxiety as to the fate of relatives and friends.

On either side of the straggling cortège the hedgeless landscape of France stretched beneath a burning August sky. The sculpted half-cut corn stood unbounded to the horizon. There were many unfamiliar sights for English eyes to peer at through the carriage curtains. Seventeenth-century travellers were fascinated by monks, an unknown sight in England now, and the wayside shrines containing holy pictures and candles. Bullock carts were frequently overtaken as they ground their way along the avenues of walnut trees, and in the fields near the road wheels of torture replaced the traditional English gibbet.

For the sake of the Queen's health the party did not go directly to Paris but made a considerable detour. At Bourbon l'Archamboult, a small spa in the heart of Bourbon country where the land begins to rise towards the mountains of the Auvergne, they rested so that the Queen could take the waters. It was a peaceful town with a twelfth-century church and a romantic castle with red-roofed turrets – an illustration from a children's fairytale set against a cool lake encircled by green trees. Bourbon l'Archamboult was a place of much needed spiritual healing.

The Queen Regent of France, Anne of Austria, acting for her seven-year-old son, Louis XIV, sent one of her favourite ladies, Madame de Motteville, to wait on Henrietta Maria. This tactful confidante of Queens became the recipient of all Henrietta Maria's trials and tribulations, real and supposed, and wrote everything carefully down for posterity. Henrietta Maria was a great trial to her ladies at this time. She was constantly in tears, yearning for the baby she had left behind in England and sick with anxiety for her husband. She could neither think nor talk of anything but her own recent griefs and misfortunes.

The Queen's health gradually improved at Bourbon l'Archamboult, and the little party began to move cautiously north towards Paris, through Orleans and Nevers. The roadsides were crowded with peasants striving to see the daughter of France who had returned in such poverty and affliction, and their loyalty and interest did much to revive Henrietta Maria's spirits. The party was joined by her brother the Duc d'Orléans and his daughter, Anne Marie de Montpensier, known as the Grande Mademoiselle. On the outskirts of the city, the Queen Regent herself awaited her sister-in-law and the two women made a triumphant entry into the city in the same carriage. Margaret, with the Queen's other ladies, was at the rear of the procession.

Paris was changing rapidly. Two new palaces, the Luxembourg and the Palais Royal, had been built recently and their gardens were now open to the public. Behind the great bulk of the Louvre to the north and east the city walls had been demolished and rebuilt further back to allow for subsequent expansion. The gates of Paris had been widened to cope with the increasing traffic. It was a crowded, bustling city. The English exiles marvelled at the confluence of people, the multitude of coaches on the streets and the innumerable accidents.

Paris was far more impressive to the eye than London. Apart from the palaces with their formal gardens, it was noted for its bridges. The Pont Neuf had twelve arches, a wide passage for coaches and a raised pedestrian way. In the centre stood a statue of Henri IV on horseback which commanded a spectacular view of the Louvre, the Ile de Palais, St Germain and Notre Dame. At the foot of the bridge was a mechanical 'water house' decorated in front with the story of Christ and the woman of Samaria pouring water out of a bucket; a dial with moving wheels and a chiming device were all worked by water pumped from the Seine. By contrast the back-street slums overflowed with people drawn from the country by the lure of the city. The overcrowding created conditions which nourished disease and a soaring crime rate; the streets were deep in mud and sewage. John Evelyn complained that Paris stank. Margaret was similarly unimpressed and initially disliked the city.

Queen Henrietta Maria and her entourage were installed in apartments in the Louvre; not the improved building we see today, but even then vast and inhospitable. It was considerably larger than anything Margaret had seen in England: its icy magnificence dwarfed the tiny, shrunken figure of the English Queen and quenched the spirits of those who attended her. The French Queen Regent found the Louvre not to her taste and was more than willing to see it occupied by the exiles, who were far from comfortable there. In parts of the palace there were piles of filth and excrement on the steps, in the corridors and behind the doors. The stench was terrible, for courtiers and servants were in the habit of relieving themselves indiscriminately around the building in a manner which shocked the more fastidious English. These insanitary conditions constituted a grave health hazard: Margaret nearly died of the 'purging Flux', and was only saved by large doses of laudanum administered by the court doctor.

The palace must have been extremely noisome to make an impression in an age not noted for its preoccupation with cleanliness. One seventeenth-century lady who caught a severe cold on her honeymoon blamed the fact that she had washed her feet on her wedding eve, and vowed never to do it again. Chamber pots and commodes were part of everyday life, and people were less embarrassed then about having to perform their natural functions in public

– even royalty occasionally received visitors enthroned upon the commode. Nevertheless, there were limits of decency which people were not expected to exceed. There was a riot at the theatre when one notable Parisian lady, having relieved herself on a chamber pot in her box, threw the contents over into the pit to get rid of the smell.

Paris was full of Royalist families who had impoverished themselves for the King's cause, and who hoped for a few sustaining crumbs from the Queen's table. But although she was soon granted a handsome allowance from the French Exchequer, every penny she could scrape together went back to her husband in England to support his continuing struggle. In the coming months Henrietta Maria and her ladies were to be found shivering in their beds at noon, starving for want of fuel and food and the money to pay for them. Margaret, maintained by the clever contriving of Elizabeth Lucas, was one of the few who managed to pay their way.

This state of affairs led to squabbles and jealousies among the courtiers, and Henry Jermyn, the Queen's favourite, was the object of much ill feeling. Madame de Motteville recorded dispassionately that 'he was a worthy man of a gentle mind which seemed very narrow and more fitted for petty things than great ones . . . he wanted money before all else, to meet his expenses, which were large'. Henrietta gave it to him. Thus when other displaced nobles walked to the Palais Royal, Jermyn dashed past in a new carriage, and his clothes and his table were always of the finest. The French were philosophical about such favouritism, but the English were furious: most of them could not forget that in 1639 he had been a mere master of the horse.

Apart from poverty, boredom was the greatest enemy at court. Once the first relief was past, the safety and inactivity of the Louvre were almost unbearable. The Queen had no money to spare for entertaining, and lacked the spirits to amuse herself. Her courtiers kicked their heels and intrigued spitefully among themselves, a pastime Margaret refused to share. She went to great lengths to avoid 'gossiping meetings', preferring to read. This, combined with her disabling shyness and the language barrier, contrived to set her apart even more from her contemporaries, and emphasised her 'difference'. She herself became an object of spite. Her constant companion was her maid Elizabeth Chaplain, who had accompanied her from England. Elizabeth was literate, respectably born – possibly the daughter of one of the yeomen on the Lucas estates – but, above all, loyal to her mistress.

When the weather was fine the ladies in waiting amused them-selves in the Tuileries garden, described by John Evelyn as 'rarely contrived for privacy, planted in the centre with elms and mul-berries, and a labyrinth of cypresses, hedges of pomegranate, foun-tains, an aviary and an artificial echo'. In the afternoons they drove out in their carriages along the Cour de la Reine, where all the fashionable went to see and be seen. Contrived by Marie de Medici, the ride was almost a mile long, entered through an arch and planted with four rows of trees, the centre being large enough to allow a hundred coaches five or six abreast to turn commodiously. The afternoon 'tour' was very much to Margaret's taste. She could observe without being observed herself and indulge her contem-plations without interruption. Margaret disapproved of any physical exertion strenuous enough to raise a sweat, and a short stroll in the garden was all the exercise she could ever be persuaded to take. Sweating, she argued in her philosophical essays, was very bad for the health, in that precious liquids were lost from the body.

The post from England arrived every Tuesday and Friday at the Rue de Quincampoix, and was eagerly awaited. In addition, couriers passed to and from London to Sir Richard Browne, the English Resident in Paris, carrying official correspondence. The Queen employed her own agents for her secret and highly sensitive letters to the King. The men who carried these communications risked their lives if they were apprehended – and many of them were; the precious letters were concealed in hat bands, waistcoat linings and sometimes in hollow canes. News was slow to arrive, delayed by the vagaries of wind and weather and the Channel crossing. The average time for a journey from London to Paris was about eight days, though in 1619 one man had gone from London to Calais and back in one day for a wager – but this was exceptional.

Apart from the writing and receiving of letters, some diversion was provided by Sir Richard and Lady Browne. Their embassy was a home from home for the exiled English, a haven of culture, where the latest information on the situation could be obtained at any time. During the interregnum, their private chapel was one of the few places where an Anglican could worship freely. Lady Browne seems to have been particularly kind to Margaret, and her comfort-able home became a refuge from the unfriendly salons of the Louvre. It is probable that Margaret used Lady Browne as the model for the character of Madame Civility in her play *The Presence*, where she figures as the matchmaker and benefactress who nurtures the romance between Mistress Bashful and Lord Loyalty.

While Margaret was struggling to adjust to life in exile, Newcastle, newly created Marquis, was coming to terms with his own changed circumstances. Things had continued to go badly for him. On arrival in Hamburg his sons had gone down with smallpox and measles. His principal seats of Welbeck and Bolsover had surrendered to Parliamentary forces, though his unmarried daughters, Jane and Frances, were apparently being kindly treated. The £90 he had brought with him was almost gone. Newcastle showed characteristic courage in adversity. Some of his personal attendants were sent home as a discreet economy, while he purchased a coach and nine Holstein horses to preserve appearances – essential if he was to secure credit to live on. Both the King and the Queen wrote kindly from Oxford and Paris respectively, though neither was in a position to repay any of the money he had invested in their cause.

With the advent of spring, the Marquis decided that an early return to England was unlikely and decided to join other Royalist refugees in Paris. He journeyed through Holland and the Spanish Netherlands, where he was received with much civility, and arrived in Paris on 20 April 1645. After obtaining lodgings for himself and his family, he went to the Louvre to pay his respects to the Queen and present her with four of his Holstein horses. Among her ladies – an entourage now much diminished by circumstance – his eye lighted upon a demure beauty who for once did not avert her eyes. Years later, in 'A True Relation', she recalled this time.

> My Lord being arrived at Paris, . . . immediately went to tender his humble duty to Her Majesty . . . where it was my fortune to see him for the first time . . . and though I did dread marriage and shunned men's company as much as I could, yet I could not, nor had not the power to refuse him, by reason my affections were fixed on him, and he was the only person I ever was in love with, neither was I ashamed to own it.

This frankness about her own feelings was something quite new and shocking. Lucy Hutchinson tore several pages from her own memoir before she allowed other members of her family to read it, even though it was not written for wider publication. Margaret's public candour, contrasting with her private shyness and her professed modesty, is a paradox – two conflicting aspects of a fascinating and complex personality.

Chapter Four

Mistress Bashful
1645

Lady Visitant: *Why, I hope you do not stay to muse upon Phantasms; faith, marriage will banish them out of your head, you must now employ your time with Realities.*
Lady Contemplation: *If I thought Marriage would destroy or curb my Contemplation, I would not marry, although my wedding guests were come, and my wedding dinner ready dressed, and my wedding clothes on.*

> Margaret Cavendish, *Lady*
> *Contemplation*, from *Plays*

Newcastle was a connoisseur of beautiful women, and Margaret certainly had great physical charm. She lacked only animation to be accounted beautiful. Her early portraits have a haunting, enigmatic quality; that, and her studied aloofness, combined to attract a man of charm and sensuality who could have had his pick of the court ladies. Newcastle was not repelled by her deep reserve, and 'did approve of those bashful fears which many condemned'. Apparently he wanted a young wife whom he could 'bring to his own humours'. Margaret says little about their courtship. But for the survival of her love letters, the Marquis' poems and some autobiographical passages in her plays, we would be ignorant of the progress of their unlikely romance.

There are considerable similarities between Margaret and New-castle's courtship and that of Lord Loyalty and Mistress Bashful in *The Presence*, published in 1668. Lord Loyalty approaches Mistress Bashful by means of a letter and some verses sent through one of the ladies in waiting. Newcastle was an accomplished flirt and may well have taken this line of approach. However, it seems more likely that, on perceiving her face in the throng around the Queen and on being told that she was the sister of his captured commander, Sir Charles Lucas, it would only have been courteous for him to have asked to be presented to her. That he afterwards sent her letters and verses we know for a fact. To Margaret, William Cavendish was already a hero ranking with Julius Caesar, Shakespeare and Plato in her esteem. It is not unnatural to suppose that, in her concern to learn of her brother's fortunes, she lost some of her fatal shyness and under the practised charms of the Marquis revealed more of herself than she was accustomed to.

However it happened and whatever was said, from that meeting each conceived an attraction for the other which gradually deepened into love. Newcastle's first wife, Elizabeth, had been dead for two years and he was now ready to marry again. Although he had two grown-up sons, his dynasty was far from secure in such precarious times. In his biography Margaret wrote, with typical practicality:

> My Lord, having but two sons, purposed to marry me, a young woman that might prove fruitful to him and increase his posterity by a masculine offspring. Nay, he was so desirous of male issue that I have heard him say he cared not (so God would be pleased to give him many sons) although they came to be persons of the meanest fortunes.

This passage, among others, has led some biographers to assume that this was a marriage motivated by convenience, despite the weight of evidence to the contrary. The truth was that, apart from the physical attraction which Newcastle felt, they shared a great many common interests: theatre, literature, music, the countryside. Both wrote – Newcastle openly, Margaret in secret. For the first time since leaving Oxford, Margaret found someone to whom she could talk without constraint. Very shortly Margaret was admitting shyly: 'I begin to like Paris because you are in it.'

In *The Presence*, Lord Loyalty contrives to meet Mistress Bashful at the home of their mutual friend Madame Civility and begins to bombard the lady with amorous verses. Something of the sort must have taken place, for the court ladies were strictly supervised by the 'mother of the maids'. Queen Henrietta Maria cared deeply about the morality of her court, and without the protection of parents and close friends meetings and communications could be effected only with difficulty. Newcastle's secretary and Margaret's maid passed continually to and fro between their lodgings. There is some evidence that Madame Civility might have been Lady Browne. She is mentioned in some of Margaret's letters, and Margaret herself admitted being 'indebted' to her for her marriage. According to John Evelyn she 'in gratitude had often and solemnly promised' £1000 to his wife (Lady Browne's daughter) when they were restored to their fortunes – money which never materialised.

Newcastle's verses are now preserved among the manuscripts at Nottingham University and are in turn witty, amorous and erotic. Their quality and style is in keeping with that of other court or

'Cavalier' poets, although less polished. What deeply romantic girl could withstand the following assault upon her sensibilities:

> I now sit down, with pen and ink and paper,
> Invoke my muse by my dim, single taper.
> Fair as yourself; for there's nothing so fair,
> Your skin is sullied by transparent air
> Well-favoured like yourself, it must be so
> For there is nothing like you that I know.
> Here is no simulising – you must know it,
> And if not that, why then you spoil a poet.

Margaret responded:

> My Lord, I think you have a plot against my health in sending so early, for I was forced to read your letter by a candle light, for there was not day enough, but I had rather read your letter than sleep and it doth me more good. P.S. If you cannot read this letter, blame me not, for it was so early I was half asleep.

Margaret's handwriting was appalling. On another occasion she put an outrageous postscript to a letter: 'Pray lay the fault of my writing to my pen.' Later she was franker and confessed: 'My handwriting is so bad as few can read it.' The Marquis was not deterred.

> It is so long, so long ago, since met
> I doubt you will me utterly forget,
> It is now how long? It is, let me see,
> Since I had letter, or did hear from thee
> I vow it is, protesting here I may,
> 'Tis since I heard from you, 'tis one whole day.

It was not long before both realised the depth of their affections. Margaret, conscious of the fact that she was accused by members of the court of 'setting her cap' at Newcastle, was more inhibited than her lover at revealing her true feelings. She writes in one letter, 'Though I give you all the love I have, yet it is too little for your merit, or could I wish for more love than ever was or shall be, yet my wish could not be so scopus [copious], but you would be still as far beyond it as your worth is above other men's.' But the following day she declares, 'I am a little ashamed of my last letter, more than of the others; not that my affection can be too large, but I fear I discover it too much in that letter, for women must love silently. But I hope you will pardon the style because the intention was good.' The standards of modesty governing the conduct of a woman affected even her expressions of affection. As late as 1696 Mary Astell could still write that modesty required that a woman should not love before marriage.

At this point some appreciation of their situation depressed their spirits. Both were penniless refugees in a foreign country, and, since the Royalist defeat at the battle of Naseby in June, hopes of an early return to England had faded for Newcastle. Although Margaret could leave the Queen at any time and go home to her family without fear of reprisal, Newcastle was banned from returning to England. He was a traitor with a price on his head.

> Dear, you nor none else know,
> Why you should love me so,
> There's nothing that can be
> Worthy of you in me.
> To you a great reproach
> To see me near your coach.
> To love me, 'tis high treason
> Against your state and reason.
> Therefore I dare not woo you,
> For fear I should undo you.

Margaret was extremely unhappy. She wrote from St Germain:·

> Pray believe that I am not factious, especially with you, for your commands shall be my law. But suppose me now to be in a very melancholy humour, and that most of my contemplations are fixed on nothing but dissolutions; for I look on this world as on a death's head for mortification, for I see all things subject to alteration and change and our hopes as if they had taken opium.

It was not only the political situation that weighed against them; there was also the difference in their social standing. Although there was considerable movement among the seventeenth-century aristocracy and the classes were not rigidly divided, Margaret, as the daughter of an ordinary gentleman, moderately wealthy but without influential connections, could not hope to aspire to the rank of Marchioness. Newcastle was one of the first-ranking men in the kingdom after the King, one-time governor of the future Charles II, and before the Civil War had been fabulously wealthy. Most of his wealth and property had come from his grandmother, the formidable Elizabeth, Dowager Countess of Shrewsbury, known as Bess of Hardwick, of whom Horace Walpole wrote:

> Four times the nuptial bed she warmed
> And every time so well performed
> That when death spoiled each husband's billing
> He left the widow every shilling.

The difference in their ages was another factor contributing to Margaret's hesitation. At fifty-three Newcastle was thirty years older than herself. He put his case vigorously:

> I know I'm old, it is too true,
> Yet love, nay am in love with you.
> Do not despise me or be cruel,
> For thus I am love's best of fuel.
> No man can love more or loves higher
> Old and dry wood makes the best fire,
> Burns clearest and is still the same
> Turned all into a living flame.
> It lasts not long, is that your doubt?
> When am to ashes all burnt out?
> A short and lively heat that's pure
> Will warm one best, though not endure.

Unable to withstand such a skilful assault, Margaret capitulated. In *The Presence* Lord Loyalty proposes to Mistress Bashful at the home of their benefactress, Madame Civility, in lines very similar to some of the letters and poems.

Lord Loyalty: Can you love an unfortunate man?
Mistress Bashful: Yes, so his misfortunes come not through his crimes. Misfortune and honesty in this age are so fixed to each other as I cannot choose one but I must take both.
Lord Loyalty: Can you love so well as to be ruined for my sake?
Mistress Bashful: If you call poverty ruin . . . I could be well content to entertain it.

The summer of 1645 was hot, and the Queen's court moved from the stifling confines of Paris to the royal residence at St Germain-en-Laye. St Germain was a beautiful château, long, low, prettily ornamented, overlooking water and flanked by the encroaching green of natural forest. Its terraced gardens, designed by Claude Millet for Henri IV, stepped gently down to the riverside. It was the perfect place to spend the sultry summer months. By the time the Queen and her ladies left Paris, Newcastle and Margaret were secretly engaged.

Margaret was fortunate to be allowed to choose her own husband. Even as late as 1688 Lord Halifax recorded in *Advice to a Daughter* that it was one of the disadvantages of her sex that 'women are seldom permitted to make their own choice; their friends' care and experience are thought safer guides to them than their own Fancies'. This fitted in with the legal notion of a woman as a perpetual minor. Another seventeenth-century lady, Dorothy Osborne, had to wait many years until the death of her father before she was able to marry the man she loved. Young people rarely married to disoblige their relatives. In promising herself to Newcastle of her own free will, Margaret was exercising an unusual liberty – though her family were unlikely to disapprove such a splendid match.

Girls were still sometimes espoused from the cradle, and marriage at twelve, thirteen or fourteen was common. John Evelyn himself married the daughter of Sir Richard and Lady Browne when she was still a child, leaving her with her parents in Paris until she was old enough to join him in England. Sometimes these young brides were taken into their in-laws' households to be brought up, and the results were not always good. One family, regretting the match they had made, attempted to starve their daughter-in-law to death before she was rescued by her own parents. Newcastle's own granddaughter-in-law, Lady Elizabeth Percy, had been married three times and widowed twice by the time she was fifteen.

When Gerard Winstanley, the Puritan pamphleteer, wrote that men and women ought to be free to marry for love, it was still a very radical notion, and although it was becoming more common the material advantages of a match still weighed much more heavily. It was not enough to be 'Heavenly Fair'; 'A hag like hell, with Gold' was more highly prized, wrote Anne Killigrew in one of her poems. Newcastle might have been expected to marry prudently to repair his shattered fortunes – his first wife had brought him £2500 a year and £6000–7000 in dower, as well as a jointure of her own for £800 a year.

Margaret's lack of dower was universally considered to be highly disadvantageous. In England the Verney sisters, better born and connected than Margaret, but also rendered dowerless by the war, had to be content with the meanest of matches. But Newcastle was romantic rather than avaricious and did not allow Margaret's lack of financial provision to influence him, even though the marriage was opposed by two of his closest friends, Lord Widdrington and Endymion Porter. Margaret had offended the latter in an unfortunate incident, but in a letter to Newcastle she denied that any incivility had been intended:

As for Mr Porter, he was a stranger to me, for before I came into France I did never see him, or at least knew him not to be Mr Porter, or my Lord of Newcastle's friend, and my lord, it is a custom I observe that I never speak to any man before they address themselves to me, nor to look so much in their face as to invite their discourse.

Her position was unenviable. Alone in a mocking and intriguing court with no family to help her, she had to make all the decisions and arrangements herself. Though not made public, their engagement was known to close friends, many of whom thought the match unsuitable and lost no opportunity to discourage the parties to it. Newcastle's friends assured him that it was folly to marry an unknown girl of gentle but unexceptional birth, with no fortune or lands or useful political connections; any one of these attributes would have been helpful in his desperate situation. Furthermore, Margaret had acquired a reputation for aloofness and stupidity, choosing to be 'accounted a fool' rather than 'to be thought rude or wanton'. Not everyone managed to penetrate to the quiet intelligence that burned beneath. In this respect, Newcastle's friends were totally correct; Margaret was not likely to be a social asset.

The women at court were motivated generally by jealousy, for Newcastle was a great matrimonial prize. The spurned court ladies could hardly control their rage when he was snatched up by a speechless, guileless, book-loving girl. Ladies Ill-Favoured and Spiteful in *The Presence* tell Mistress Bashful that 'The Lord of Loyalty is none of the chastest men . . . he loves variety too well to tie himself to one.'

Newcastle had inherited Bess of Hardwick's sensual nature as well as her money. While his first wife was alive there had been rumours of an affair with the Countess of Rutland, and poems among the manuscripts preserved at Nottingham hint at other liaisons. Envious ladies in waiting were quick to capitalise on his reputation. Margaret, thoroughly confused, wrote sadly:

I fear others foresee we shall be unfortunate, though we see it not ourselves, or else there would not be such pains taken to untie the knot of our affection. I must confess, as you have had good friends to counsel you, I have had the like to counsel me and tell me they hear of your professions of affection to me, which they bid me take heed of, for you had assured yourself to many and was constant to none.

Newcastle protested the enduring quality of the love he had for her, and Margaret ignored the warnings and reaffirmed her attachment. 'My Lord, I have received your letter which seems to satisfy me against the noise of a court.' Her great joy in Newcastle's love spilled over on to the page:

There is nothing will please me more than to be where you are . . . my Lord, the reason I had to conceal our affections was because I thought it would be agreeable to your desire, but for my part I would not care if the trumpet of fame blew it throughout all the world, if the world were ten times bigger than it is.

There are indications from the letters that Newcastle wanted Margaret to consummate the marriage before all the formalities were completed. Before Hardwicke's marriage act, which set out for the first time the requirements for a legally valid marriage, union was legally enforceable if a betrothed couple had sexual intercourse – a betrothal being regarded as a contract to marry, completed by the physical act. But it was also very easy for someone rich and powerful to wriggle out of such an agreement. Margaret, perhaps remembering her mother's experiences, refused to share his bed until all the papers had been signed and the formal ceremonies completed. If Newcastle was an impatient lover, Margaret was anxious and insecure.

Some of the court ladies, having failed to drive a wedge between the Marquis and his lady in waiting, tried to make mischief with the Queen, who as yet had not been apprised of their intentions. Someone betrayed Margaret's discreet meetings and correspondence to Henrietta Maria and she was enraged, partly by the duplicity of their conduct and partly by the inequality of the match. Margaret wrote from St Germain:

I have not been with the Queen as yet, by reason I am not well, but I hear she would have me acknowledge myself in a fault and not she to be in any . . . I heard not of the letter, but she sayeth to me she had it in writing that I should pray you not to make her acquainted with our desires . . . I hope the Queen and I are friends, she sayeth she will seem so at least; but I find if it hath been in her power she would have crossed us.

In another troubled missive Margaret, with her customary common sense, discussed ways to mollify the Queen.

My Lord, I know not what council to give concerning the Queen, but I fear she will take it ill if she be not made acquainted with our intention [to be married], and if you please to write a letter to her and send it to me, I will deliver it that day you send for me. I think it no policy to displease the Queen, for though she will do us no good, she may do us harm.

In the same letter, Margaret shows signs of breaking down under the strain of her position. With Newcastle in Paris and Margaret at St Germain it was easy for misunderstandings to arise. She was deeply disturbed by the viciousness of the opposition to her attachment, and, without Newcastle to support and reassure her, almost overwhelmed by it. She offered to free him from his engagement: 'Pray my Lord, consider well whether marrying me will not bring a trouble to yourself, for believe me, I love you too well to wish you unhappy, and I had rather lose all happiness myself than you should be unfortunate.' Newcastle's responses were growing so ardent that she was forced to write a postscript to her letter: 'My Lord, let your eye limit your poetry.'

Margaret must often have wondered if she was doing the right thing. She claimed that she 'dreaded marriage' and her writings later on reveal that, despite her happiness with Newcastle, she heartily endorsed the view of contemporary philosophers that marriage was an unsatisfactory relationship for women. Lawes' *Resolution of Women's Rights* in 1632 described wedlock as a 'locking together' of man and wife into one person, but as

> when a small brook or little river incorporateth with Rhodanus, Humber or Thames, the poor rivulet loseth her name; it is carried and recarried with the new associate . . . a woman as soon as she is married is called covert, in latin nupta that is 'veiled'; as it were clouded and over-shadowed; she hath lost her stream.

But to be unmarried in seventeenth-century England was unthinkable for a woman, for there was no place in society for the spinster: she could no longer enter a convent and spend her life usefully studying, teaching or nursing. The unmarried girl remained at home, a social anachronism, a burden first to her parents and then to her brothers. Even the laws of inheritance did not provide adequately for the notion of a single, independent woman, but considered her always as the dependant of a man.

Another seventeenth-century lady, Alice Thornton, who intended to remain single, was dissuaded on religious grounds:

> For my own particular, I was not hasty to change my free estate without much consideration, both as to my present and future

. . . yet might I be hopeful to serve God in those duties incumbent on a wife, a mother, a mistress and governess in a family, and if it pleased God so to dispose of me in marriage, making me a more public instrument of Good to those several relations, I thought it rather duty in me to accept my friends' desires for a joint benefit than my own single retired content.

Margaret too had considered the possibility that she might remain single. Some years later, when her sister Anne wrote to ask Margaret's advice on her proposed marriage, she replied (in a letter she published in *Sociable Letters*);

There is so much danger in marriage, as I wonder how any dare venture . . . all wives, if they be not slaves, yet they are servants, although to be a servant to a worthy husband is both pleasure and honour. A happy marriage is very happy, but an unhappy one is hell. Where there is doubt the best is to be mistress of yourself, which in a single life you are.

Only the strength of Margaret's love for Newcastle could overcome so deep an aversion to marriage, and she made him aware of his unique position: 'I must tell you I am not easily drawn to be in love, for I did never see any man but yourself that I could have married.'

The court planned to return to the Louvre in time for the celebration of the marriage of Princess Marie of Mantua to the King of Poland, an elderly gentleman of raddled countenance, incapacitated by gout. Margaret offered to stay behind in order to reduce the gossip, but Newcastle repudiated this suggestion. Queen Henrietta Maria's retinue was by now greatly diminished. Some ladies had been seduced by the comforts of home, others had married, and yet others had fallen victim to the Queen's stringent economies. The Grande Mademoiselle wrote in her diary with not a little spiteful glee that 'nothing marked the loss of her dignity more than the appearance of her retinue'. It was a thinly spread, shabbily attired court that returned to the Louvre in the autumn of 1645.

All Paris turned out to see the arrival of the Polish embassy, which was as colourful and entertaining as a Mardi Gras. First came the footguards in red and yellow, with mounted officers in Turkish jackets embroidered with jewels; then companies in green and grey with richly caparisoned horses, some of which had their skins dyed red. They were followed by the Polish seigneurs with suites and liveries dressed in rich silver and gold brocade, and diamonds scattered liberally about their persons with barbaric disregard for style. Madame de Motteville reported that they wore no linen underneath, and slept, not in sheets like civilised Europeans, but naked under robes of fur. Their heads were shaved but for one lock at the top, dangling down behind like a squirrel's tail. Amid the pomp and bustle and celebration Margaret's faithful maid, Elizabeth Chaplain, went to and fro between her mistress, Lady Browne and the Marquis, who wrote:

> The Princess Mary marries King of Poland
> And you my dear do marry Prince of Noland
> She hath a portion, I hope you have none,
> She hath a dower, but your dower's gone,
> She doth embrace all this world's full delight
> And you take me to bid the world goodnight
> She will possess what height of courts can be
> But you take up your cross to follow me
> Leave court, your parents, brothers, sisters, friends
> Only for me, and hath no other ends.

Shortly after Princess Marie's much-publicised nuptials in November, Margaret left the service of the Queen and she and Newcastle were quietly married in Sir Richard and Lady Browne's private chapel by Sir John Cosin, Anglican chaplain to the Queen's court. The date is not recorded, but by 20 December Elizabeth Lucas, not a little pleased by her daughter's good fortune, wrote Newcastle a dignified epistle:

> You have been pleased to honour me by your letters, my daughter much more by marriage, and thereby made her extremely happy, for often times they come not together, but by yourself she hath attained to both.
>
> The state of the Kingdom is such yet that I confess her brother cannot give unto her that which is hers, neither can I show my love and affection towards my daughter as I would in respect of the great burdens we groan under. God deliver us, and send us a happy end of these troubles.

Newcastle, in a more buoyant mood, wrote in one of his poems:

> Let Care go kill Cats, what comfort's in Sorrow?
> Therefore let tomorrow care for Tomorrow.

Chapter Five

Married Poverty
1646 – 8

Mistress Reformer: *Madam, now you are become mistress of a family, you must learn to entertain visitants, and not be so bashful as you were wont to be.*
Lady Bashful: *Alas, Mistress Reformer, it is neither their birth, breeding, wealth, or title that puts me out of countenance, for a poor cobbler will put me as much out of countenance as a prince, or a poor seamstress as much as a great lady.*
Mistress Reformer: *What is it then?*
Lady Bashful: *Why, there are unaccustomed faces, and unacquainted humours.*

> Margaret Cavendish, *Love's*
> *Adventures*, from *Plays*

The wedding ceremony was private and few details have survived. It would have been attended by Newcastle's close friends Lord Widdrington and Endymion Porter, his brother, two sons and members of the household. Margaret had no relatives to support her and promised Newcastle that she would bring only those friends whom he chose. Marriage in exile, in poverty, hundreds of miles from close relatives and friends, was a sober affair. John Evelyn, married about the same time in the same chapel to Lady Browne's daughter, was accompanied by only five or six friends and the ceremony was followed by a quiet family celebration at the fashionable St Cloud.

Margaret's play *The Bridals*, published with *The Presence* in 1668, describes the wedding celebrations of Lady Coy and Lady Virtue. The heroines are shy and serious, like their creator. Unaccompanied by their parents, they choose a quiet marriage and refuse to be 'dressed up as if for a pageant show'. In the play Margaret describes how the bride is prepared for bed by her friends and relatives after the wedding meal. The bride's stocking has to be flung for some hopeful lady to catch and her hairpins thrown away to ensure a happy marriage. It was also traditional to play practical jokes on the couple, but it is unlikely that anyone at the Newcastles' wedding would have ventured to sew the sheets together or tie a bell under the bed.

The bridegroom, attended by his friends, was attired in a separate chamber, and after a decent interval knocked upon the bride's door and demanded admittance. Once she had been placed between the sheets by her maids the door was opened and the bridegroom got into bed beside her. A 'sack posset' – a kind of wine cup – was drunk by the couple and a piece of the bride cake broken over their heads. Margaret objected to the latter because it left crumbs in the bedclothes. Finally the chaplain blessed the bed and the couple were left alone, while musicians rendered an Epithalamium – a nuptial song – outside the door.

The Bridals, for which Newcastle wrote the Epithalamium, describes the bedding ceremony of Lady Coy, whose shyness matches Margaret's own. Lady Coy, like Margaret, dreads marriage and confesses that she is 'afraid to lie with a man'. It is some time before her attendants can prevail upon her to remove her outergarments and get into bed. Three times the bridegroom comes to the door and is turned away. Only when his patience is exhausted does he finally gain admittance. It is one of Margaret's best dramatised episodes and, given her propensity for autobiographical narrative and her earlier confession that she 'dreaded marriage and shunned men's company', suggests that she wrote the scene from her own experience.

Most of Margaret's biographers have assumed that she was frigid, or at the very least sexually cool, but there is ample evidence that she was not. Part of their argument rests on her statement that she was a stranger 'to amorous love', with all its overtones of incontinent sexual desire. But it is these overtones which would have made Margaret so anxious to disclaim any knowledge of 'amorous love' in order to reinforce the image she wished to put over of virtue, modesty and chastity. Her love for Newcastle, she claimed, was 'grounded in merit', a deep and enduring affection. The distinction she draws is of a woman who *loves* rather than one who is in love. This does not preclude sexual passion. Lucy Hutchinson, writing of her love for Colonel Hutchinson, also denies 'amorous love' for much the same reason.

The correspondence between Margaret and Newcastle before marriage is by modern standards remarkably frank, at least on Newcastle's part: in one poem he refers to masturbation. Although Margaret requests that he 'limit his poetry' she is not particularly disturbed by it, and her response to his suggestion that they consummate their relationship is practical rather than outraged. In her later work she discusses sexuality in a frank and matter-of-fact fashion, advocating that wives should 'act the courtesan' in order to keep their husband's affection, adding that such conduct is not shameful in a lawful relationship. Newcastle seems to have been quite happy with her responses, and the amount of time he spent in her company called forth sarcastic comments from contemporaries. It seems quite possible that, despite her shyness and modesty, Margaret achieved a fulfilling sexual relationship under the tutelage of her much more experienced husband.

For Margaret the marriage had brought problems other than sexual adjustment. She had entered a large masculine household with well-established loyalties, all rubbing elbows in cramped lodgings, and short of money as well as space. Apart from her husband there were his brother, Sir Charles Cavendish, his two sons, Henry and Charles, their tutor, and Newcastle's steward, secretary and other household servants. With deep feeling Margaret observed in *The World's Olio* 'that when a second wife comes into a family all the former children and old servants are apt to be factious and do foment suspicions against her, making ill constructions of all her actions, were they never so well and innocently meant, yet they shall be ill taken'. Although Margaret got on well with Newcastle's brother, striking up an affectionate relationship, there was hostility from Newcastle's sons; and though she was on friendly terms with Newcastle's secretary, John Rolleston, and the tutor, Dr Benoist, she was never accepted by the other servants, a situation which continued to cause problems throughout her married life.

Once again it was her 'bashful disposition' and inability to mix which caused the trouble, and perhaps Elizabeth Lucas' instructions to her children to avoid familiarity with their servants. Margaret's social inadequacy led to disastrous errors, one of which was recorded in *Sociable Letters*: when musing on a friend's good and bad points she drew up a list of each, and was so pleased with her account of the Lady A.N.'s virtues that she decided to send it to her. Unfortunately she put the wrong sheet of paper in the envelope. When she read her friend's reply and realised her mistake,

> I was as if I had been Thunder-Stricken, my Blood flushing so violently into my Face, my Eyes flashed out fire like Lightning, and after that fell such a Shower of Tears as I am confident there were more Tears shed than Letters Written.

Margaret solved the problem by withdrawing into herself, spending much of her time alone in her room, living in the inner world from which all her fancies sprang. If there had been an establishment for her to manage, a natural role for her to fill, her personality might have developed along different lines – as she herself freely admitted. As it was, Margaret found herself with little privacy and nothing to do. Just as the idle hours of her childhood and adolescence had been used to fill sixteen 'baby books' with rambling prose, so she began to occupy her time setting down her innermost contemplations. Although she published nothing until 1652, *The World's Olio* was completed some time between 1646 and 1651 – being written 'before I went into England'. The bulk of poems and philosophical musings published in England in 1652 and 1653 also argue literary activity over a much greater period of time.

Paris in the 1640s was an exciting place for a writer, and particularly for a woman. Twenty-five years had elapsed since Marie de Gournay had published her controversial feminist tract in which she claimed intellectual equality for men and women and made the radical assertion that sex was a physical distinction, which did not affect the mind. Feminist and anti-feminist arguments were regularly and thoroughly aired in a much more serious way than in England. John Swetnam's *Arraignment of lewd, idle, froward and unconstant women*, printed in 1615, and Esther Sowernam's indignant reply, are not to be compared with the sophisticated logic of Marie de Gournay and her French contemporaries, which had grown out of a tradition of debate which dated back to Christine de Pisan in the fifteenth century.

The 1640s were the high summer of the Parisian salon. In the Rue St Thomas de Louvre, not far from Margaret's lodgings, Catherine Vivonne, the cultured Marquise de Rambouillet, held court, and she had many imitators. Among them were Madame de La Fayette, who published the remarkable *Princesse de Clèves* in 1678, and Madeleine de Scudéry, whose romantic novels were very popular, particularly *Artamène ou le Grand Cyrus*, which included a discussion of women's education. Although there was much to ridicule among the affected *précieuses* and *savantes* who frequented the salons, these did provide places where men and women could meet and converse on equal terms, on subjects previously the prerogative of men, and in particular the new science propounded by Descartes. These educated and scientifically minded women provided further examples for Margaret of what could be achieved: the publication and acceptance of their work gave her the precedents she needed and which were lacking in England.

In 1647 le Moyne published his *Gallerie des Femmes Fortes*, a collection of short biographies of heroic women which showed how women could be strong and active while remaining essentially feminine. The idea of the heroic woman was much in vogue at the time, influenced by the examples of Marie de Medici, Anne of Austria and, across the Channel, the memory of Queen Elizabeth I. In addition le Moyne depicted Judith, Semiramis, Joan of Arc and, controversially, Lucrezia Borgia. The idea of the *femme forte* was, not unnaturally, well received at the French court. It found particular favour with Queen Henrietta Maria's niece, the Grande Mademoiselle, who decided to model herself on heroic lines, donned armour and fought at the head of her troops in the French civil wars of 1648–53 known as the Fronde.

It is difficult to determine how aware Margaret was of the intellectual activity and reassessment of women going on around her. She did not understand French well enough to read much of what was written, and it is unlikely that she visited the salons. But the ideas that they stimulated were in the air to be inhaled, like smoke, and they appear frequently in her published work. Although le Moyne's book was not translated into English until 1652 it was the subject of discussion everywhere, and in a letter Margaret records a lively debate on the moral dilemma of Lucrezia Borgia, which argues a familiarity with his work. Margaret shows herself to be conversant with all the feminist arguments current at the time, many of which concerned the problems of biblical interpretation. In *The World's Olio* she fiercely refuted the theory that the Bible gives proof that woman is inferior to man, echoing Marie de Gournay and anticipating the great French feminist Poulain de la Barre, whose works appeared after her death:

> Some say a man is a nobler creature than a woman because our Saviour took upon him the body of a man; and another that man was made first; but these two reasons are weak, for the Holy Spirit took upon him the shape of a dove which creature is of less esteem than mankind; and for the pre-eminency in Creation, the Devil was made before Man.

Feminists made much of the fact that Eve was made after Adam and was therefore the pinnacle of creation, a view originally propounded by Cornelius Agrippa in the sixteenth century. His works were well known in both England and France, and the numerous translations which continued to appear are evidence of their influence.

Margaret's personal life during 1646–7 was acutely affected by lack of money. France was growing increasingly impatient with the large numbers of penniless refugees attached to the Queen's court.

Henrietta Maria could spare them nothing, for all her money went to the King in England. She denied herself food, clothing and fuel for his cause and expected others to do likewise. A Parliamentary spy wrote that he knew not how the exiles lived. The Queen's favourite, Henry Jermyn, alone prospered.

In England, too, things were going badly. By March Newcastle's old charge, the Prince of Wales, had taken refuge in the Scilly Isles. Among the staff who accompanied him was a new secretary, Richard Fanshawe, and his wife Anne. The Fanshawes had narrowly escaped from Ireland with their lives; in her memoirs Anne records how she was warned by a Parliamentary friend and drove out of town in a borrowed horse and cart in the early hours of the morning. She had begun to think that they 'should all like Abraham live in tents all the days of our lives'. While the Fanshawes camped in a damp cottage in the Scillies with the sea breaking over their doorstep, Newcastle's credit ran out in Paris.

One evening the steward apologetically informed the Marquis that he was unable to provide dinner for him because his creditors would not trust him any longer. Newcastle, preserving his outward calm, turned to his wife and humorously informed her that she would have to pawn her clothes to provide money for food. Margaret sensibly pointed out that her dresses would fetch very little. Instead she sent for her maid Elizabeth and directed her to pawn the various trinkets she had been given by her mistress from time to time. There was no mention of Margaret pawning her own jewellery, but it seems probable that anything that could be spared had already been pledged.

The following day Newcastle called his creditors together and addressed them with such persuasion that they extended their credit once more. It was a performance he had to repeat with wearisome regularity over the next few years. Margaret acted in a practical fashion: after redeeming the small items of jewellery so obligingly pledged, she sent Elizabeth Chaplain back to England to ask her brother for anything that remained of her marriage portion. Newcastle also despatched Dr Benoist, his sons' tutor, to see what could be borrowed from friends, but he returned shortly afterwards almost empty-handed. Most of Newcastle's old friends had lost their fortunes and estates in the struggle with Parliament, and some were afraid, their eyes so fixed on self-preservation that they 'dared not relieve so notorious a traitor', as he was regarded by the Cromwellians in England. There was other dismal news. The King was in the hands of the Scots, the Prince of Wales now in Jersey, and

Parliament was ruthlessly putting down any remaining pockets of resistance.

While in England, Dr Benoist had been approached with offers of marriage for Newcastle's two sons, Charles (Viscount Mansfield) and Henry. This gave the boys a welcome excuse to escape from an uncongenial situation: cramped lodgings in Paris under the close eye of father and tutor were not the best surroundings for two lusty young men used to the freedom of great estates in which to ride and hunt. They seized the opportunity and departed almost immediately. Once in England they were granted a pardon on the grounds of their minority, and extricated themselves discreetly from the proposed betrothals in order to shift for themselves. Newcastle was therefore relieved of the expense of feeding them and Margaret was spared the problem of playing mother to children almost as old as herself.

But as one anxiety was smoothed away, another replaced it. Margaret had been married now for several months and there was still no sign of pregnancy. The long cycle of hope and despair began, month after month, under the close scrutiny of servants and friends. To be barren was accounted a great disgrace. It was also equated with sin, as a contemporary prayer for the childless in Samuel Hieron's *A Helpe unto Devotion* shows: 'It is just, I confess . . . to punish my barrenness in grace and my fruitlessness in Holy things, with this want of outward increase.' But despite Margaret's apparent infertility, her relationship with Newcastle was blossoming. A letter to her beloved sister Catherine, published in *Sociable Letters*, revealed:

> Though I thought it was impossible I could love any creature better than you, yet I find by experience I do, for since I am married I love my husband a degree above you . . . But you may say, if my love was troublesome to you, what is it to my husband? I must tell you that I have some more discretion now than I had then . . . But though I do not ask my husband so many impertinent questions as I did you, yet my love to him is not less watchful, careful, fearful, but rather more if it can be, and all the powers and endeavours of my life are ready to serve him.

The exiles' lives were brightened momentarily in August 1646 by the arrival in Paris of Charles, Prince of Wales. He was officially received by his cousin, the seven-year-old King Louis XIV, and there were three days of festivities, balls and masques. Charles was no longer the sweet-tempered boy who had once advised Newcastle affectionately not to take Physick 'for it doth always make me worse' (Ellis, *Original Letters*). He had commanded troops in battle, skilfully evaded attempts to render him a political pawn, bedded his first woman and resisted the persuasions of his own formidable council. He was now a man, and his outwardly pleasant, rather indolent demeanour hid a firm resolve and a stubborn will.

Inevitably there were clashes between the Prince and his intractable mother, but Henrietta Maria soon found that she could not bend her son to her purposes as easily as she had his father. When she raged and insisted, he became polite and withdrawn, but he did not give in. The Queen turned, as in the past, to Newcastle, and asked him to use his influence over the Prince. Newcastle gallantly accepted the charge, but he had been succeeded in the Prince's council by Edward Hyde, Earl of Clarendon, and though he could and did offer gratuitous advice, he had no more influence than the Queen.

By 1647, sufficient funds were available to enable the Newcastles to rent a house in the fashionable area between the Louvre and the Palais Royal. Rents were high in Paris; houses were built by the merchant classes to rent to the aristocracy and there was much competition for them. A good house in the Faubourg St Honoré might cost as much as £1000 a year.

Margaret now had a small establishment to run, and space and privacy in which to write. The Marquis bought a couple of horses on credit from friends and began to practise the art in which he excelled: the schooling of horses, which we now call *haute école*. The Newcastles were still convinced that their exile was only a temporary inconvenience. In January the King was handed over to Parliament by the Scots. He escaped, but by the summer had been recaptured and immured in Carisbrooke Castle. While he lived, there was still hope that he might be freed and restored to his throne, and various uncoordinated intrigues were afoot to achieve this end.

Paris was full of congenial, if impecunious, company, and some of the most interesting members of its society met around the Newcastles' table. The poet Edmund Waller claimed that he had met Hobbes, Descartes and the eminent mathematician Gassendi there. Both Descartes and Gassendi were friends of Newcastle's brother Charles, who was himself a first-class mathematician. Thomas Hobbes had been tutor to Newcastle's cousin, the young Earl of Devonshire, at Chatsworth and was an old acquaintance who had often stayed at his own family seat, Welbeck. He was in Paris writing his *Leviathan*, and according to Margaret many of the ideas embodied in it were discussed over supper. Descartes brought the gossip of the salons. Favourably inclined towards the education of women, he was a friend and correspondent of Anna van Schurman, whose *Question Célèbre*, published in Paris in 1646, was being avidly read and discussed.

Margaret does not appear to have taken much part in these discussions. She claimed not to have spoken more than twenty words to Hobbes, and conversation with Descartes was limited since he was by reputation a man of few words and Margaret understood little French. She had to rely on her husband to report their exchanges, but she was always in the background, listening to what she could and forming her own opinions and ideas. On one occasion Newcastle propounded the astonishing idea that all stars were actually suns and that each sun had planets above and below, as our sun has. He argued that they could not be seen because, being planets, they had only reflected light which could not be perceived at so great a distance. This provoked lively discussion, particularly when Newcastle proposed that life might exist on these hypothetical and invisible bodies. Then, seeing that Margaret was following their arguments, the men asked her for her opinion. She blushed, as usual, and neatly sidestepped the question by saying that if they, being learned and witty men, could not decide the issue, it was impossible for her to do so. As she recorded in her biography of Newcastle: 'Then they laughed and said they would discourse of women. I said I did believe they would find women were as difficult to be known and understood as the Universe.'

Though Margaret was free to dispute with her husband in private the theories she heard expressed by their guests, the inequality of discourse that existed between men and women prevented her from challenging them publicly. Well-bred women were supposed to remain silent, listening and learning. Their minds and their discourse were so inferior through lack of education that intelligent men shunned their conversation. A contemporary witticism said that unmarried men avoided the conversation of women because it was morally dangerous; married men had no need of it because they had a surfeit at home; and educated men scorned it because women were so ignorant.

At first Margaret accepted this position, being conscious of her own intellectual inferiority. She wrote hesitantly in the Preface to *The World's Olio* that 'It cannot be expected I should write so wisely or so wittily as men, being of the effeminate sex whose brains nature has mixed with the coldest and the softest elements.' But this was not a viewpoint she could sustain even to the end of the essay. She constantly castigated women for the silliness of their conversation, and in a later essay in *Divers Orations* urged women to increase their wit by conversing 'in Camps, Courts and Cities, in Schools, Colleges and Courts of Judicature'. It was not nature that was at fault, but 'Custom and Use'.

On a personal level 1647 was a distressing year for Margaret. First her niece, then her eldest sister, Mary Killigrew, died of consumption. Six months later Margaret's mother, Elizabeth Lucas, whose health had been broken by all that she had endured, died suddenly. Margaret recorded that 'one might think death was enamoured with her, for he embraced her in a sleep, and so gently as if he were afraid to hurt her'. Then news arrived that Margaret's eldest, illegitimate, brother Sir Thomas had died as a result of a head wound sustained in Ireland. Denied the comforts of family mourning and oppressed by problems of her own, Margaret became the victim of deep depression. Her despair found its way on to the page, in a series of morbid verses later published in *Poems and Fancies*.

> Upon the hill of sad melancholy
> I did a silent, mourning beauty spy
> Still as the night, not one articulate noise
> Did once rise up, shut close from the light of joys
> Only a wind of sighs which did arise,
> From the deep cave, the Heart, wherein it lies
> A veil of sadness o'er her face was flung
> Sorrow a mantle black about her hung.

The roots of her depression were complex: the long separation from her family, the strain of living in an alien country, bereavement, the shame of living at the mercy of creditors and the growing conviction that she was infertile. Friends tried to draw her out. One caller was turned away, and another's invitation refused, as *Sociable Letters* reveals:

> You were pleased to invite me to a ball, to divert my melancholy thoughts, but they are not capable of your charity, for they are in too deep a melancholy to be diverted . . . besides my very outward appearance would rather be an obstruction to your mirth . . . for a grieved heart, weeping eyes, sad countenance, and

black mourning garments will not be suitable with dancing legs. I am fitter to sit upon a grave than to tread measures on a carpet . . . my mind is so benighted in sorrow, that it hath not one lighted thought. It is all put out with the memory of my loss.

Her depression was also held to be responsible for her failure to conceive. Newcastle had made no secret of his desire for sons to 'increase his posterity', and Margaret in her loving desire to serve him would have given anything to provide him with heirs. But after two years there were still no signs of pregnancy, and Newcastle was worried enough about both her mental and gynaecological states to write to the King's doctor, Sir Theodore Mayerne, in London. The elderly physician counselled patience. 'It is difficult to beget heirs with good courage when one is melancholy', he wrote. However, he put no faith in Margaret's swallowing his medication, or heeding his instructions. He knew her disposition from his attendance on the royal household, and was well aware that she had her own ideas on health, a regime which included fasting and frequent purges. Other doctors were consulted and a series of bizarre remedies for infertility prescribed, including rams' excrement. Margaret was also urged by friends and family to take more exercise and spend less time bent over her books. The link between the womb and the brain was imperfectly understood before the advent of twentieth-century scientific knowledge, and it was widely believed that the source of female creativity, both physical and mental, was the womb. It was also thought to be the seat of female neuroses, according to Pope's 'The Rape of the Lock':

> Parent of vapours and of female wit,
> Who give th' hysteric or poetic fit;
> On various tempers act by various ways,
> Make some take physic, others scribble plays;

The words 'know' and 'conceive' had both intellectual and sexual meanings: too much mental activity, it was felt, could damage a woman's ability to breed. This idea was very persistent, and as late as 1904 Herbert Spencer in *The Principles of Ethics* referred to the dangerous effects of 'Excessive Cerebral Activity in Women . . . The reproductive capacity is diminished in various degrees – sometimes to the extent of inability to bear children.' Education was thought to be particularly dangerous for pubescent girls.

Margaret bowed down beneath her misfortunes and prepared to endure, writing in 'A True Relation' that 'Heaven hitherto hath kept us, and though Fortune hath been cross, yet we submit and are both content with what is and cannot be mended, howsoever it doth pinch our lives with poverty.'

Chapter Six

Royal Vagrants
1648 – 51

Sweetheart, we are beggars, our comforts 'tis seen
That we are undone for the King and the Queen
Which doth make us rejoice, with Royal Brags,
That now we do foot it in Royal Rags,

We cannot borrow, nor take up of trust
So Water we'll drink and bite a hard crust,
Let Care go kill Cats, what comfort's in Sorrow,
Therefore let tomorrow care for Tomorrow.

William Cavendish, Portland Mss

In 1648 France began to experience the first civil disturbances that heralded the Fronde. An extract from *Sociable Letters* emphasises how distressingly familiar it all was for Margaret.

> I am so full of fear as I write, for all this city hath been in an uproar; the common people gather together in multitudes, pretending for the right of their privileges, but it is thought the design is to plunder the merchants' houses and the churches. To make it the more fearful the great bell, which is only rung in time of danger, sounds dolefully. My maids, being possessed with the like fear, come often to me with maskered faces and tell me divers reports; some that the army is coming to destroy the city, and others that the soldiers have liberty to abuse all the women, others that all in the city shall be put to the sword. The best report is that all shall be plundered – but as for this last . . . my husband and I are safe, for we are plunder free, having had all our goods and estates taken from us in our own country.

In England things were equally unsettled, and a series of uprisings triggered by the King's intrigues from Carisbrooke seemed to indicate to his supporters in exile that the time was right to mount another offensive against Parliament. On 9 March the Prince of Wales called a council at St Germain which Newcastle was invited to attend. Queen Henrietta Maria, Prince Rupert, the Marquises of Worcester and Ormonde, and Lord Jermyn were also present.

Newcastle was certain that the Scottish army was now the only instrument available to put the King back on his throne. The Queen opposed him, but the Prince's other advisers shared Newcastle's opinion. Faced with such united opposition Henrietta Maria countenanced a dialogue with the Scots, but she did not trust the Prince and feared that he might be persuaded to agree to unacceptable religious concessions. She asked Newcastle to follow him to Holland, still believing that the presence of his old governor might exercise a restraining influence on the Prince's actions. In the event Charles, who had little liking for the counsel of old men, easily evaded his reluctant mentor.

In view of the political unrest in France the Newcastles were glad to leave, but were at first unable to do so because Newcastle's debts remained unpaid. He applied to the Queen, who promised to stand surety for him. His creditors, however, doubted that the Queen would discharge her obligation, and Newcastle was obliged to add his word to hers. He remained, in effect, still liable for his own debts, and in addition he was forced to borrow £300–400 more from friends for the expenses of the journey. As Margaret had foreseen, the Queen was little use to them, despite the fact that they had beggared themselves in her service. The amount of money borrowed by Newcastle and others like him was staggering, and it was no wonder that the wealthy merchants who lent the money occasionally became jittery. They depended for their security on the Restoration of the King, and political fluctuations in England affected their willingness to lend. On the morning of the Newcastles' departure all their creditors made ceremonial visits to wish them well, and were received with formal courtesy. The comic aspects of this situation cannot have escaped the man who had once spent £15,000 on a single entertainment for his sovereign in the more affluent days before the war, and who now had not a single penny in his pocket that had not been borrowed.

Newcastle left Paris in the same state as he had entered it, and in the same vehicles. First came his coach, containing Lord Widdrington, Sir Charles Cavendish, Elizabeth Chaplain, the steward, the secretary and other personal servants; then Newcastle and Margaret in a 'chariot' built (fortuitously) for two; this was followed by three wagons of luggage, and the whole escorted by servants on horseback. Their route took them through the Spanish Netherlands, ruled at that time by Don John of Austria, the brother of the King of Spain. Newcastle had been favourably received on his way from Hamburg to Paris four years earlier, and found that his welcome was still warm. They arrived at Cambrai in darkness after a long and tiring journey, to find the Governor of the town waiting to receive them by the light of flaming torches. He presented the Marquis with the keys of the city and invited him and his entourage to a formal entertainment in his honour. Tired with the long day's racking in an unsprung vehicle, Newcastle declined as tactfully as he could. The torch-bearers were then ordered to escort them to their lodgings. The Governor sent wine and provisions and instructed the landlord to make no charge for his guests. They met with similar hospitality all along their route, proudly recorded by Margaret as evidence of the esteem in which her husband was held.

After the stench of Paris, the narrowness of its streets and a view hedged in by high buildings, the Low Countries afforded a pleasant contrast. The towns and cities were clean, with wide, paved streets shaded by lime trees, and beyond them travellers were struck, then as now, by the extreme flatness of the landscape, the vast expanse of sky relieved only by the windmills on every horizon, and the masts of the merchant ships tied up behind their owners' houses. Between the sails of ship and mill, belltowers marked out a profusion of churches, bearing witness to the religious tolerance that existed there; the ever-present breeze was full of the chiming of their carillons. Margaret, who always preferred the country to the town, was delighted.

At Rotterdam Newcastle contacted a friend, Sir William Throckmorton, who sent them to lodge with a Mrs Beynham, widow of an English merchant. Once settled there, Newcastle enquired about the Prince and discovered that he had already embarked without disclosing his destination. Mindful of Henrietta Maria's charge, Newcastle valiantly hired a ship and victualled it, but was easily dissuaded by Margaret from setting off 'on so uncertain a voyage, to seek a needle in a bottle [bale] of hay'. Lord Widdrington and Sir William, not subject to such matrimonial constraints, did set out but were forced to return after near-shipwreck off the coast of Scotland without ever sighting the Prince's ships.

Charles had gone straight to Helvoetsluys, where his brother James had arrived after escaping from England dressed as a woman. James had brought with him several ships which had defected from the Parliamentary Navy, and was in high spirits. After dealing with a mutinous crew and settling the awkward problem of precedence between his brother and Prince Rupert, Charles set sail on 14 July. His advisers were still unable to agree over what concessions, if any – particularly the taking of the oath of the Covenant – the Prince should make to the Scots over points of religion. After failing to raise the siege of Colchester, Charles successfully blockaded the mouth of the Thames, but by the time agreement had been reached with the Scottish spokesman Lauderdale, it was too late to achieve anything effective. Northern Royalists refused to join the invading Scots without the Prince at their head, and without their support Cromwell easily defeated the Scots army at Preston. The Welsh risings were also efficiently suppressed. The struggle in Essex, organised by Margaret's brother Sir Charles Lucas, was more protracted.

On the evening of 1 June 1648 George Goring, Earl of Norwich, was routed by General Fairfax near Maidstone. Keeping some three thousand men with him, he managed to retreat across the Medway to London where he was joined by a party of about fifty 'gentlemen'. He marched his small force northwards into Essex, where they joined up with the strong Royalist troop headed by Sir Charles; they were now about four thousand strong and included another Civil War veteran, George Lisle. Fairfax was pressing hard on their heels, and so, after a long march, it was decided to make a temporary halt at Colchester.

After a short skirmish, the city unwillingly became a Royalist garrison. Fairfax surrounded it almost immediately and began a determined assault on the hastily erected defences. Margaret's old home, St John's, became the scene of a fierce battle for possession. Defenders were driven from the outer and inner courtyards, until finally a hundred of them were forced to take refuge in the gatehouse. Even this had to be abandoned when an enemy grenade ignited the magazine and blew out the wall. The Parliamentary troops completed the work begun seven years earlier and pulled down anything that remained of the house. In a final act of barbarity the vaults of St Giles' church were broken open and the bodies of Elizabeth Lucas and Mary Killigrew dismembered and scattered around the church. Small items of jewellery on the corpses were stolen, and the soldiers made game with the dead ladies' 'hair in their hats'.

Royalist troops led by Sir Charles retreated behind the town walls. Fairfax managed to thrust his way through one of the town gates behind them, but was repulsed, as recorded by Matthew Carter, with heavy loss of life. 'Their bodies in the streets and hedges, as infallible witnesses of what had been done; yawning out their souls to receive their arrears in another world, for their religious rebellion in this.' The Parliamentary commanders decided to subject the city to a siege and starve the garrison out: the blockade was so effective that the Royalists were able to make only one more sally before supplies were cut off. The watermills for grinding corn were situated outside the city and quickly burned by Fairfax, who also occupied the waterworks. The town was surrounded with siege works, well supplied with cannon and mortars mounted in pairs. From then on the outcome was never in doubt.

Sir Charles Lucas, George Lisle and Lord Norwich held on to the last, vainly hoping for relief from the north. By 20 July they had begun to kill their horses for meat, and a few weeks later were eating dogs and cats. The starving citizens of Colchester were mainly Parliamentary sympathisers and therefore hostile to the garrison; the Royalists were vulnerable to enemies inside as well as outside the walls, and had to contend with frequent insurrection.

In the latter days of the siege Whitelocke's *Memorials* tells us that there was a leakage of men from the town 'weary of eating horseflesh . . . 20 or 30 a day run from the enemy and the last day a whole guard together came from them'. There was dysentery in the town. On one occasion a woman with five children, the youngest at her breast, came out of the town and fell on her knees before the guards, begging leave to pass the line, but she was forced to go back again. Lord Norwich reputedly told a band of starving women to eat their children, to which they replied that they would put out his eyes. On 21 August, five hundred women came out of the town towards the Parliamentary forces. The Colonel ordered a cannon to be fired over their heads, which they ignored. His men then fired muskets primed only with powder, and finally he ordered his men to catch and strip them, which made them run. The town refused to readmit the women. Fairfax demanded that they must – the blood of these innocent people being on their hands. Those who managed to escape from the town confirmed that all the dogs and cats and most of the horses had been eaten. When one of the sentries' horses was killed, many risked their lives to try to obtain pieces of the meat even when it began to stink.

Fairfax bombarded the city with propaganda as well as shot, and it was in this fashion that the officers learned of the Scots' defeat at Preston. On 26 August mutiny broke out in the junior ranks. A council of war was held, and it was decided that there was no alternative but to surrender. Fairfax's terms were stiff – the rank and file would be granted 'fair quarter', but the officers surrendered to the mercy of Parliament.

The strength and duration of the Royalists' resistance provoked Generals Fairfax and Ireton to an act of revenge. On the evening of 28 August 1648, after a brief court martial, Sir Charles Lucas and Sir George Lisle, two of the ablest officers who ever bore arms for the King, were led from Colchester Castle on to the green and shot, according to William Lilly, 'for some satisfaction to military justice, and in part of avenge for the innocent blood they had caused to be spilt, and the trouble, damage and mischiefs they had brought upon that town, that country and kingdom'. As Sir Charles fell, Lisle caught him in his arms in a last embrace. In a Royalist pamphlet, 'The Loyal Sacrifice', he is depicted ordering the firing squad to fire, declaring defiantly: 'Your shot, your shame; our fault, our fame.'

News of her brother's death and the defilement of her mother's tomb were brought to Margaret in Rotterdam. Her grief was terrible, and she expressed it in a series of melancholy poems dedicated to her dead relatives. Graphic descriptions of sorrow and depression are to be found in many of her later works, whose titles often reflect past experiences. The heroine of *Youth's Glory and Death's Banquet* (1662) describes how 'Black despair like melancholy night, muffles my thoughts, and makes my soul as blind.'

Margaret had suffered much more than her husband through the Civil War. While he lost only property and income, some of which he eventually recovered, his family remained unscathed. Margaret's losses were irrecoverable. She had lost her home – it was now too ruined to be rebuilt – and several of her closest relatives. The family, once so tightly knit that they thought and acted almost as one person, was now scattered, and the members fending for themselves as best they could. Margaret's remaining brother John, Lord Lucas, was forced to compound for his Essex estates – a system whereby Cavaliers paid a proportion of the value of their property as a fine and took an oath of allegiance to the Commonwealth – and took charge of Margaret's unmarried sister Anne. Her two other sisters, including Catherine Pye, remained in London.

In December 1648 the King was moved from Carisbrooke to Windsor to stand trial. The significance of this ominous event was not immediately apparent to the exiles. In Rotterdam Newcastle was optimistically hoping for a successful outcome to the Prince's venture and living in some state, keeping open house and table at others' expense with reckless prodigality. Margaret kept to her room, too depressed to socialise. Eventually Newcastle's money ran out. While in Rotterdam he had spent £2000 borrowed from the Marquis of Hereford and Earl of Devonshire, and £1000 more from other sources – most of it had gone on entertaining. Now that his pockets were to let once more he decided that he would have to find a more economical place to live. He left Margaret with Mrs Beynham in Rotterdam and travelled to Antwerp, which had taken his fancy as he passed through the Spanish Netherlands on his way to Holland. His purse was so empty that he was forced to stay at a public inn.

Endymion Porter, the ex-groom of the bedchamber to King Charles, who had often carried messages to England for the Queen, heard that Newcastle was in town and insisted that he come and share his lodgings. Newcastle was reluctant at first, but Porter would not take no for an answer. While he was there, Newcastle was told that Rubens' widow was thinking of leasing the painter's old house – a substantial property in its own gardens – and he went immediately to view it.

Rubens' house, built on his return from Italy, was large but not comparable to Welbeck Abbey or any of Newcastle's other properties back in England. It was a house more befitting a wealthy merchant than a Marquis. But there was nothing like it anywhere else in the Netherlands – it was an architectural fantasy in which the Renaissance style was only barely discernible. There was a great deal of Italian influence in Rubens' design, some of it hardly practical – open staircases were not ideal for the Flemish winter. The house surrounded a courtyard. On one side was the baroque building that Rubens had used as a studio, on the other the living quarters, which extended across the entrance to connect with the studio at first-floor level, and were constructed in traditional Flemish brick. Around the courtyard gods and goddesses rioted in stone; Pan, Neptune, Hera and Zeus posed endlessly. From the walls Margaret's favourite philosophers, Plato, Seneca and Socrates, looked down. Frescoes depicted scenes from mythology – the sacrifice of Iphigenia, the toilette of Venus, the judgement of Paris. On the portico leading to the garden were cartouches containing an appropriately admonishing quotation from the poet Juvenal, 'One must pray for a sane spirit in a healthy body, for a courageous soul, which is not afraid of death, which is free of wrath and desires nothing.'

Inside, the floors were bare, tiled in black and white downstairs and upstairs in more traditional terracotta. The fireplaces were of herringbone brick tiled in the traditional blue and white, and the walls were half panelled, half hung with gilded Flemish leatherwork.

Rubens' studio was an ideal receiving room with a separate ante-chamber and another large room over, reached by an open staircase from the entrance. The domestic apartments were on three floors – modest, medium-sized rooms, wonderfully lit by tall leaded windows. From the largest of the ground-floor rooms an imitation Pantheon with circular roof and gilded niches opened out; it is shown in some engravings decked out as a chapel. Above it was the large bedroom with its ornate domed ceiling in which Rubens had died. Today the house has been carefully restored, but remains substantially the same as it was in the seventeenth century. All the rooms look out on to a walled garden, which in contemporary paintings was shown filled with a riot of mature trees and plants. A line of poplar trees grew along one side, and Tudor-style enclosures and arbours covered with roses filled the middle, which was entered through a rustic gate. Beyond it was a formal garden with statues and fountains, and, most important of all from Newcastle's point of view, space to erect a building where he could school his horses.

William Aylesbury, brother-in-law to the Earl of Clarendon and agent to the Duke of Buckingham, lent Newcastle £200 to pay for the lease. Aylesbury had some standing in Antwerp, and his gesture established Newcastle as creditworthy among the merchants of the city. He was then able to buy furnishings and provisions and other necessities, and to send for Margaret and the rest of his household.

Antwerp was described by John Evelyn as a town of handsome and convenient lodgings. It was heavily fortified, and the citadel was 'the most matchless piece of modern fortification' Evelyn had ever seen. Very little of it now remains, but the docks still dominate the city and you can still smell the sea. In the 1650s Antwerp was suffering from the aftermath of the war and the River Schelde was still closed. It was also sparsely populated. Margaret counted only four other coaches besides her own making the obligatory afternoon 'tour'. This was Margaret's only glimpse of life outside her garden: when the weather permitted, the nobility went out in their coaches 'to see and be seen'. They circled the square of guild houses with their high stepped façades surmounted with the gilded symbols of their function – figures, animals, ships – and drove past the massive bulk of the cathedral – a fantastic conglomeration of roofs of differing heights, towering, lacy spires and Turkish onion domes, its flanks packed tight by tiny shops. From the square the coaches processed down the long avenue of limes to the white marble market cross, past the three-hundred-windowed Palace of the Oosterhuis, the offices of the Dutch East India Company, a symbol of past prosperity. Antwerp's current prosperity, like that of the exiles, was at a very low ebb.

The horizon was a fantastic vista of steep grey roofs with rows of tiny dormer windows, gilded weathervanes, spires, turrets, towers and minaret-like domes, a jumble of baroque and Flemish vernacular. Beyond the city a featureless landscape thick with poplars and willows, with marshes and reedbeds clattering with wildfowl, stretched on every side.

On 30 January 1649 the King was executed in London, though the news took some days to reach the continent. The future looked very bleak indeed. Although the shock waves of the King's death were felt throughout Europe, sympathy was all that was offered to the new King, Charles II. The European kingdoms were still recovering from the Thirty Years' War, just concluded, and some were already preparing the ground for an accommodation with the English Parliament for reasons of their own.

The Royalist press was doing its best to capitalise on the horror felt by the English people for the execution of their lawful King. For a time he became more popular in death than he had ever been in life. Pamphlets like 'The Loyal Sacrifice', depicting the brutal execution of Lucas and Lisle, were on sale, and the *Eikon Basilike*, a small book of King Charles' favourite devotions, became a bestseller. But there was little hope of any revival. The ordinary people were exhausted by the Civil War, and the remaining Royalists poor, disunited and closely watched by Cromwell's agents.

After waiting on the new King at The Hague to swear an oath of fealty, Newcastle went back to Antwerp where, Margaret wrote in her biography, 'he lived as retiredly as it was possible for him to do'. Privately he still put much faith in the Scots, and while Margaret arranged her new household, he and the King's other advisers discussed ways of using the Scots to their advantage. At that time the Scots were divided into three factions – the Covenanters, the most extreme Protestants; the Engagers, led by the Duke of Hamilton; and a small group of non-adherents who were fervently Royalist, represented by James Graham, Marquis of Montrose.

In January 1650, Charles sent Montrose to Scotland to see what support could be raised for another English invasion. Montrose, perhaps scenting danger, went first to call on Newcastle in Antwerp to ask his advice. Margaret relates that Newcastle was cautious. He advised against so rash an undertaking without money, arms, ammunition and secure places for his men to rendezvous. The

Marquis' forebodings were not without foundation, for while Montrose was in Scotland attempting to raise a force, Charles began negotiating with the Covenanters.

Newcastle was summoned to attend the King's Council, whose members included the King's brother-in-law, William of Orange. Newcastle, recognising that it is sometimes necessary 'to light a candle to the devil', could perceive no other way but to make an agreement with the Scots upon any condition. He and the Prince of Orange persuaded the King that, once installed on his throne by a Scottish army, he could do as he pleased. So, on 27 April, Charles agreed to swear the Oath of the Covenant. In doing so he betrayed Montrose, who was captured by the Covenanters and put to death.

In 1651 Charles crossed the border into England at the head of a Scottish army and was proclaimed King at Penrith in Cumbria. But the English did not flock to his banner as expected. They were weary with war, suspicious of the King's accommodation with the Covenanting Scots, and had fallen into an exhausted peace. The Parliamentary forces were better organised and better motivated. The Earl of Derby, whose wife had defended Latham House with such spirit, was defeated by Lilbourne at Wigan almost as soon as he landed. He was executed shortly afterwards, first writing, as Whitelocke related in his *Memorials*, 'a handsome, passionate letter to his lady to comfort her, and advised her, as then matters stood, to surrender the Isle of Man upon any condition'.

Charles arrived at Worcester on 22 August with sixteen thousand exhausted troops and was easily defeated by Cromwell, after a furious battle that turned into a massacre. Major General Harrison wrote to Parliament, as recorded in Whitelocke's *Memorials*, that

> all things were then in confusion; Lords Knights and gentlemen were plucked out of holes by the soldiers. The common prisoners they were driving to the cathedral church in Worcester; and what with the dead bodies of men and the dead horses of the enemy filling the streets, there was such a nastiness that a man could hardly abide the town.

The walls of Worcester were pulled down and the ditches filled up. Late on 3 September Charles crept out of the city by the back gate and made his famous escape from England disguised as a servant. When he heard of the defeat Newcastle fell into so violent a passion that Margaret feared for his life. The failure of this uprising meant that there could be no early end to their exile or their penury.

Chapter Seven

Musing on Phantasms
1652 – 3

And if a Lady dress, or chance to wear,
A Gown to please herself, or curl her hair,
If not according as the Fashion runs,
Lord, how it sets a-work their Eyes and Tongues!
Straight she's fantastical, they all do cry,
Yet they will imitate her presently,
And for what they did laugh at her in scorn,
With it think good themselves for to adorn.

Margaret Cavendish, *Nature's Pictures*

By 1652 the exiles had been living on credit and the generosity of friends for eight years and their financial situation was desperate. Clarendon wrote:

> I do not know that any man is yet dead for want of bread, which really I wonder at . . . I am sure the King himself owes for all he hath eaten since April, and I am not acquainted with one servant of his who hath a pistole in his pocket. Five or six of us eat together, one meal a day for a pistole a week, but all of us owe for God knows how many weeks to the poor woman that feeds us.

News reached Antwerp that Newcastle's sequestered estates were to be dispersed, and it was decided that Margaret and Sir Charles Cavendish should return to England to see whether anything could be salvaged from the wreck of his fortune. Pensions for maintenance and support were being granted to the wives of those Royalists who had been denied the right to compound, and Margaret hoped to obtain a small annuity to relieve their penury. Under the laws of sequestration a woman could very rarely be declared a 'delinquent' in her own right. Legally she was a minor and her husband was answerable for her crimes; she could not, however, be made responsible, or suffer, for her husband's. Therefore allowance was made for wives and children of Royalist delinquents to receive support from their sequestered estates.

The task of negotiating with the Commonwealth was often given to the wives of exiled Cavaliers. Endymion Porter's wife Olivia and Ralph Verney's wife Mary both came over to England and secured passes enabling them to settle their husbands' affairs and, if possible, arrange a composition for their estates. Tragically Porter, that 'fat amiable Catholic', as Clarendon described him, died within months of his return to England, before he could enjoy the fruits of his wife's labours.

Although Sir Charles was allowed to compound for his estates, he initially refused to do so. It was a matter of principle. To be forced to pay for something that was already his and humble himself before Parliament, confessing his 'errors' and professing penitence, was more than he could bring himself to do. The alternative, however, was to lose his estates outright. Edward Hyde, Lord Clarendon, was staying in Antwerp at the time and he lent the weight of his argument to Newcastle's in order to persuade Sir Charles to do the politic, if unpleasant, thing. According to Clarendon, Sir Charles declared that he would rather 'submit to nakedness or stoning in the street' than subscribe to the Covenant. Common sense eventually prevailed when he realised that it might be possible to provide assistance for his brother once he was in possession of his own estates.

The journey to England was more risky than usual, although less eventful than Margaret's outward voyage had been. In addition to the usual hazards of wave and weather, privateers lurked in the Channel to harass shipping. But some of them were in the service of King Charles and had they been attacked it is possible that they would have fared well: one gentleman set upon by pirates was saved by his acquaintance with the Marquis of Newcastle, for the men were some of his whitecoats turned pirate in the service of the King. Even after passengers had reached the safety of port with their goods intact, Parliamentary agents were waiting to go through their luggage in much the same fashion as modern customs officers, but far less scrupulous about confiscation. In order to leave the port and move from one place to another, permits were required, though these were easily counterfeited, and if not available, wrote John Evelyn, 'money to the searcher and officers was as authentic as the hand and seal of Bradshaw [Head of the Council of State] himself'.

Margaret and Sir Charles soon had so little money left that they were forced to stop in Southwark and pawn his watch before they could finish their journey. With the aid of Newcastle's old steward they took modest lodgings in Covent Garden – not particularly fashionable, but suitable for persons in reduced circumstances. It would have been unwise for Margaret – the wife of such a notorious delinquent – to stay with her sisters.

Margaret had a sorrowful reunion with the remnants of her family and was often in their company revisiting old haunts, though there is no record that she ever visited Colchester again to see her mother's and brother's desecrated graves. In London there were fewer diversions for the visitor. The Spring Gardens had been closed – it was rumoured that Mrs Cromwell had been insulted there, but this may not have been the only reason. The Gardens had been going steadily downhill throughout the 1640s and had acquired a lewd reputation. Mulberry Gardens were, however, still open, and it was still possible to go to Hyde Park to picnic or to pick cherries as they had done before the Civil War. In the evenings there were other, private, entertainments. Although the public performance of music was forbidden, concerts were often held in people's houses, and even Cromwell had been known to stroll uninvited through the open doors of a private house, drawn by the music. Margaret was sometimes a guest at the house of the composer, Henry Lawes, where Puritans and Royalists mingled freely. Music was very much part of Margaret's life. She had a clear, sweet voice, well suited to the native English airs which Lawes set for solo voices and which were now replacing the madrigal in popularity. Margaret loved lyric poetry, writing in *Sociable Letters* that 'sweet words are better than a sweet sound, and when they are joined together it ravishes the soul'.

Shortly after her arrival Lawes gave a concert for the tenth anniversary of the marriage of Newcastle's second daughter Elizabeth, Countess of Bridgwater, and her husband. The Earl of Bridgwater had once performed in Milton's masque *Comus* – with music by Lawes – at Ludlow Castle to honour his father's appointment as Lord President of Wales. He had been in prison for his part in the Civil War, and was now keeping a strictly neutral stance. Margaret had not met her step-daughter before. The girls, Elizabeth, Jane and Frances, were of an age to have known their own mother well and therefore inclined to be critical of this strange, tongue-tied creature, only a little older than themselves and, it seems, already becoming addicted to the extravagances of dress that were to become legendary. 'Rumour,' wrote Margaret in 'A True Relation', 'did dress me in a hundred several fashions.' She disdained the fashion of the day, preferring to design her own dresses with the emphasis on comfort and suitability. Clothes, she insisted, should suit their purpose, whether it was for warmth, modesty or adornment. She hoped to be a leader of fashion, and took delight in looking different.

On Sundays it was always possible to find somewhere to listen to an Anglican service, though church services were proscribed and their participants ran the risk of arrest, the Book of Common Prayer being regarded as the mass in English. Church celebrations and feasts such as Christmas Day were forbidden. The churches had been purged of idolatrous ornament and ritual – St Martin's in the Fields became simply a meeting house and was called plain Martin's in the Fields. Although Anglican clergy were still allowed to preach, they shared their pulpits with lay preachers of dubious accomplishments whose message was often as much political as religious. Texts such as 'Now the Saints were called to destroy temporal governments' were a favourite at this time, anticipating and then subsequently justifying Cromwell's purge of Parliament and the so-called Rule of the Saints. Some of the preachers were women, including one of Margaret's friends who came to visit her and begged her opinion on extempory prayer. Margaret went to one of her services, and her description in *Sociable Letters* is worth quoting in full because it demonstrates her skill in mimicry and her ability to observe and record.

Since I last wrote to you, I have been to hear Mrs P.N. preach, for now she is, as I did believe she would be, viz a Preaching Sister. After she had sighed and winded out her Devotion, a Brother stood up and preached thus as I shall briefly relate to you. 'Dearly beloved Brethren and Sisters who are gathered together in the Lord with Purity of Spirits to Preach his word amongst us, we are the chosen and elect children of the Lord who have glorified Spirits and sanctified Souls, we have the Spirit of God in us, which inspires us to pray and to preach, as also to call upon his name and to remember him of his promise to Unite and Gather us together into his New Jerusalem.'

So, after the Holy Brother had done his praying, Mr N.N. who was there pulled off his Periwig and put on a night cap, wherein he appeareth so like a Holy Brother as they took him for one of their sect and he preached . . . but before he had quite ended his Sermon the Holy flock began to Bustle and at last went quite out of the room so that he might have prayed by himself had not I and two or three ladies more that were of my company stayed, and when he had done his short prayer he told me and the other ladies, that he had done that which the Great Council of State could not do, for he had by one short discourse dispersed a company of Sectaries without Noise or Disturbance.

In March General Ireton, Cromwell's son-in-law, who with Fairfax had been responsible for the execution of Lucas and Lisle, was given a state funeral through the streets of London, having died of plague in Ireland the previous November. Few mourned him. His funeral motto of '*Dulce et decorum est pro patria mori*' was translated by Royalists to mean 'It was good for his country that he should die.' In the same month there were total eclipses of both sun and moon, which seemed to symbolise for many the eclipses of the natural order of Church and State. Such was the superstitious fear they aroused that many people fled the capital.

England in the aftermath of the battle of Worcester was bewildered and confused. Active Royalists had either been imprisoned or fled into exile. Richard Fanshawe had been captured, and his wife Anne went every evening to stand beneath his window, whatever the weather. The cause seemed hopeless. The underground Royalist movement was fragmented and lacked leadership. Ordinary people witnessing the abolition of the House of Lords, the creation of a new flag and the renaming of the ships of the fleet complained, said the newssheet *Mercurius Pragmaticus*, that Old England was 'grown perfectly new, and we in another world'.

The events of the 1650s puzzled even the most intelligent people of the period. Something had been set in motion which was now out of control, wrote Gerard Winstanley in *The True Leveller's Standard Advanced*, and was 'running up like parchment on fire'. The House of Lords had been abolished; only a truncated House of Commons, nicknamed the Rump Parliament, remained and England was now a Commonwealth, governed by a Council of State. Between Worcester and the expulsion of the Rump even Cromwell was living in a strange state of unease. Although he was undoubtedly the most powerful member of the Council of State, he occupied no official position giving him overall authority among his peers apart from the Captain Generalship of the army. It was difficult for him to control and administer the policies he believed were vital to the health of the new state. The failure of the Commonwealth to devise any effective democratic system of executive government, with a recognisable hierarchy and proper accountability, was one of the reasons for the slide back towards autocracy which occurred during the next decade.

In February 1652 the Act of Oblivion was passed, designed to bury past grievances except against those declared guilty of treason. This left the way open for the exclusion of all those Royalists – like Newcastle – whom the government wished to penalise.

While the Parliamentary bureaucratic machinery began the slow task of assessing the Cavendish property, Margaret addressed herself to the renewal of old friendships breached by the Civil War. Her views, published in *Sociable Letters*, were admirable, if unrealistic:

> I hope I have given the Lady D.A. no cause to believe I am not her friend, though she has been of Parliament's and I of the King's side, yet I know no reason why that should make us enemies . . . for though there has been a Civil War in the kingdom and a general war amongst men, yet there has been none amongst women. Her ladyship is the same in my affection as if the kingdom had been in a calm peace.

These naïve sentiments betrayed how utterly out of touch Margaret had become with life and thought in England in the eight years that she had been in exile. Divisions had cut too deeply into English society for the wounds to heal quickly.

During the interregnum, between the execution of Charles I in 1649 and the Restoration of his son in 1660, London was a dull place to be, for all stage plays and other public entertainments were banned. People met quietly, secretly, in their own houses, aware that the tentacles of the Council of State extended even there. Besides being careful from a political point of view, Margaret had also to be careful of her reputation. She had been unpopular at court, and as a married lady unaccompanied by her husband her comings and goings were eagerly noted, driving Margaret to write indignantly in 'A True Relation': 'I never stirred out of my lodgings unless to see my brothers and sisters, nor seldom did I dress myself, since he I only desired to please was absent.'

Margaret was deeply affected by her separation from Newcastle. This misery and the nervous anxiety occasioned by her efforts to raise money made it difficult for her to sleep. She occupied the long hours before dawn in her room above the perpetually noisy streets of Covent Garden writing poetry by candlelight. In the year and a half that she was in England she completed a volume of poetry and composed a book entitled *Philosophical Fancies*. The results of Margaret's nocturnal musings are startling and sometimes grotesque. She wrote on 'Burning – why it Causes Pain', 'Flame Compared to the Tide of the Sea', 'The Circle of Honesty Squared',

'The Arithmetic of Passions' and 'The Head of a Man Compared to a Hive of Bees'. They are full of curious and bizarre conceits:

> Death is the Cook of Nature and we find,
> Meat dressed several ways to please her mind,
> Some meats she roasts with fevers, burning hot,
> And some she boils with dropsies in a pot.
> Some are consumed for jelly by degree,
> And some with ulcers, gravy out to squeeze
> Some as with herbs she stuffs with gouts and pains,
> Others for tender meat she hangs in chains.

There are similarities between some of her poems and those of Marvell, whose work had not been published at that time but may have been circulating in manuscript. Particularly striking is the resemblance between her 'Dialogue Between the Body and Mind' and Marvell's 'Dialogue Between the Soul and Body', which was written some time between 1645 and 1652 but not printed until 1681. Both, however, were drawing on Renaissance ideas and the medieval tradition of debate, and the choice of subject matter may be coincidental. However it does show that Margaret was familiar with these traditions and influenced by the same ideas as her contemporaries.

Margaret's poetry is uneven in quality, but this did not worry her. She sought a 'natural' style – metre and prosody seemed pedantic. One of the poems expounding this poetic ideal also demonstrates its limitations:

> Give me a free and noble style, that goes
> In an uncurbed strain, though wild it shows,
> For though it runs about it cares not where
> It shows more courage than it doth of fear.
> Give me a style that nature frames not art,
> For art doth seem to take the Pedant's part.

Margaret's fairy poems are, in contrast, particularly delicate. Queen Mab's palace is made of 'Hodmandod Shells', her bed carved from a cherry stone with sheets of 'the Skin of Dove's Eyes made'. Margaret was quite prepared to believe that fairies existed, and Newcastle's brother, Sir Charles Cavendish, could not resist teasing her a little.

> Sir Charles into my chamber coming in
> When I was writing of the Fairy Queen,
> 'I pray,' said he 'When Queen Mab you do see

Present my service to Her Majesty,
And tell her, I have heard fame's loud report
Both of her beauty and her stately court.'

When I Queen Mab within my fancy viewed
My thoughts bowed low fearing I should be rude
Kissing her garment thin, which Fancy made,
Kneeling upon a thought like one that prayed
And then in whispers soft I did present
His humble service which in Mirth was sent.

Also interesting is Margaret's use of domestic imagery in her poetry. There are poems entitled 'Nature's Wardrobe', 'An Olio dressed for Nature's Dinner', and a love poem composed entirely of food called 'Nature's Dessert':

Sweet marmalade of Kisses, newly gathered,
Preserved children which were never fathered.
Sugar of Beauty, which away melts soon
Marchpane of youth, and childish macaroon;
Sugarplum words, which fall sweet from the lips
And Wafer-promises mouldering like chips.
Biscuits of love, which crumble all away
Jelly of pear which shaked and quivering lay.

Among the best poems is the 'Dialogue between Mirth and Melancholy', in which Melancholy is the victor.

Then Melancholy with sad and sober face,
Complexion pale, but of a comely grace
With modest countenance thus softly spake,
May I so happy be your love to take?
True I am dull, yet by me you shall know,
More of yourself and so much wiser grow;
I search the depth and bottom of mankind
Open the eye of ignorance that's blind.
All dangers to avoid I watch with care,
And 'gainst evils that may come prepare.
I hang not on inconstant fortune's wheel
Nor yet with unresolving doubts do reel.
I dwell in groves that gilt are with the sun
Sit on the banks by which clear waters run,
In summer hot down in a shade I lie
My music is the buzzing of a fly
Which in the sunny beams doth dance all day

And harmlessly doth pass the time away.
I walk in meadows where grows the fresh green grass
In fields where corn is high I often pass . . .
Thus I am solitary, live alone
Yet better loved, the more that I am known
And tho' my face ill favoured at first sight
After acquaintance it will give delight,
Refuse me not, for I shall constant be
Maintain your credit and your dignity.

There are striking resemblances between this poem and Milton's 'L'Allegro' and 'Il Penseroso'. An article in *The Connoisseur* in 1775 suggested that Milton borrowed the idea from the Duchess, and some early Victorian critics put forward the same theory. Modern scholarship, however, dates Milton's poems earlier than Margaret's.

One short poem, not unlike Newcastle's in style, gives some idea of what Margaret was capable of:

Oh love, how thou art tired out with rhyme,
Thou art a tree whereon all poets climb,
And from thy tender branches every one
Doth take some fruit which Fancy feeds upon:
But now thy tree is left so bare and poor,
That they can hardly gather one plum more.

This poem is very important as a statement of Margaret's intentions as she began to develop her talent. She was gradually becoming determined to be different, to abandon that tree 'whereon all poets climb'. As a woman she was expected to write of love, romance, nature, religion. There was no real tradition of women's writing in England, but her precursors – Mary Sidney, writing towards the end of the sixteenth century, and Elizabeth Falkland and Mary Wrothe in the early years of the seventeenth – had led the public to expect such subjects from a woman's pen. As Margaret herself observed: 'Our sex is more apt to read than to write, and most commonly when any of our sex doth write they write some Devotion, or Romances, or Receipts of Medicines, for Cookery or Confectioners, or Complemental Letters, or a copy or two of Verses.'

Margaret purported to abhor romance, and despised women who spent their days reading the seventeenth-century equivalent of Mills and Boon. 'The chief study of our sex is Romances, wherein reading they fall in love with the feigned Heroes and Carpet Knights with whom their thoughts secretly commit adultery,' she wrote in *Sociable Letters*. She herself craved stronger meat and, like Charlotte Brontë, each time she took up her pen she refused to think always of what was 'feminine' and 'becoming'. But in expressly denying a woman's role she also denied and distorted a large part of her talent. She had the ability to become a first-class writer of fiction – the power of her imagination as revealed in her earliest writings is acute. A poem describing an imaginary world, 'In an Earring', and another describing worlds within worlds like a nest of boxes are both brilliant fantasies well thought out, and then justified by a third poem admonishing the reader that 'Nothing doth so hard to Nature's Eyes, As to believe Impossibilities'. She was also capable of minute, honest observation. Not for her the glorification of country life exemplified in 'Come Live with Me and Be My Love'; Margaret's shepherdesses refuse to trip lightly through green pastures – their complexions are yellow from the sun, their lips cracked by the wind, and they have dirty hands.

When Margaret abandoned love in favour of originality it was in fact a useful ploy. Donne, Marvell and Milton were all well known, and Margaret's verses would not have merited a second glance except for their extraordinary subject matter and the fact that they were written by a woman. Having denied herself romance, she wrote on subjects not obviously suited to poetic treatment and quite definitely regarded as the exclusive preserve of the men – outrageous verses on the lode stone, on whether fish have brains and whether the stars are fiery jellies or chips off the sun; she discussed the motion of the planets, vacuums, the shape of atoms, the 'attraction' of the earth and the nature of wind and weather.

> Who knows but Thunders are great winds, which lie
> Within the middle vault above the sky,
> Which wind the sun on moisture cold begot,
> When he is in his region Cancer hot.
> This child is thin and subtle, made by heat
> Its thinness makes it agile, agile, strong
> Which by its force doth drive the clouds along
> And when the clouds do meet, they each do strike
> Flashing out fire, as do flints the like.
> Thus in the summer thunder's caused by wind
> Vapour drawn so high, no way out can find.
> But in the winter, when the clouds are loose
> Then doth the wind on earth keep rendezvous.

She was also simultaneously developing these ideas in her book *Philosophical Fancies*; exploring theories gleaned from Hobbes and Descartes, examining arguments between Newcastle and Sir Charles on the discoveries of the chemist Van Helmont, and defending some of the ideas expressed in her poems. In both this work and the poems she attacked fanciful notions with vigorous common sense:

> There have been many learned and studious men, which have been accounted sages of former, present and it may be also of future times; but in my opinion they have had very improbable, and I may say very extravagant opinions in Natural Philosophy, as for example that thunder is caused by frozen clouds and roves of Ice falling upon each other. If so, most of the creatures upon the earth would be knocked on the head in times and places of thunder, for I cannot perceive but clouds and roves of ice should fall down upon the earth more forcibly than hail or snow, for the natural air cannot uphold those solid clouds of ice when they cannot uphold light flakes of snow and small hail.

It would be fascinating to know how much contact Margaret had with the work of the Puritan poets Marvell and Milton while she was in London, or whether she met Mrs Katherine Philips – known as the 'Matchless Orinda'. She may also have seen the English translations of le Moyne's *Gallerie des Femmes Fortes* and Cornelius Agrippa's *Female Pre-eminence*, which were published during her stay.

At some point in 1652 she took the very important decision to publish, or 'put forth', as she phrased it, her poems and philosophical pieces. Margaret's writing was dramatically different from that of other women before her, not only in the range and type of subject matter – philosophy, essays, literary criticism, stories, plays – but in the way she wrote. Margaret did not write just for her own pleasure, but with the aim of printing and distributing her works. She had no intention of scribbling in her closet and hoping for her husband, or one of her other relatives, to print the results after her death.

Chapter Eight

In Search of a Tradition
1652 – 3

I am obnoxious to each carping tongue
Who says my hand a needle better fits,
A poet's pen all scorn I should thus wrong,
For such despite they cast on female wits;
If what I do prove well, it won't advance,
They'll say it's stol'n or else it was by chance.

Anne Bradstreet, *The Tenth Muse*

Margaret, although only a spectator of the changes taking place in England and a firm adherent of the Royalist cause, was nevertheless able to absorb and evaluate the new ideas generated by the political situation. During the Commonwealth tremendous developments in political thought were put forward by Hobbes, Winstanley, Milton and many others. In 1651 Milton published *The First Defence of the People of England*, in which he argued that Commonwealth is superior to monarchy on the grounds that it is more democratic and can therefore never deteriorate into tyranny. He also published a tract on divorce – allowed for the first time. Winstanley, the Leveller pamphleteer, argued for true equality, universal education including book learning, and vocational training for both men and women. He also wanted to abolish the clerical monopoly of biblical interpretation.

Not all of them agreed about the class system on which the government of the kingdom depended. The Levellers argued that the removal of the king was of little effect if the aristocracy remained intact and repressive. Hobbes stated that absolute liberty and property were incompatible. He believed that if everyone was equal there would still have to be an overriding umpire, otherwise anarchy would result. Milton defended the Commonwealth, and at the same time affirmed in *Paradise Lost* that 'Orders and Degrees Jarr not with Liberty, but well consist.'

Little was said about the enfranchisement of women. In *Sociable Letters* Margaret argued that they were neither citizens nor subjects.

And as for the matter of Governments, we Women understand them not, yet if we did, we are excluded from intermeddling

86

thereto; we are not tied, nor bound to State or Crown; we are free, not Sworn to Allegiance, nor do we take the Oath of Supremacy; we are not made Citizens of the Commonwealth; we hold no offices, nor bear we any Authority therein; we are accounted neither Useful in Peace, nor Serviceable in War; and if we be not Citizens in the Commonwealth I know no reason we should be Subjects to the Commonwealth; and the Truth is, we are no subjects unless it be to our Husbands.

Winstanley's statement of the common hope that 'this Commonwealth's freedom will unite the hearts of Englishmen together in love' was not coming true. The various factions all disagreed over key points as well as political philosophy. Obvious reforms like that of the tithe system were never made, because no one could agree on new systems to replace the old. Most people were not even sure within themselves of the right course to take.

According to William Lilly, the fashionable astrologer, Parliament began to grow 'odious unto all good men, the members whereof became insufferable in their pride, covetousness, self-ends, laziness, minding nothing but how to enrich themselves'. Not all MPs were corrupt; there remained, wrote William Lilly, a kernel of 'very able, judicious and worthy patriots' who felt unable to challenge the majority and who 'by their silence, only served themselves; all was carried on by a rabble of dunces, who . . . voted what seemed best to their non-intelligent fancies'.

Bulstrode Whitelocke, chronicler of events during the Commonwealth, wrote that dissatisfaction focused on the Rump. In November 1652 Cromwell, walking alone in St James's Park, met Whitelocke and desired to have some private discourse with him. It was important, he said 'that the Lord having given us an entire conquest over our enemies we should not now hazard all again by our private janglings, and bring those mischiefs upon ourselves which our enemies could never do'. Parliament was daily 'breaking forth into new and violent parties and factions'. They were making too many 'delays of business and design to perpetuate themselves and to contrive the power in their own hands'. Nor could they be 'kept within the bounds of justice and law or reason', being answerable to no one but themselves. Whitelocke states that it was during this conversation that Cromwell posed the question: 'What if a man should take it upon him to be King?' Dismayed, Whitelocke replied that 'all those who were for a commonwealth (and they are a very great and considerable party) having their hopes frustrated, will desert you, your hands will be weakened, your interest straitened, and your cause in apparent danger to be ruined'. His advice was not well received, and Whitelocke records that there was a certain coolness in the Captain General's manner towards him from that day on.

On 20 April 1653 Cromwell, hearing that Parliament was discussing a bill to prolong its own life when he had been given to understand that they were about to terminate their existence, was so enraged by their duplicity that he entered the Chamber with three files of musketeers and, after a furious speech in which he accused them of being drunkards, whore masters, corrupt and unjust men, turned them all out of the House and, Whitelocke wrote in his *Memorials*, bade his men take away 'that fool's bauble, the Mace'. The Rump disappeared, unlamented, and a few days later a facetious notice was pinned to the door: 'This House is to be Lett; now Unfurnished.'

Margaret's attitude to politics was cynical. 'The truth is,' she wrote in *Divers Orations*, 'many politicians will be apter to dissolve than to agree to make good laws and will sooner cause a destruction than govern a commonwealth.' Her quick ear picked out the absurdities of Puritan speech, enabling her to mimic them cruelly in her plays and letters.

She made several attempts to write about the Civil War and her experiences. The earliest, *Phantasm's Masque*, is an allegorical autobiography – the 'Voyage of a Ship under which the Fortune of a Young Lady is Expressed'. It anticipates her more successful venture in prose, and has some good lines, although the use of a ship as a metaphor for Margaret herself was unoriginal. An ambitious poem on the origin and progress of the Civil War, published in *Poems and Fancies*, begins pretentiously: 'There was an Island rich by nature's grace'. It continues with rather strained imagery – 'armies of waves in troops, high tides brought on' – and soon the island becomes a place

> Where malice boiled with rancour, spleen and spite,
> In war and fraud, injustice took delight,
> Thinking which way their lusts they might fulfil,
> Committed thefts, rapes, murders at their will,
> Parents and children did unnatural grow
> And every friend was turned a cruel foe
> Nay, innocency no protection had,
> Religious men were thought to be stark mad,

Frontispiece of The World's Olio, *1671 edition, engraved by Abraham van Diepenbeke, showing Margaret Cavendish in her closet. Reproduced by permission of the British Library.*

The Loyal Sacrifice, *1648: a pamphlet depicting the execution of Sir Charles Lucas and Sir George Lisle by Thomas Fairfax after the Siege of Colchester. Reproduced by permission of the British Library.*

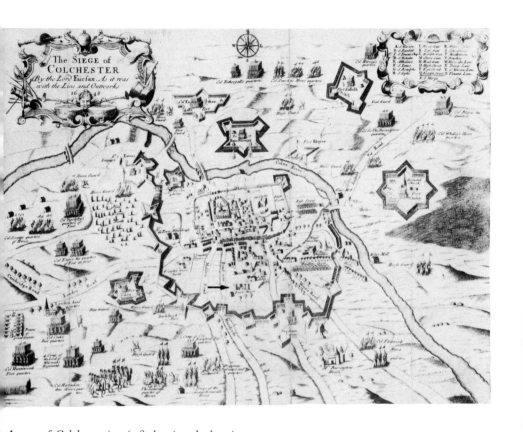

*A map of Colchester in 1648 showing the location
of St John's Abbey, the 'Lucas House' which was
totally destroyed during the Siege of Colchester.
Reproduced by permission of the British Library.*

On the following pages:
*Margaret Cavendish, Duchess of Newcastle, by
Sir Peter Lely, 1663–4. From a private
collection.*

*William Cavendish, 1st Duke of Newcastle. This
is a copy of the Van Dyck original at Welbeck
Abbey. It was commissioned by Edward Hyde,
Earl of Clarendon, when the Duke was installed
as Knight of the Garter in 1661. It now hangs in
the Palace of Westminster. Reproduced by
permission of the Earl of Clarendon.*

Margaret Daughter
to Tho. Lucas Es. of

Parties de La maison HILWERVE Anuers. 1694

*Welbeck Abbey. One of several engravings by
Abraham van Diepenbeke for William
Cavendish's manual of horsemanship* Methode et
invention Nouvelle de dresser les Chevaux,
*1658. Reproduced by permission of the British
Library.*

On the previous pages:
*The Rubenshuis, engraved by J. Harrewijn in
1692. This house was rented to the Duke and
Duchess of Newcastle by Rubens' widow and was
their home during their years of exile.*
© *Museum Rubenshuis, Antwerp.*

In witches, wizards they did put their trust,
Extortion, bribes were thought to be more just
Like Titan's race all did in tumults rise
And 'gainst the heavens utter blasphemies.

'Witches and wizards' may be a sneering reference to William Lilly and Elias Ashmole, the noted astrologers known to be consulted by many leading Puritans. There was a great vogue for astrology at the time. Whitelocke sent his urine to be analysed regularly by William Lilly, who had also been present at the siege of Colchester to advise Fairfax. Lady Eleanor Davies had also achieved much credibility with Queen Henrietta Maria before the outbreak of Civil War, correctly predicting her pregnancies and the assassination of Charles' favourite, the notorious womaniser Buckingham. Both she and William Lilly wrote books on the subject. Margaret did not believe in astrology, nor in the supernatural nor the existence of witches, and she wrote scathingly about those who did. Her common sense would not allow her to believe that all who were born at the same moment could possibly be the same or have the same fate.

When not sitting, as she called it, at the Well of Helicon, in Greek mythology sacred to the Muses, much of Margaret's time was occupied with the problem of Newcastle's relief. Sir Charles successfully compounded for his estates, meeting the fine of £5000 by selling off land. So many others were doing so at the same time that the land market was at rock bottom. It was common for purchasers to bribe surveyors to undervalue estates still further. Jewellery and silver could also be had for a fraction of their pre-war value. There was a fortune to be made for anyone in a position to indulge in long-term speculation; many an eighteenth-century gentleman owed his wealth to the wit of his forefathers during the interregnum.

While Margaret and Sir Charles waited to gain entrance to his estates, they struggled to obtain credit from friends in order to live. Many feared to assist them, lest it should prejudice their own compositions. Eventually the time came for Newcastle's estates to be sold, and Margaret was taken by her brother John to Goldsmiths' Hall to claim a portion for her support.

Margaret's petition was summarily dismissed; the reason given was that she had married after her husband had been made a delinquent. She privately maintained that it was because he was one of the greatest traitors to the state, and possibly this and the lack of young children to be provided for influenced the court's decision. Margaret found the public proceedings embarrassing and distressing, and after forbidding her brother to argue the case further asked him, in mingled rage and humiliation, to escort her out of the building.

After the failure of her mission Margaret was uncertain what to do next, being, as she wrote in 'A True Relation', 'unpractised in public employments, ignorant of the humours and disposition of those persons to whom I was to address my suit and not knowing where the power lay'. Margaret's pride forbade her to crawl, and so Newcastle's suit went unpursued. Had she had the courage to take her suit to the highest level, like Betty Mordaunt, she might have been more successful. Elizabeth, Viscountess Mordaunt was the wife of John Mordaunt, a staunch Royalist condemned to death in 1658. He was reprieved after Betty appealed personally to Cromwell. Anne Verney and Lady Isabella Twysdale were also successful in personal petitions.

The Civil War and the Commonwealth gave women the opportunity to do many things that lay outside their normal experience. Many of the political pamphleteers were female, and women formed a large percentage of the membership of the Puritan sects. They had a share in their management and the formulation of doctrine that had never been allowed in the Anglican Church, besides having the right to preach. In the absence of their husbands and fathers women on both sides of the divide found themselves doing jobs usually reserved for men. Many of them, like Margaret, had to deal with the legal and bureaucratic machine in the place of husbands who were either in prison or in exile.

Paradoxically, Margaret disapproved of the new licence and the way women conducted themselves in their new roles, writing in *The World's Olio*:

> The customs of England being changed as well as the laws where women become Pleaders, Attorneys, Petitioners and the like, running about their several causes, complaining of their several grievances, exclaiming against their several enemies, bragging of their several favours they receive from the powerful; thus trafficing with idle words bring in false reports and vain discourse; for the truth is our Sex doth nothing but jostle for the pre-eminence in words . . . but if our Sex would but well consider and rationally ponder they will perceive and find that it is neither words nor place that can advance them but Worth and Merit.

Why such an insistent advocate for greater freedom for women should condemn those who exercised such freedom is difficult to assess. It may have been the manner in which it was exercised which was under attack. Margaret was always a severe critic of women's behaviour. She felt that women would have to be very careful in the use of new rights and privileges if they were ever to be taken seriously and win the respect of men.

While in a state of despair following the committee's refusal, Margaret received news from Antwerp that Newcastle required immediate relief if he was not to starve, for his creditors had once more run out of patience. It was Margaret's recurrent nightmare, she wrote in her biography, that he would be sent to the debtors' prison 'where sadness of mind, and want of exercise and Air, would have wrought his destruction'. Sir Charles resolved if possible to buy his brother's two principal residences of Bolsover and Welbeck, at the cost of selling off more of his own land. He then settled these estates on Newcastle's sons, with the proviso that they return them to their father should the opportunity arise. Margaret went diligently every day to Drury House, where the committee for compounding were sitting, to discover how the rest of his estates were being disposed of, and to make careful notes of their new owners. Before Sir Charles could raise the money Bolsover was sold to a speculator who intended to pull down the building and use the materials – some fine dressed stone and a large quantity of lead. It was eventually bought back, though at a much higher price, notwithstanding that part of it had already been demolished. Welbeck was also secured, but not Newcastle's town house in Clerkenwell. Sir Charles could now be reasonably confident that, despite the ruin of the estates, some small portion might be spared from the rents to provide his brother with an assured, if meagre, income. His sons also sent him money, and his eldest daughter Jane, now married to Charles Cheyne, sold jewels and some silver plate left to her by her grandmother and sent the proceeds to Newcastle for his immediate relief. Meanwhile, the Marquis had called his creditors together and used his eloquence to extend their credit; his pride by now worn almost as thin as their patience.

The Nominated Parliament – nicknamed the Barebones Parliament after one of its members, Praisegod Barebones – replaced the discredited Rump, and once more there were high hopes. However, this blatant abrogation of constitutional power and Cromwell's growing dictatorship worried many who, like Milton, had believed that Commonwealth could not descend into tyranny, but who had failed to resolve the problem of an equal over equals. Colonel Hutchinson, a committed Parliamentarian whose estates marched with Newcastle's, was particularly disgusted at Cromwell's exercise of arbitrary power. He saw Cromwell's support by the army in a sinister light. According to Hutchinson's wife Lucy, Cromwell 'grew wanton with their power and invented a thousand tricks of government which when nobody opposed they themselves fell to dislike and vary every day . . . He makes up several sorts of mock Parliaments but not finding one of them absolutely for his turn, turned them off again.' Furthermore he 'set up a company of silly mean fellows . . . as governors in every country' and 'at last took it upon himself to make Lords and Knights and wanted not many fools . . . to accept of and strut in its mock titles'. Far from the Commonwealth of social equality they had fought for, they discovered that they had created another monarch who was gathering his own court around him and setting up his own instruments of tyranny. From limited suffrage they had sunk to no suffrage at all.

In 1653, during her last months in England, Margaret prepared her volume of poems and her *Philosophical Fancies* for publication. It was this act, rather than the writing of them, which was so universally condemned. Even male writers rarely published, but circulated their work in manuscript. Anne Winchelsea observed in her *Poems* that women needed not only the 'skill to write', but also the 'modesty to hide'. Women might write, but to publish their work was the equivalent of Lady Godiva's ride through the streets of Coventry. It was an extension of the idea that women inhabited a purely private sphere, while public life belonged to men. In *Epistle to a Lady* Pope gave clear expression to these views:

> But grant in public, men sometimes are shown,
> A woman's seen in private life alone;
> Our bolder talents in full light displayed
> Your virtues open fairest in the shade.

One event which may have precipitated Margaret's decision was the publication of the Puritan Anne Bradstreet's *Poems* in 1650, but the French influence must also have been strong.

There were certainly few English precedents for Margaret's action. Most of the texts we know today were private documents, diaries, memoirs, letters, devotions, known only to the family and a few close friends. Occasionally a small volume would be published by loving relatives as a memorial after the author had died. Even so dedicated and accomplished a poet as Katherine Philips disclaimed the intention of writing for public view; she thought the occupation 'unfit for the sex to which I belong'. When the first edition of her poetry appeared in print she was so distracted that she became ill and claimed vehemently that it had been published without her knowledge or permission. She declared that she had never 'writ any line in my life with any intention to have it printed'. This 'cruel accident' not only affected her health, but, she wrote in a letter to her husband, prevented her from making a visit to London: 'I must never show my face there or among any reasonable people again.'

Margaret made no modest pretence of her intentions. She was, as her maid Elizabeth eulogised, 'The First', and all who came after must own her 'as their pattern'. Her motives were clear; thirty years later Mary Astell confessed to a similar motive and in *A Serious Proposal* exhorted women to 'exalt and establish your fame'. It was a way of escaping the terrible anonymity of women's lives. Margaret's books were her posterity, bearing her own particular stamp, for 'Fame is a report that travels far and many times lives long, and the older it grows the more it flourishes and is the more particularly a man's own than the child of his loins.' This brand of immortality, she argued, should be extended to women.

It would be too simplistic to ascribe her longing for fame only to her lack of offspring. The truth was that she possessed a great natural gift and an insatiably curious mind, both totally frustrated by the restrictions placed on her sex. 'That my ambition . . . is restless and not ordinary I cannot deny; and since all heroic actions, public employments (as well civil as military) and eloquent pleadings are denied my sex in this age, I may be excused for writing so much.' If other idle women followed her example, she wrote, it would be preferable to them 'winding up the thread of their lives in snarls and unsound bottoms'. In 1697, in the second part of *A Serious Proposal*, Mary Astell urged women to do likewise, whatever the risks.

> Are you afraid of being out of the ordinary way and therefore admir'd and gaz'd at? . . . She shall never do anything praise-worthy and excellent who is not got above unjust censures, and too steady and well resolv'd to be sham'd from her Duty by the empty laughter of such as have nothing but airy Noise and Confidence to recommend them.

Margaret's deliberate publicity-seeking seems at odds with her extreme shyness, which, she wrote, rose often in blushes and contracted her spirits to a chill paleness when confronted with strangers. Her need to speak and to be heard was greater than her fear of public censure.

Margaret dedicated her *Poems* to Sir Charles Cavendish, with whom she had developed a very close relationship. Described by Aubrey in his *Brief Lives* as a 'little, weak, crooked man', he had great personal courage and despite his physical disability he had fought alongside Newcastle in the Civil War. This clever, scholarly gentleman took the place of Margaret's serious elder brother John, the person to whom she had always turned when she wished to have something explained. Sir Charles encouraged Margaret's literary productions, and his help was gratefully acknowledged.

The volume of *Poems* and *Philosophical Fancies* were copied by an amanuensis and sent to the printers with Newcastle's permission. Margaret awaited their publication with trepidation, anticipating the public condemnation that was sure to follow. She armed herself as if for a battle, directing her book of *Poems* 'To all Noble and Worthy Ladies'. Using the very arguments she professed to have abandoned, she exhorted them to

> condemn me not as a dishonour of your sex for setting forth this work, for it is harmless and free from all dishonesty, besides, Poetry which is built upon Fancy, women may claim as a work belonging most properly to themselves . . . but I imagine I shall be censured by my own sex; and men will cast a smile of scorn upon my book, because they think thereby women encroach too much upon their prerogatives, for they hold books as their crown and the sword as their sceptre, by which they rule and govern . . . Therefore pray strengthen my side, in defending my book for I know women's tongues are as sharp as two-edged swords. And in this battle may your wit be quick and your speech ready and your arguments so strong as to beat them out of the field of dispute. So shall I get honour and reputation by your favours – otherwise I may chance to be cast into the fire. But if I burn, I desire to die your martyr.

Margaret was right to anticipate that the most fervent condemnation would come from her own sex when she led the movement from private to public life. John Evelyn's wife's attitude was typical.

Women were not born to read authors and censure the learned, to compare lives and judge of virtues, to give rules of morality and sacrifice to the Muses. We are willing to acknowledge all time borrowed from family duties misspent; the care of children's education, observing a husband's commands, assisting the sick, relieving the poor and being serviceable to our friends, are of

sufficient weight to employ the most improved capacities amongst
us. If sometimes it happens by accident that one of a thousand
aspires a little higher, her fate commonly exposes her to wonder,
but adds little to esteem . . . A heroine is a kind of prodigy; the
influence of a blazing star is not more dangerous or more avoided.

As Mary Evelyn's letter was written in 1672, it is possible that
Margaret was in her mind when she wrote it.

Another literate lady, Dorothy Osborne, wrote to her lover
William Temple:

Let me ask you if you have seen a book of Poems newly come
out, made by my lady Newcastle. For God's sake if you meet
with it send it me, they say it is ten times more Extravagant than
her dress. Sure, the poor woman is a little distracted, she could
never be so ridiculous else as to venture at writing books – and
in verse too. If I should not sleep this fortnight I should not
come to that.

The publication of her books was a pinnacle of achievement for
Margaret and she gloried in it, writing in *Sociable Letters*: 'I love
those best which I create myself, and Nature hath taught me to
prize whatsoever is my own most, though of small value, than what's
another's, though of greater worth.'

Chapter Nine

By a Woman Writ
1653 – 5

Did I my lines intend for public view,
How many censures would their faults pursue,
Some would, because such works they do affect,
Cry they're insipid, empty, uncorrect.
And many have attained dull and untaught
The name of Wit, only by finding fault.
True judges might condemn their want of wit
And all might say, they're by a Woman writ.

Anne Winchelsea, *Poems*

In 1653, having been back in England for a year and a half, Margaret received some disturbing news from Antwerp: 'Some intelligence which I received of my lord's being not very well.' Whether this communication concerned his physical health – he was now sixty – or the 'weakness of the flesh and disturbance of the soul' referred to in one of his early unpublished poems, is unclear. Margaret was consistently over-anxious for the health of those whom she loved and was concerned enough, despite the unfinished nature of her business, to pack and depart hastily for Antwerp.

It is not unreasonable to wonder whether the passionate Newcastle had taken a mistress during his wife's long absence. Margaret admits in his biography that he was 'not addicted to any manner of Vice, except that he has been a great lover and admirer of the Female Sex'. There are hints of infidelity during his first marriage, but no obvious scandals. Court gossip clearly thought him to be a womaniser, though such promiscuity was accepted as normal in a man of his position. Newcastle outlined the situation in a frank poem called 'Love's Constellation', written to Margaret before their marriage. The aristocratic gentleman

> Thinks greatest ladies prostitute must be
> Unto his will, though under honour's locks
> Courts these, but with a whore doth get the pox,
> Or else his high ambition ends in stench,
> Lays his great fury with a kitchen wench

96

> Or else doth worse for to save charges and
> Like a good husband makes for whore his hand.

There are a series of undated, short, erotic poems, similar in handwriting, ink and paper to others written during his marriage to Elizabeth Basset, which concern various household servants, maids and laundresses and which make one wonder whether Newcastle, like the gentleman depicted in Margaret's plays and stories, laid 'his great fury' with his own female servants. The double standard of sexual morality prevailed.

In one of her published letters, often autobiographical and almost always expounding her own views, Margaret reveals a pragmatic attitude to what she privately regarded as an obnoxious situation.

> W.C.'s lady hath heard of her husband's mistress, but she seems not to be angry at it, but talks of it with great patience, saying that if her husband takes pleasure in variety he will be more delighted with her wit than with his mistress' beauty . . . Besides, said she, Wit attracts the mind more to Love than Beauty to Admiration, and if my husband loves me best I am well content he should admire her beauty most.

There was little that a woman could do.

Sir Charles Cavendish had intended to escort Margaret back to Antwerp, but unfortunately he became ill with an 'ague' – a form of malaria – more severe than usual and the doctors recommended that he should go to the country to convalesce. Margaret travelled back accompanied by four menservants and four maids. She felt guilty about leaving Sir Charles in such poor health, but subsequently, in 'A True Relation', excused her abrupt departure on the grounds that 'I should have been a trouble rather than any ways serviceable, besides more charge the longer I stayed', and it was obvious that her conscience troubled her. Sir Charles' constitution had never been strong, and shortly after Margaret's return 'his ague did put out the Lamp of his life'.

Back in Antwerp, joyfully reunited with her husband, words continued to pour from Margaret's pen. She wrote so fast in order to keep up with the fancies in her brain that her handwriting, always a 'ragged rout', as she described it in 'A True Relation', became at times totally illegible. It was the only activity that gave her any real pleasure. Newcastle, anxious for her health, begged her to take more exercise, but she paid little heed. A letter written in Antwerp probably refers to her: 'When she is sick, promises if ever she recover she will take the air and use exercises, but being restored to health, she forgets her promise, or only looks out of a window for once or twice and walks two or three turns a day in her chamber, which is as little exercise as she can do.'

Margaret disapproved of exercise, and regarded any pastime which produced perspiration as downright harmful. Dancing was unbecoming to the gravity of the married state, swimming incurred more risk than advantage, and those that played at tennis impaired their health and strength, she declared in *Sociable Letters*, and wasted 'their vital spirits through much sweating . . . There can be no recreation in sweaty labour.' When Newcastle became ill after becoming overheated exercising his horses, it only served to prove her point.

Margaret's shyness and dislike of meeting people did not improve as she grew older, and exaggerated her naturally reclusive disposition. In *Sociable Letters* she explained that her personality 'not merry, makes me think myself not fit for company'. The occasional social forays she made only confirmed her in her habits. When she could bring herself to speak it was usually at the wrong moment and with a complete disregard for tact. Invited to a christening, she listened to the other women gossiping (something she could not endure) and remarked that they should not complain of their husbands' faults, 'for if they had faults it was the wives' duty not to divulge them, and if their husbands would speak of them and tell their faults it was likely they would equal their husbands . . . if not surpass them'; but the ladies being 'heated with wine, and then at my words, with anger fell into such a fury with me as they fell upon me, not with blows but with words, . . . I became as silent as if I had been dead . . . and came away, and it hath so frighted me as I shall not hastily go to a gossiping meeting again.' Margaret found it difficult to talk to other women, having little in common with them. They were unlikely to want to discuss Plutarch's *Lives*, or Harvey's discovery of the circulation of the blood, and she was unable to join in the anecdotes about housewifery and child-bearing – that useful bridge between women of any class or culture. She was also impatient with the stupidity and complacency of women, feeling that such frivolous behaviour only fuelled men's arguments that, just as women's bodies were weaker than men's, so were their minds. She was scathing about their habits and employment; in the play of the same name Lady Contemplation says: 'Many of our effeminate sex do hurt the lungs with over-exercising of their tongues not only with licking and tasting of sweetmeats, but with chattering and prating, twitling and twatling.'

The reunion with Newcastle once again failed to produce the desired pregnancy, and Margaret came to terms with her infertility with remarkable resolution.

> A woman hath no reason to desire children for her own sake, for first her name is lost to her . . . in her marrying . . . also she hazards her life in bringing them into the world, and hath the greatest share of trouble in bringing them up; married women desire children as maids do husbands, more for Honour than for comfort or happiness, thinking it a disgrace to live old maids, and so likewise to be barren.

But there is a note of bitterness in some of her letters when she writes of pregnant women who spend exorbitant sums on bedlinen for their lying in, and behave in an affected manner. Of one woman she wrote in *Sociable Letters*,

> I had not seen her since she was a Wife and had been Married which was some four Weeks ago, wherefore I did not know she was with child, but the rasping wind out of her Stomach as Childing-women usually do, making Sickly Faces to express a Sickly Stomach and fetching her breath short and leaning out her Body, drawing her Neck downward and standing in a weak and faint Posture as great bellied wives do bearing a heavy Burden in them, told me she had been with child a fortnight, though by her behaviour one would not have thought she had above a week to go.

Increasingly Margaret sought honour in literature. Her books, large volumes handsomely bound in leather, were now available to the public, and people's response to their contents was, just as she had feared, as bigoted as it had been to the mere fact of their publication. On 7 May 1653 Dorothy Osborne wrote to her lover that she had managed to obtain a copy of the poems and was 'satisfied that there are many soberer people in Bedlam, I'll swear her friends are much to blame to let her go abroad'. Edmund Waller declared that he would give all his own compositions for her verses on 'The Death of a Stag', adding that 'Nothing was too much to be given, that a lady might be saved from the disgrace of such a vile performance.' Others, conversely, said that they were too good to be written by a woman. Newcastle was a well-known poet and playwright – two of his plays had been published before Margaret left for England –

and so his hand was suspected. These paradoxical quibblings moved Margaret to write a passionate, exasperated epistle, published in *Observations on Experimental Philosophy*:

> But though the world would not believe that those conceptions and fancies which I writ were my own, but transcended my capacity, yet they found fault, that they were defective for want of learning, and on the other side they said I had plucked feathers out of the universities, and thought it impossible that a woman could have so much learning and understanding in terms of art and scholastical expressions, so that I and my books are like the old apologue in Aesop, of a father, and his son, who rid on an ass through a town when his father went on foot. The old man received so many blemishes and aspersions for the sake of his ass, that he was at last resolved to drown him when he came to the next bridge. But I am not so passionate to burn my writing for the various humours of mankind, and for their finding fault, since there is nothing in this world, be it the noblest and most commendable action whatsoever, that shall escape blameless.

Margaret herself was to blame for some of the criticism she incurred. She refused to edit her work, declaring that there was 'more pleasure in making than in mending'. She begged the reader's indulgence for her errors, adding flippantly that in any case, 'I had nothing to do when I wrote it, and I suppose those have nothing or little else to do that read it' – an attitude not calculated to impress her critics. Newcastle himself was too amiable and careless in his own literary endeavours to discipline his wife's effusions. After the death of Sir Charles there was no one else whose judgement she trusted. Her years at court had hardened her to public criticism, though it never ceased to give her pain.

Margaret's lack of education and limited field of reference constituted another flaw. Educated people were supposed to have a great range of knowledge and experience, not only of the world of letters but of politics, law, religion, philosophy and science. This was gained at university, the court and by travelling. Margaret was at a disadvantage, barely able to write a legible hand or spell a word the same way twice in one sentence.

Whatever his peccadilloes, Newcastle was, in Margaret's words, 'a kind husband and a constant friend', though his embarrassment must at times have been acute as his wife became the subject of public debate on account of her literary activities. Pepys described Newcastle as 'an ass', not just for allowing his wife to make an exhibition of herself, but for 'suffering her to speak of him' in her books. A cruel anecdote ascribed to Newcastle on the subject of clever women may well be true. On being complimented about his wife, he is reported to have said: 'A wise woman is a very foolish thing.' But he saw, better than anyone, the intellectual qualities that his wife possessed and knew what she was striving to achieve. He never begrudged the money spent on printing her books and, despite his financial situation, when she returned to Antwerp, he bought Margaret the perfectly matched pearl earrings and necklace she wears in all her portraits. Queen Henrietta Maria herself had nothing finer.

In some quarters Margaret's open publication was welcomed, despite the ridicule it attracted, but she was sceptical that her example would do anything to better the lot of women. In *Sociable Letters* she said: 'You write in your last letter that I had given our sex courage and confidence to write, and to divulge what they writ in print, but give me leave humbly to tell you, that it is no commendation to give them courage and confidence if I cannot give them wit.' She used 'wit' in the old sense of 'intelligence'. The stupidity and silliness of women in general was an obstacle to their advancement for which she could see no cure – 'women breeding up women, one fool breeding up another, and as long as that custom lasts there is no hope of amendment', says Lady Sanspareille in *Love's Adventures*.

The lack of levity and the apparently joyless lifestyle of female intellectuals like Bathsua Makin, Mary Astell and even Katherine Philips was apt to give ordinary women the impression that intellect and pleasure were antipathetic. Part of their fault lay in their isolation – in Margaret's case self-imposed. Those who had attained these mental acquisitions, wrote Mary Berry in *Home Life of English Ladies in the Seventeenth Century*,

> instead of becoming more agreeable or more intelligent members of society, were in general so estranged from the world and its ways and from the duties of their sex and situation that their example was little likely to be followed by others, whose more natural dispositions inclined them to please and to live like the rest of the world.

The pressure on women to display a 'natural disposition' was enormous, and those who could not conform became outcasts. Elizabeth Elstob, the famous Anglo-Saxon scholar, died dirty and unkempt among her books, Katherine Philips was rumoured to be a lesbian,

Mary Astell was described as a man-hating spinster, Aphra Behn and Mary Manley were reputed to be whores, and Margaret Cavendish herself was nicknamed 'Mad Madge'. The ideal was Lady Langham, who was praised by Mary Berry for using her 'knowledge and learning only to capacitate her to make the best improvement of her husband', from whom 'she was ever ready to receive instruction'.

It was also believed – a belief fostered by men – that men preferred empty-headed, pliable women, unable to think for themselves. 'To make women learned and foxes tame' had the same effect, to make them more cunning, and incurred 'all those inconveniences which some have fancied, so necessarily accompany a Learned Wife', wrote Samuel Clarke in 1683 in *The Lives of Sundry Eminent Persons*. In Gisborne's *Duties of Women* they were urged to consider the importance of their roles as wives and mothers, and 'the real and deeply interesting effects which the conduct of their sex will always have on the happiness of society . . . It is like the dew of heaven which descends at all seasons, returns after short intervals and permanently nourishes every herb of the field.' The Angel in the House, Virginia Woolf's domestic adversary, the male ideal of submission and self-sacrifice, had been born.

Antwerp had become a very sociable place crowded with English refugees. The four coaches that Margaret had remarked rapidly expanded to more than a hundred, vying for room on the narrow streets with the pedlars' carts, drawn by five or six dogs, and the merchants' wagons. Margaret, perforce, had to become a hostess. Edward Hyde, Lord Clarendon, came occasionally to visit his wife and family – Anne Hyde, who later became the controversial Duchess of York, counted Margaret a friend. The Queen of Sweden visited the city and exchanged courtesies with the Newcastles. When the King passed through with his entourage he was entertained to dinner. He received Margaret kindly, afterwards gambling in a light-hearted fashion with Newcastle, though neither of them had anything of value left to stake.

The long-term prospects looked bleak and Margaret was pessimistic about the possibility of a Restoration. Her 'doubts and fears' were not shared by Newcastle, who gently chided her for them. He always believed that the divisions within the Commonwealth would eventually bring it down. Not everyone was so optimistic, and the royal family was having a particularly hard time. King Charles wandered around Europe like a gipsy, sometimes alone, sometimes accompanied by his sister, the Princess of Orange, who was now also displaced following the death of her husband. France had begun its own overtures to Cromwell, and bribed Charles with a pension – which arrived at erratic intervals and sometimes not at all – to live outside its boundaries. There followed a number of depressing years at Spa and Aachen (where he complained that it cost fivepence a night for board and lodging), in the Spanish Netherlands, at Düsseldorf and at Cologne, where his lonely figure was observed walking ceaselessly through the streets in the icy weather.

On Friday, 16 December 1653, at 1 p.m., Oliver Cromwell was installed as Lord Protector of England with all the pomp of a coronation. Arrayed in black velvet amid the scarlet-clad Aldermen of London Cromwell solemnly accepted the Great Seal, the Sword of State and the Cap of Maintenance proferred by the Lord Mayor. London buzzed with rumours that Cromwell would shortly assume the crown: it was even said that he had commissioned jewellers in Cheapside to make him one.

Yet things were not quite so settled as they seemed. Newcastle was right in believing that 'it was impossible for the Kingdom to submit long under so many changes of government'. Endymion Porter's son was involved in an abortive plot to assassinate the Protector, and another unsuccessful assassin was executed in 1654. Cromwell lived in such fear of his life that he was careful to vary his routes whenever he travelled about the city, and used back streets in preference to the main thoroughfares. It was even rumoured that he had several bedchambers prepared for him each evening, selecting one at the last moment and entering with his own key.

Newcastle resigned himself to his lot, living, Margaret wrote in her biography of him, 'as much to his own content as a banished man could do'. All his children were now married and he had grandchildren whom he had never seen. He applied himself to the pursuit of 'Mannege', and his expenditure on horses occasionally irritated Margaret when she thought the money could have been better spent. Newcastle had become the leading international authority on the art of horsemanship, displacing Pluvinal whose methods he discredited, claiming that they spoilt more horses than they trained. He occupied his spare time in setting down his own ideas in a book published in 1658, entitled *La Méthode Nouvelle et Invention Extraordinaire de Dresser les Chevaux*. This was no amateur production, but a learned exposition of one of the foremost accomplishments of a gentleman. Its publication, on the best paper in an enormous leather-bound volume with engravings by Diepenbeke, cost £1300, and Newcastle was forced to acknowledge that he could not have printed it without the assistance of his friends.

They were now living partly on credit and partly on money from England. Sir Charles Cavendish had left to Newcastle in his will a small amount of money which was promptly 'sprinkled' among the creditors. Welbeck and Bolsover were now settled on Newcastle's sons and providing a small income, but it was never more than about £2000 and not enough to support Newcastle's lifestyle. A large part of his income was spent on horses. Although the two Barbary horses he had purchased in Paris died, he quickly borrowed enough money to buy more, eventually bringing the numbers up to eight. Men came from all over Europe to see him put them through their paces. On one day Margaret counted as many as seventeen coaches at the door. The Spanish court of Don John of Austria, brother to the King of Spain, also paid a visit to the house and pressed Newcastle with invitations to come to Spain, which he tactfully refused. He also turned down large sums of money to sell the horses he had trained, declaring that he would not part with any of them however impecunious he became.

One of Margaret's first tasks on returning to Antwerp was to resuscitate work that she had penned over the previous five or six years and which had been locked up in a trunk while she was in England. Reading it through, she subsequently wrote in its Preface, she 'judged it not so well done but a little more care might have placed the words so the language might have run smoother', but at last it went out into the world as it was, lest correction should spoil her 'following conceptions'. Margaret's secretary had the job of preparing her books for the press. She had trouble, particularly in Antwerp, finding someone with sufficient scholarship to understand her philosophical work and sufficient tenacity to decipher her handwriting. This, she wrote, was 'a great disadvantage to my poor works, and the cause that they have been printed so false and so full of Errors'.

She called her new book *The World's Olio*, an olio being a kind of spicy stew, and it was an apt title for a collection of fragments, essays and sketches on a number of unconnected subjects. It was dedicated to Fortune, 'that powerful Princess', and the contents included thoughts on the translation of the scriptures, madness, dancing, society and Harvey's discovery of the circulation of the blood, with essays on vulgar discourse and on physick – 'The reason why one and the same quantity shall purge some to Death and others it will never move.' There are some memorable phrases, such as 'Wine though it begins like a friend, goeth on like a fool.' Margaret was against sending girls to boarding schools – like pears or apples 'they should be bred singly'. Such girls, like 'meat dressed at a cooks' shop which smells of the dripping pan, have a smack of the board school about them'. There are allegories and a few brief historical sketches, including lives of Queen Elizabeth I and King James.

Margaret's first attempt at literary criticism, a defence of Shakespeare, was good enough to be included later in the Oxford University Press anthology, *Shakespeare Criticism*. It is one of the earliest and best examples of serious consideration of his work. She sets out to refute the charge that Shakespeare's plays are made up only of 'clowns, Fools, Watchmen and the like'. Margaret argues that

> so Well he hath Expressed in his Plays all Sorts of Persons, as one would think he had been Transformed into every one of those Persons he hath Described and as sometimes one would think he was Really himself the Clown or Jester he Feigns, so one would think, he was also the King, and Privy Counsellor; . . . nay, one would think that he had been Metamorphosed from a Man to a Woman, for who could describe Cleopatra better than he hath done, and many other Females of his own Creating . . . and in his Tragic Vein, he presents Passions so Naturally, and Misfortunes so Probably, as he Pierces the Souls of his Readers with such a True Sense and Feeling thereof, that it Forces Tears through their Eyes, and almost Persuades them, they are Really Actors, or at least Present at those Tragedies. Who would not Swear he had been a Noble Lover, that could Woo so well? And there is not any person he hath Described in his Book, but his Readers might think they were Well acquainted with them.

Though some of the essays are entertaining, the most interesting discourse in the book is contained in one of the Prefaces. Margaret continued the habit, begun in *Poems and Fancies*, of prefacing her work with defensive epistles, apologising for and justifying her creations. This volume of poems had only seven; some of her later works had as many as twelve. The long preface to *The World's Olio* deals with the problem of male/female equality. Margaret's attitude at this time was slightly ambivalent, and the inconsistencies in the piece reflect the divided state of her own mind. She personally believed that men and women were born equal and that women wanted only education in order to prove themselves so. On the other hand she still lacked the confidence to challenge outright the arguments – mainly scriptural, but also scientific – in favour of male supremacy.

The historical precedents for female inferiority were formidable and persuasive:

> What woman was ever so strong as Sampson, or so swift as Hazael, . . . what woman was ever so wise as Solomon or Aristotle, so politic as Achitophel . . . so demonstrative as Euclid . . . so inventive as Seth or Archimedes? It was not a woman that found out the card and the needle, and the use of the lodestone . . . What woman was such a chemist as Paracelsus; such a physician as Hippocrates, such a Poet as Homer, such a painter as Apelles?

If there had been such women, they had left no traces to encourage Margaret or her contemporaries. Elizabeth Barrett Browning's heartfelt cry 'I look everywhere for grandmothers and see none' applied even more to Margaret and her generation. Faced with such awesome historical evidence, Margaret began *The World's Olio*: 'It cannot be expected I should write so wisely or wittily as men, being of the effeminate sex, whose brains nature has mixed with the coldest and softest elements.' These scientific arguments, based on the science of humours, were joined to the biblical evidence to persuade women that not only were they inferior to men physically and mentally, but it was a fact ordained by Almighty God. 'According to the description in the Holy Writ which saith "God made two great lights; the one to rule the Day and the other the Night;" so Man is made to govern Commonwealths and Women their private families.'

It was virtually impossible for a woman to challenge these assumptions without also challenging the validity of Holy Writ and the teachings of the Church. The feminists of the seventeenth century argued almost exclusively for equality of education for women without attempting to overthrow this basic concept. Even such ardent feminists as Bathsua Makin and Anna van Schurman stopped short of asserting female equality with men. They believed, as Margaret had been brought up to believe and wrote in *The World's Olio*, that 'Nature hath made man's body more able to endure labour, and Man's brain more clear to understand and contrive than woman's; and as great a difference there is between them as there is between the longest and strongest willow compared to the strongest and longest oak.' Yet some women could be

> far wiser than some men; like Earth, for some ground though it be barren by Nature, yet being well mulched and manured may bear plentiful crops . . . when the richer ground shall grow rank

and corrupt . . . for want of tillage; so women by education may come to be far more knowing and learned than some rustic and rude bred men.

Margaret's experiences in the Civil War, her own observations of her mother's skill and of Henrietta Maria's statecraft, and her exposure to feminist ideas in Paris reinforced her private belief in a female birthright which had been sold out. Her views become increasingly radical.

True it is, our sex makes great complaint, that men from their first creation, usurped a supremacy to themselves, although we were made equal by nature, which tyrannical government they have kept ever since so that we could never come to be free, but rather more and more enslaved, using us either like children fools or subjects . . . and will not let us divide the World equally with them, as to govern and command to direct and dispose, as they do; which slavery hath so dejected our spirits, as we are become so stupid that Beasts are a degree below us, and men use us but a degree above beasts, whereas in Nature we have as clear an understanding as men; if we were bred in schools to mature our brains and to manure our understandings that we might bring forth the fruits of knowledge.

Chapter Ten

Dull Manage
1655 – 7

Alas! a woman that attempts the pen
Such a presumptuous creature is esteemed
The fault can by no virtue be redeemed
They tell us we mistake our sex and way;
Good breeding, fashion, dancing, dressing, play,
Are the accomplishments we should desire;
To write, or read, or think or to inquire,
Would cloud our beauty, and exhaust our time,
And interrupt the conquests of our prime,
Whilst the dull manage of a servile house
Is held by some our utmost art and use.

Anne Winchelsea, *Poems*

Margaret's domestic responsibilities occasionally invaded her contemplations, and her guilt at their neglect caused her temporary unease. She now had her own household, and this included a number of 'maids of honour' attendant on her rank. These were usually girls of good family whose parents sent them to live in a noble household to wait upon the lady of the house and acquire a final polish in the social graces – much as some parents send their daughters to finishing school today. Margaret spent little time with her maids. When not in Newcastle's company she shut herself in her room to write. Her unusual lifestyle and her dislike of the company of 'gossiping women' caused her to neglect her duties towards her maids, with some unfortunate results.

The garden of the Antwerp house was surrounded by other dwellings – at the rear was the practice yard of the Company of Archers and on either side the private gardens of neighbours. Margaret's pretty waiting women were much spied on as they chattered in the garden. There was also a gate which connected with their next door neighbour's garden, and although locked it had a hole in it enabling this gentleman to peep through. He was evidently much enamoured of one of the maids, leaving notes and bunches of flowers in the hole for her to take, and on one occasion throwing a knotted handkerchief containing sweetmeats up into her open bedroom window. Unfortunately he was discovered by his wife, who confronted Margaret and her maid angrily and accused them of encouraging his approaches.

The maid defended herself fiercely. She had not encouraged him in his advances. They had been a source of amusement among the girls – one can imagine them giggling over his amorous missives. The handkerchief had been kept only because they could see no sensible way of returning it. The sweets had been eaten because it seemed a pity to waste them. But the charges made against Margaret by her neighbour weighed more heavily. Margaret recorded that she told her that her waiting maids

> were spoiled with idleness, having nothing to do but to dress, curl and adorn themselves, and they, excusing themselves, laying the blame upon me that I did not set them to any employment . . . the truth was, they oftener heard of their lady than heard or saw her themselves, I living so studious a life, as they did not see me above once a week, nay many times not once in a fortnight.

Margaret resolved to rectify this state of affairs and sent for her housekeeper. She first discussed the possibility of ordering spinning wheels and learning to spin flax with her ladies. But the housekeeper smiled 'to think what uneven threads I would spin. "You will spoil more flax than get cloth by your spinning" she said, "It being an art that requires practice to learn it."' When Margaret suggested the making of silk flowers, such as she had seen her sisters make, the housekeeper declared that she and her ladies could not make them as well or as cheaply as those who made it their trade – besides doing them out of valuable business.

> Then I told her I would preserve, for it was summer time and the fruit fresh and ripe upon the trees. She asked me for whom I would preserve, for I seldom did eat sweet-meats myself nor made banquets for strangers, unless I meant to feed my household servants with them. Besides, said she, you may keep half a score servants with the money that is laid out in sugar and coals which go to the preserving only of a few sweetmeats that are good for nothing but to breed obstructions and rot the teeth.

When Margaret explained her dilemma, and the nature of her neighbour's accusations, her housekeeper diplomatically replied that 'neighbours would find fault where no fault was'. Her maids could not 'employ their time better than to read, nor your ladyship better than to write, for any other course of life would be unpleasing and unnatural to you', she related in *Sociable Letters*. Margaret retired thankfully to her chamber, leaving her housekeeper once more in complete command of the domestic offices – a situation that suited them both.

Margaret was occasionally tempted to leave her room by the need for her fancy to find new material to work on, and go out into the town. Apart from her short daily 'tour' in her coach, she loved to visit the annual Shrovetide Carnival which was colourful and bizarre enough to fascinate the curious. The streets were thronged with people in fancy dress – sometimes men in women's dress and vice versa. On Ash Wednesday everyone daubed a black mourning cross on their foreheads. There were sideshows – rope dancers, private stage players, mountebanks, monsters and exotic animals such as dromedaries, lions and baboons. Street displays were put on by jugglers and tumblers, an art in which the Dutch excelled. On one occasion Margaret's attention was arrested by a woman covered all over with hair; the sight troubled her so much, she recalled in *Sociable Letters*, that she had to 'kick the image out of her mind like a dog'. She was, on the whole, rescued from exploitation by her common sense. When a man was brought before her claiming to be more than a hundred years old, Margaret observed that under the beard and long white hair he was not quite so old as he seemed, and she believed that 'he made himself older by his own report . . . being a poor man, and got money by showing himself'. The private stage players interested Margaret most. One particularly good troupe was led by an Italian mountebank called Jaen Potage, and included two women. Margaret had never seen women act on a public stage before – it was unknown in England before the Restoration – though women had taken part in privately enacted masques. She hired a private room overlooking the street where they performed so that she could watch them every day, but her amusement was cut short when they were ordered out of town by a magistrate for their peripheral activities, which included the selling of physick and other patent medicines.

One of the Newcastles' neighbours was a wealthy Portuguese merchant called Duartes, who lived in some state with his sisters. With these women, Eleanora, Katherine and Frances, Margaret found the kind of friendship she had been looking for. She discussed with Eleanora the philosopher's stone and the distillation of elixirs. They disagreed over alchemy, Eleanora being of the opinion that gold could be made by chemistry, Margaret that it could only be found in the earth. Newcastle too found their company congenial, and they were entertained to dinner. Senor Duartes set some of Newcastle's verses to music, and sometimes the sisters played and Margaret was persuaded to sing some of the simple ballads of Henry Lawes, learnt while she was in England. On Sundays they worshipped in Clarendon's private chapel, but otherwise they went out very little. Newcastle's obvious pleasure in his wife's company aroused some comment, but says a great deal about the happiness of their marriage.

In 1655 Margaret was once again at work on another book, and was now much more skilled in the art of ordering her thoughts and getting them down on paper. She often composed aloud, walking round her room, finding that when some of her thoughts were 'sent out in words, they give the rest more liberty to place themselves in a more methodical order'. She wrote everything down herself, but had trouble keeping pace with her thoughts, she admitted in 'A True Relation', 'the brain being quicker in creating than the hand in writing or the memory in retaining, many fancies are lost, by reason they oft times outrun the pen'. Unkind gossip related that she kept several of her waiting maids (or even Newcastle's secretary, John Rolleston) in adjoining rooms both day and night, and whenever she cried out 'I conceive, I conceive' they had to rush through and write down whatever had sprung into her mind.

Nature's Pictures, published in 1656, was one of Margaret's most successful books. It was a collection of stories and anecdotes strung together by an artificial thread, and this anecdotal structure suited her very well. A company of people sit around the fire in winter, and to pass the time they decide to tell stories, some in verse, some in prose, an idea which obviously owes a lot to Chaucer. There is also a small piece contributed by 'my lord Newcastle', entitled appropriately 'The Beggar's Marriage'. Appended to all the others is a story 'in which there is no feigning' – a 'True Relation' of her own birth, breeding and marriage.

This dignified and revealing epistle, in which she analyses her personality with remarkable insight, ends with a plea to the reader. She hopes that he 'will not think me vain for writing my life, since there have been many that have done the like . . . both men and women, and I know no reason I may not do it as well as they'. It was also a plea for indulgence in breaching that anonymity which was the height of good manners in a woman.

Some censuring Readers will scornfully say, why hath this lady writ her own life? Since none cares to know whose daughter she was, or whose wife she is, or how she was bred, or what fortunes she had, or how she lived, or what humour or disposition she was of? I answer that it is true, that 'tis to no purpose to the Readers, but it is to the Authoress, because I write it for my own sake, not theirs, . . . to tell the truth lest after ages should mistake in not knowing I was daughter to one Master Lucas of St John's, . . . second wife to the Lord Marquis of Newcastle.

Margaret was striking a blow for all those women who lived out their lives in quiet anonymity, and who have left us largely ignorant of the intimate, day-to-day details of their lives. It is sad that in speaking out for herself she still felt that she had to define herself in terms of her relationship with men.

It is difficult to know how much credence to give Margaret's account of herself. Much of it, however, can be verified from other sources. Newcastle comments more than once on her shyness. Harder to understand are the claims to modesty in a volume which exposes her innermost thoughts to the critical public eye. This deliberate act, which seems to negate her own analysis of her personality, is a paradox which will probably never be resolved. Prevented from intellectual communication with others by both her sex and her nature, she achieved it through the printed page, realising with her pen the eloquence denied her tongue.

There are the usual prefaces to the book, often more interesting than the text because they reveal more of their author. This time Margaret used them to explain her desire for 'extraordinary Fame', and to defend her use of English rather than Latin for her published work. Latin, as the natural medium for the printed word, was falling into disuse even for scientific works. Descartes published in French in order to be accessible to everyone and especially to women. Margaret celebrated her much maligned native language 'which is, at this time, extremely enriched with the wise and lawful plunder of others; and is like mithridite and cordial waters, which are much the better for being compounded of the choicest ingredients'. She also aimed for a simple, plain style, scorning the 'high words and mystical expressions' of an earlier fashion.

In *Nature's Pictures*, Margaret displayed the acute observation of incident and character that distinguish her story-telling. It begins simply with the group of people deciding to tell each other tales,

> And drawing lots, the Chance fell on a Man
> Who, having Spit and blown his Nose, began:

There is a story about a coachman and a carter who fall out over who should give way to whom in a narrow lane. The coachman considers himself a class above the carter; the carter considers business more important than pleasure. Two women fight in the marketplace, and as the observers try to separate them they are drawn into the fray until a full-scale riot ensues. In another tale a venial landlady vets all her lodgers to make sure they are young, lusty, single and male. There are stories of matrimony, of unfaithful husbands who get their wives' maids with child, of husbands who divorce their wives and then regret their actions.

The Discreet Virgin decides that it is better to become an ape leader than the wife of a drunkard, or an affected man who modishly plays with his cloak, or a man who carelessly lolls about in company with his feet raised on the furniture within the scent of a lady's nose. Men, she declares, stand selfishly before the fire to warm their breeches and block out the heat; men are vainer than women and change their fashions more often; men meet every day in taverns to sit and gossip over wine; men 'are like flies bred out of a dunghill buzzing idle about . . . when women are like industrious ants . . . always employed to the benefit of their families'.

Not many of the stories have plots; some have morals, while others are mere excuses for observation or to express an opinion. Some are pure fantasy, like the man who consults a witch because he wishes to travel to the moon. There is also a cautionary tale entitled 'Assaulted and Pursued Chastity', written to show 'young women the dangers of travelling without their parents, husbands, or particular friends to guard them; for though virtue is a good guard, yet it doth not always protect their person' – a sentiment that is valid for women today. Margaret's women disguise themselves as men, an expedient which possibly only made them vulnerable to advances of a different kind. As Pepys observed, a pretty young man was as unsafe as his female counterpart, though Margaret in her naïvety was probably as hazy about the nature of pederasty as was the famous diarist. The common custom of mixed bedrooms at wayside inns increased the hazards for an unaccompanied young person of either sex.

Although childless herself, Margaret none the less gave common-sense instructions on the care of children. They must not, she wrote emphatically, 'be deceived with lies, lest they learn to deceive with lyings, or frighted with Hobgoblins', nor laid on tables or stools, but on a blanket on the floor to roll and kick freely in order to develop their limbs. They should be kindly used, prudently bred and not overfed.

The first of Margaret's 'superwomen' appears in *Nature's Pictures*. This character, variously named Lady Sanspareille, Mlle Ambition, Lady Victoria and Lady Perfection, recurs frequently in her plays and stories. These women rise from humble beginnings and are scorned at first, but their brilliance and wisdom are always recognised in the end; they have all the learning, education and fame that Margaret herself desired. The She-Anchoret in *Nature's Pictures* is the central character in an overlong story in which she retires to contemplate in a cave like a hermit and is besieged by people who have come from all over the world to consult her about their problems. She dispenses wisdom and justice in some extremely turgid prose, completely at odds with the lightness of touch evident in the rest of the book. Such women were not entirely unknown in Renaissance and Jacobean drama; Shakespeare's Beatrice and Portia, Dekker's Roaring Girl and Milton's unyielding Lady from his masque *Comus* were all familiar to Margaret. Her characters are different because they are the central figures in the drama – there are heroines but no heroes, and her heroines are always superbly educated. Margaret poured in everything she had ever heard of heroic women, and all she had ever dreamed of doing herself.

In some of the stories Margaret attacked the double standard of sexuality that she and other women were forced to accept. 'The Matrimonial Agreement' propounds the novel notion of an agreement between the parties to a marriage that if the husband is unfaithful he must forfeit his estates to his wife. Eventually the wife becomes ill, and the husband inevitably begins to absent himself from her side.

> The husband returning home one day from jolly company, whose discourse had been merry and wanton, he met with his wife's maid at the door, and asked her how her mistress did. She said 'Not very well.' 'Thou lookest well,' said he and chucks her under the chin. She, proud of her master's kindness, smirks and smiles upon him, insomuch that the next time he met, he kissed her.

The husband is then abroad on business and persuaded by friends that 'Wives are only to keep our home, to bring us children – not to give us laws.' Very soon he is carousing and whoring with the rest. His wife discovers a letter from one of his mistresses in a cabinet, but instead of asking him to forfeit his estates she blackmails her husband into allowing her the same life of pleasure and licence that he is enjoying.

Another cautionary tale describes a much more familiar situation. A wife decides to punish her unfaithful husband by taking a lover. Her husband responds by divorcing her for adultery, being 'willing to make a cuckold, yet he was not willing to be made one himself'. The giddy Lady Isabella Thynne, one of Margaret's companions at the court of Queen Henrietta Maria, was the subject of a divorce case in 1653, having been persistently unfaithful with the Marquis of Ormonde – one of Newcastle's friends. Divorce 'a mensa et thoro' was merely separation from bed and board, with no remarriage. Those who did remarry, like the scandalous Lady Penelope Rich, were regarded as bigamists. In certain restricted cases annulment could be obtained, and for the very wealthy a proper divorce by Act of Parliament. The Cromwellian Marriage Act of 1655 permitted the innocent party of divorce proceedings to remarry, but this bill did not outlast the Commonwealth. Milton's The Doctrine and Discipline of Divorce advocated desertion, adultery, cruelty, impotence and incompatibility as grounds for divorce, citing Old Testament authorities. It was nevertheless biased towards men; the right to put away a husband was not recognised – Eve being an equal inferior as far as Milton was concerned.

Margaret's heroines are no patient Griseldas, prepared to suffer unlimited domestic humiliation. This was the first time that the sexual inequalities between men and women had been dealt with in fiction in such a direct and open fashion. Margaret's treatment of the subject is so detailed and sensitive that it must spring from the close observation of the experience of friends, or perhaps her own. If Newcastle was unfaithful, he was very discreet. Her life at court, and the observation of the marital hypocrisy all around her, would have been sufficient to provide her with the material for her stories and plays. One particularly notorious incident concerned the Earl of Dorset, who brought his mistress Lady Penistone to Knole and forced his wife to entertain her. Lady Isabella Thynne was also living on the continent with the wife of her lover, the long-suffering Elizabeth Ormonde. Margaret may have been thinking of these women when she wrote of a woman forced by her husband to wait upon his mistress. He has threatened to divorce her, despite her innocence, and she complains that if he does she, and not he, will be 'left to the censure and scandal of the World'.

Though Margaret's heroines rebelled against sexual injustice, her advice to women actually in this situation was to endure, and to 'wink' at their husband's adultery. For a wife to do otherwise was to do 'herself double injury, by her Husband's inconstancy, and then by her own Grief, Rage and Fury'.

Some of the stories in *Nature's Pictures* are written in verse, and Margaret managed to achieve a reasonable standard of taut narrative and an acceptable marriage of language and form. In 'A Description of Love and Courage',

> The Vizzard of the Lord fell off at length;
> Which, when the bridegroom saw with vigorous strength,
> He ran upon him with such force that he
> Struck many down to make his passage free.
>
> The trembling bride was almost dead with fear,
> Yet for her husband had a listening ear . . .
>
> Wounded they were, yet was each other's heart
> So hot with passion that they felt no smart.

Had Margaret been living a hundred years later she might easily have rivalled Mrs Radcliffe. Her prose pieces show the same distinction. In 'The Speculators' she builds up a nice atmosphere of anticipation:

> A man, having occasion to travel, being in the heat of Summer, for more ease took his journey when Night was running from Day, for fear the glorious Sun should overtake her. And looking earnestly, to observe how her darker clouds returned, or were illuminated at last in the dawning before the Sun appeared in Glory, he thought he saw something appear in the Air, more than usual, which Fancy of his caused him to alight from his Horse and, fastening his Bridle to a Bush, himself went and lay upon his back on the ground, that he might fix his eyes on the Strange sight more steadfastly.

These stories show a talent for rendering personal experience and observation as fiction. Her greatest achievement is 'The Contract', a long story which uses narrative, dialogue, letters and a judicial judgement. It describes a match made by two old men between their children. One of them subsequently dies, and his son decides not to honour the agreement. However, later on, after he has married someone else, he meets the girl and falls in love with her. This meeting takes place at a court masque, attended for the first time by Lady Delicia. Her gaucherie and sense of awe are vividly described. Like the shy Margaret Lucas at Oxford, she knows no one. 'When the Company was called to sit down that the Masque might be represented, every one was placed by their Friends, but she being unaccustomed to those Meetings knew not how to dispose of herself . . . and therefore she stood still.' When Lady Delicia sees the Duke she immediately falls in love with him, and their parting is particularly poignant. 'Heaven direct you for the best, said she, it is late, Good night. You will give me leave said he, to kiss your hand? I cannot deny my hand, said she, to him that hath my heart.' Eventually the Duke's marriage is annulled on a legal technicality and the lovers are reunited.

This is one of the earliest examples of English fiction, antedating Aphra Behn's *Oroonoko* by nearly thirty years, and its length and form deserve closer consideration in the development of the novel. If Margaret had persevered she might have written fiction of some importance, but she had already decided that fiction was in some way immoral and that real virtue lay in truth. She was also about to abandon poetry, that medium, she wrote in *Poems and Fancies*, 'so suited to a lady's pen', following the advice of Epicurus, one of the Greek philosophers whom she was now reading in translation in Thomas Stanley's *History of Philosophy*. Like Plato, Epicurus was of the opinion that 'a wise man will not labour in composing fabulous poems'. The way of truth lay in philosophy.

Chapter Eleven

Philosophical Opinions
1657 – 60

2nd Philosopher: *Nature thou doest us wrong, and art too prodigal to the effeminate sex; but I forgive thee, for thou art a She, Dame Nature thou art; but never showed thy malice until now. What shall we do?*
3rd Philosopher: *Faith, all turn gallants, spend our time in vanity and sin, get Hawks and Hounds, rich clothes and feathers, waste our time away with what this man said, or what that man answered, backbite and rail at all those that are absent, and then renounce it all with new oaths à la mode.*

> Scene contributed by William
> Cavendish to Margaret Cavendish,
> *Youth's Glory and Death's Banquet,*
> from *Plays*

The seventeenth century saw tremendous developments in scientific knowledge – the observations of Galileo, Robert Hooke's discovery of the microscope, Harvey's discovery of the circulation of the blood, Boyle's law, the mathematics of Sir Isaac Newton and the establishment of the Royal Society. This institution, dedicated to scientific experiment and demonstration, was a purely masculine one whose proceedings were barred to women.

Margaret's interest in natural philosophy had begun when the Newcastles were living in Paris and visited by Descartes, Hobbes and Gassendi. She was introduced to the subject by her husband. A letter still survives from Newcastle to Hobbes, written in 1648 in Paris, concerning 'perspective glasses' which Hobbes had bought for him. Although Newcastle did not have the taste for scholarship that his brother possessed, both of them had a deep interest in the sciences and the Marquis eventually became a founder member of the Royal Society. Before the Civil War he had made experiments at Bolsover with his chaplain, Dr Payn, examining the characteristics of sulphur and saltpetre. He had also had animated discussions with Hobbes at Welbeck on the subject of light.

Margaret was drawn to the subject by her own natural curiosity, and then driven on by the knowledge that she was the only woman working in an exclusively masculine field. Here was the chance to achieve the fame she so ardently desired. Dismissing the 'fantastical notions' of many of her male contemporaries, all amateurs like herself, she began her own search for Perfect Truth.

The sciences were not then divided up as they are now; knowledge was still regarded as a whole indivisible mass. The term 'philosophy' was loosely used to describe any kind of intellectual enquiry, and its roots were classical. At the Reformation, the rediscovery of the Greek philosophers displaced by the spread of the Christian Church, and the discovery of the New World, combined to produce an upsurge of scholarship. Philosophy, according to Socrates, was the true way to happiness and all learning merely reminiscence, a rediscovery of that first knowledge lost by the soul on its implantation in the body.

Like many other seventeenth-century ladies, Margaret seized on reason and contemplation as paths to scientific discovery, as if by thinking and imagining she could solve the problems of the universe. Initially she relied on snippets of information gleaned from conversations with her husband and his friends; later she read more, though only those works available in translation. She was greatly influenced by Plato, and gained reassurance from him, through Thomas Stanley's *History of Philosophy*, that the 'contemplative life is best and to be preferred before the active'. Margaret was also fully conversant with Democritus' theories concerning atoms and vacuums, and with Epicurus, reflections of whose work appear frequently in her own, and whose basic precepts chimed so happily with her disposition that he might have been addressing her directly:

> Happy are they, who are of such a disposition of Body or Mind, or born in such a country, as they can either of themselves, or by the instigations of others, addict themselves to Philosophy and Perfect Truth, by attainment whereof, a man is made truly free or wise, and absolute Master of himself.

The great medieval philosophers had all been theologians, bound by the restrictions of the Church, and much seventeenth-century philosophy wrestled with the problems of reconciling discovery by revelation with discovery by reason. Francis Bacon in the sixteenth century had been an empiricist, firmly on the side of reason, but he had departed from the old logic based on syllogism, and stated that conclusions should be reached from the much wider bases of experimentation, observation and experience.

The difficulties of reconciling the new philosophy with the teachings of the Church are illustrated by the fate of Galileo, forced to recant his findings and kept under house arrest until he died in

1642. He had been visited by Descartes and Hobbes in the late 1630s, and through them Margaret was familiar with his discoveries and his problems. She specifically avoided theology in her own work 'for Philosophy is built all upon Human Sense, Reason and Observation, whereas Theology is only built upon an implicit faith', as she wrote in *Philosophical and Physical Opinions*, a new edition of her *Philosophical Fancies*, which had appeared in 1655. Her views occasionally aroused controversy. One correspondent wrote that because Margaret believed that Nature was eternal, without beginning or end, and that matter was infinite, she had made Nature into God. Margaret wriggled out of that with difficulty, affirming her belief in God as a spiritual, immaterial being beyond matter, and admonished her critic that natural philosophy must be viewed 'by the Light of Reason only and not of Revelation'. Man's curiosity was God-given, Margaret argued, and the search for knowledge could not be wrong. *Philosophical and Physical Opinions* ended with a prayer:

> Oh pardon Lord, for what I now here speak
> Upon a guess, my knowledge is but weak;
> But thou hast made such creatures as Mankind,
> And gav'st them something which we call a Mind.

These volumes were the first scientific works to be published by a woman in England. Their value is difficult to determine – ideas which seem ridiculous to us today were considered quite credible to Margaret's contemporaries. The subject matter is alien and often difficult to understand – but no more so than that of many other seventeenth-century philosophical publications – and is illuminated by her infectious enthusiasm. The importance of natural philosophy, which included physics, chemistry, biology and mathematics, was self-evident to Margaret, who wrote in *Observations on Experimental Philosophy*:

> Without Natural Philosophy men could not tell how to live, for it doth not only instruct men to know the course of the Planets and the Seasons of the Year but it instructs men in husbandry, architecture and navigation as also combination and association – but above all it instructs men in the rules and arts of physick; indeed all arts and science are produced in one kind or another from Natural Philosophy.

The French influence was particularly important for Margaret. The *femmes savantes* of the French salons had a special interest in science: Descartes was a frequent salon visitor and his work was often discussed. His great contribution to the seventeenth-century debate was the *Discourse on Method*, which laid down basic rules to govern observation and experiment. The technique was called the chain of reasoning. Each problem had to be divided up into as many parts as possible and dealt with one by one, beginning with the simplest component. The slightest doubt meant that the premise had to be rejected.

Fontenelle's *Discovery of New Worlds*, published in Paris in 1686, is interesting because it features a *femme savante* very like Margaret herself. Fontenelle insists that she is a fiction, created to 'give encouragement to the Ladies', but he asks: 'And why may not there be a Woman like this imaginary Marquise? Since her conceptions are no other than such as she could not choose but have?' The book consists of a dialogue between the author and a Marquise who is scientifically knowledgeable but still young enough to require instruction, and who asks questions very similar to those asked by the young Marchioness of Newcastle. Aphra Behn translated the book in 1688, inveighing against the author for making the Marchioness say either 'very many silly things' or make observations as learned as any philosopher. Like Margaret, Aphra opposed the idea that the new sciences were a male preserve. The scholar Glanville, a friend and correspondent of Margaret's, also translated Fontenelle's discourse. He made the Marquise a Countess, but her remarks are so like some of Margaret's written comments on the motion of the earth, travelling to the moon and the benefits of a 'Shepherd's Life' for scientific contemplation, as to be more than a coincidence.

Much of Margaret's philosophical work consists of analysis and discussion of both old and new ideas. She found it difficult to accept the idea of a vacuum, as postulated by Democritus. 'If a vacuum be allowed, how can a place be, and no matter, for nothing is nothing?' Similarly she struggled with the concept of atoms, writing with exceptional insight to a puzzled correspondent:

You desire me to explain that chapter of atoms which is before my book of *Philosophical Opinions*, but truly I cannot explain it more clearly than I have done, which is that I thought this world could not be made out of atoms, but if it was made by atoms, they must be both the architects and materials, neither could they do that work unless every atom was animated with life and knowledge, for an animated substance is a living, knowing substance, which life and knowledge is sense and reason, and thus every atom must have a body, which is a substance, and that substance sense and reason, and so probably passions and appetites as well as wit and ingenuity to make worlds and worlds of creatures.

The logical extension of this view was that all substances made from atoms – even vegetables – must have sense and knowledge. How was it possible to tell, she asked, 'For shall we say . . . that a man doth not know, because he knoweth not what another man knoweth.'

Public reception of her work was predictable and very far from Newcastle's witty fantasy on the philosophical triumphs of Lady Sanspareille in the scenes he contributed to her plays. Her attempts to enter the scientific debate and make a serious contribution to knowledge served only to increase her reputation for eccentricity. *Nature's Pictures*, deserving of a better fate, was similarly scorned. Men figured badly on its pages, and it was understandable that it did not find favour with male critics. Life from a woman's point of view was totally unacceptable, and although women could identify with the characters in Margaret's tales they hesitated to defend her in case they too were branded as 'ridiculous'.

There were exceptions, however. Her views on witchcraft sparked off the correspondence with Joseph Glanville, who sent her his own publications. At this time there was considerable disagreement between scholars on the subject. Margaret agreed with those members of the Royal Society who felt that it was necessary to separate scientific enquiry from astrology, alchemy, witchcraft and superstition. Her common sense would not allow them to exist, except in people's minds. She stated firmly that those who believed in witchcraft and those who believed themselves to be witches or wizards could do great harm.

Other letters are less free from the taint of patronage. Oxford University wrote that 'We have a manuscript Author in Bodlei's Library who endeavours to show "That Women Excell Men"; your Excellency has proved what he proposed, has done what he endeavoured, and given a demonstrative argument to convince an otherwise unbelieving world.' Trinity College, Cambridge, wondered 'how it came to pass that Eloquence, Poetry, Philosophy, things otherwise most different, should without the help of a Tutor, without the Midwifery of a University, at length agree in a Woman'. Queen's College, Oxford, paid a similar compliment: 'Your works will be a just foundation of a lasting immortal honour to yourself;

but I fear a reproach to our sex and us, when Posterity shall consider how little we have done with all our Reading and Industry and how much your excellency without them.'

By far the most interesting correspondence is a publication by a man called Du Verger in 1657, entitled *Humble Reflections on Some Passages of the Marchioness of Newcastle's Olio*. It referred to an essay on monasticism. Du Verger wrote that he admired her *Olio* tremendously, but soon came to passages so unsound 'that I may not say wholly corrupted, that my stomach began to rise and loathe what formerly it so much liked'. He defended the monastic life with scriptural authority and the seal of antiquity's approval, as he did the writings of the saints, including the homilies of the fourth-century Father of the Church St John Chrysostom. Margaret had written that 'Like drones they [monks] suck up the honey they never took the pains to gather.' Du Verger pointed out that that could apply to many others in society, and wholly refuted her allegation that 'They are an idle, lazy and unprofitable people.' As for the fact that 'they go not to wars to adventure their lives', not everyone, he said, was suited to the sword. Margaret also attacked nuns, declaring that 'there are as many kept barren as would populate whole nations'. Monastics were 'covetous and cheaters', and more damning, they sold redemption from sin. Du Verger defended Catholicism as well as monasticism – Catholics, he said, were obedient to St Paul's counsel and walked in the steps of their forefathers. He quoted at length from Papal Bulls on the subject of redemption.

All these letters were published by Newcastle in 1676, after Margaret's death, in a volume entitled *Poems and Letters in Honour of the Incomparable Princess Margaret, Duchess of Newcastle*. It includes sycophantic eulogies addressing her as Princess of Philosophy, Chief of Women, Minerva, Athene, the Muses and Aristotle as well as his Lyceum. Some are in verse.

> Now let enfranchised Ladies learn to Write
> And not paint white and red, but black and white,
> Their bodkins turn to Pens, to Lines their Locks,
> And let the Inkhorn be their Dressing Box,
> Since Madam, you have scaled the walls of Fame
> And made a Breach where never Female came.

They are stiff with hyperbole and lavish compliment.

> Had Spenser lived your works t' have seen
> You must have been his Fairy Queen . . .

And had you liv'd when Ovid writ
You'd been the subject of his wit.

Margaret had no way of balancing the extremes of criticism and compliment. She suffered from the problems of the woman writer of her period, unable to belong to a coterie as men did, with all its mutual support, and denied, by her situation in Holland, the company of other like-minded women. Paris had its Hôtel de Rambouillet, London the salon of Katherine Philips, Margaret only her imagination. Her fancies were like 'sparkling fireworks . . . or rather stars, set thick upon the brain, which gives a twinkling delight unto the mind'. Contemplation, she has Lady Solid say in her play *The Several Wits*, was the only way of life: 'Indeed few doth live as they should, that is to live within themselves; The Soul that keeps at home . . . only views the world for knowledge . . . as out of a window on a prospect . . . it is industrious for its own tranquility, fame and everlasting life.'

The winter of 1657–8 was the severest within living memory, and a bitter north-easterly wind blew for almost six months. John Evelyn wrote that 'The crow's feet were frozen to their prey; islands of ice enclosed both fish and fowl frozen, and some persons in their boats'. As late as June there was an extraordinary hailstorm, and in August severe gales devastated crops and property, blowing ships inland. The newssheets complained all winter of a lack of news, 'the ways being full', and when the snow melted, of floods. Across the flat reaches of Holland and the Spanish Netherlands the cold was 'as sharp as an axe', and Margaret's house with its open Italian staircase and bleak tiled floors was comfortless. 'Though I sit so near the fire as I have burned a part of my clothes, yet the cold is so furious as it doth not only freeze the ink in the standish, but in the pen I am writing with, so that I am but a cold writer, nay the very thoughts seem to be frozen in my brain.' Despite the cold, Margaret was at work on another book, using a medium that gave full scope to her wide-ranging talents.

While writing *Nature's Pictures* she had conceived the idea of publishing a book of letters, some fictional, some actual, written to an anonymous friend and strung together to form a kind of narrative. This idea was not entirely new – James Howell had already used it in his *Familiar Letters*, but it was original enough to capture Margaret's imagination. The use to which she puts the letters is, however, original and reveals the possibilities of the epistolary form as a narrative device. Margaret described them as 'rather scenes than Letters, for I have endeavoured under the Cover of Letters to Express the Humours of Mankind, and the Actions of Man's Life by the correspondence of two Ladies living at some short Distance from each other'. The letters are to portray their daily lives, entertainments, private opinions, gossip and public affairs. Published in 1664 as *Sociable Letters*, the result is an entertaining, idiosyncratic view of life as a Royalist exile. Margaret's innermost thoughts are revealed through the intimate, person-to-person style. The letters recount her feelings on the death of her mother and her opinions on fashion, sex and politics, and contain vivid descriptions of life in Antwerp which force the reader to regret Margaret's refusal to continue writing fiction.

Antwerp was snowbound for much of the winter and Margaret described how from her windows she watched

> the young men and their mistresses ride in sleds by torchlights . . . every sled having a fair lady . . . sitting at one end of the sled, dressed with feathers and rich clothes, and her courting servant like a coachman, or rather a carter, bravely accoutred, driving the horses with a whip, which draw the sled upon the snow with a galloping pace, whilst footmen run with torches to light them.

Many of these gallants 'for want of skill' overturned the sleds and tumbled their mistresses into the snow. Margaret was secretly envious of their freedom and high spirits. Although the cold was so great that she was as unwilling to leave her fireside 'as criminals are to go to their execution', Newcastle managed to persuade her to accompany him in their coach, warmly mantled in furs with hot bricks at her feet, to watch the skaters on the frozen River Schelde. Confronted by the pretty scene she was seized with a desire to join them and slide freely on the glittering expanse. She was prevented by her own timidity and by her views on what was 'fitting' for a lady of her station. So, having 'neither the agility, art, courage nor liberty', she was forced reluctantly to return home and contemplate wistfully on 'a river, lake or moat, frozen in my brain into a smooth glassy ice, whereupon divers of my thoughts were sliding'. In the privacy of her closet, with her pen in her hand, she had fewer inhibitions and was less afraid of making a fool of herself.

King Charles visited Antwerp again in February 1658 and the Newcastles gave a ball in his honour. Poverty and exile were forgotten in one of the brilliant displays of hospitality for which the Marquis had been famous before the war, though this could not compare with the lavish entertainment created for Charles I at Welbeck which involved a masque by Ben Jonson and cost Newcastle £15,000. However, huge fires were lit in every grate and Rubens' beautifully proportioned reception rooms cleared for dancing and banqueting. According to a member of the King's entourage, a 'little room' was 'well filled with most of the English here and some of the town'. The King's two brothers, James and Henry, were present, and his sister the Princess of Orange and her retinue, which at that time included Anne Hyde, daughter of the Earl of Clarendon, King Charles' chief adviser, whose beauty had already attracted James' eye. Clarendon was conspicuously absent, his excuse that the ladies might have led him out to dance. He was in fact just recovering from a bad attack of gout, but many other reasons could have accounted for his absence. The King was brought into the banqueting room 'with loud music' and a Major Mohun 'in a black satin robe, and garland of bays' delivered a speech in verse composed by Newcastle 'wherein as much was said of compliment to his Majesty as the highest hyperbole could possibly express'.

They danced for two hours and then 'my Lady Moore, dressed all in feathers' sang one of Newcastle's songs set to music by Nicholas Lanier, master of the King's music. The banquet was brought in on eight enormous chargers, each one requiring two men to carry it. This was the first time Margaret had entertained on this scale and it must have caused some domestic anxiety. However, their staff was supplemented for the occasion by various 'gentlemen of the court' who served food and drink, and the whole entertainment was supervised by Newcastle's experienced steward. The guests then danced until midnight, and the evening was so successful that the King remarked jestingly to Margaret, she recorded, that 'he perceived my Lord's credit could procure better meat than his own,' a statement that contained much truth. Apart from money received from his own children, Newcastle was also being helped by Francis Topp, an English merchant who had married Margaret's maid Elizabeth. Newcastle was now able to buy in cash from the markets rather than on credit, thus saving a considerable amount in interest charges.

In England the bitter weather affected the Protector's health. Cromwell opened Parliament on 20 January and cut his speech short on the grounds of infirmity. Throughout the rest of the year his health was uncertain, although he could still summon up the old strength when goaded into action. The House of Lords, abolished since 1649, was reconvened by Cromwell in January as the Second

Chamber or Upper House. It was a nominated assembly, but the majority of the original peers, although summoned, declined to attend. Within a few weeks Cromwell dissolved Parliament again in one of his lightning strikes. There were more Royalist arrests and executions. It was said that Cromwell entertained people to dinner and teased them with news of where they had been and what they had said, and how they had drunk the King's health. No one felt safe. The Countess of Derby wrote in a letter: 'We know little news, and it is dangerous to ask for any. We live in times in which the most insignificant person may do harm, and very few have the power to do good.'

In August the Protector's favourite daughter died after a protracted and painful illness. His grief overcame his frail health and he collapsed. Although visibly ageing, troubled with kidney stones and gout, these were fairly normal complaints for a man of sixty and not of themselves life-threatening. No one at that time took into account the effect of the considerable stress, both public and private, under which he had been for some years. The sole government of England had been in his hands, and momentous decisions such as the refusal of the crown, eventually offered by Parliament, had taken a great toll of his stamina. Throughout August his health waxed and waned; sometimes he appeared close to death, at other times well enough to have dinner with Fairfax. At the beginning of September his condition worsened suddenly, and on the afternoon of the 3rd, seven years to the day after his great triumph at Worcester, he died.

Cromwell was given a state funeral befitting a monarch, but the passing of his immense personality seemed to wake the kingdom from its apathetic unity. There was a mood of change. John Evelyn witnessed Cromwell's obsequies and wrote that 'it was the joyfullest funeral that ever I saw'. Across the Channel the exiles were dancing in the streets. Charles had remained in Antwerp throughout the summer of 1658, but was in Hoogstraten on a hunting trip when he received the news. There was speculation as well as joy, and Royalist agents went to and fro with a new sense of urgency and purpose, their message increasingly one of hope as the months went past.

Cromwell had made no preparation for a successor, but those present at his deathbed believed that he had assented to the suggestion that his son Richard should succeed him. It was an unfortunate choice. Of Cromwell's two sons Richard was the weaker, a mild-mannered, indecisive man, fonder of hunting and hawking than of politics, and with a tendency to get into debt. There was no suggestion of the Protectorate passing to another member of the

Council of State: a dynastic form of succession was the only kind they knew or would accept. Besides, there were few who might have been deemed suitable. Self-made men of power and authority tend to surround themselves with people who are unlikely to compete with them, and so it was with Cromwell. Of those with the ability to rival the Protector, Lambert was languishing at Wimbledon, Fleetwood haltered by marriage to Bridget Cromwell, and the perennially cautious Monck biding his time in Scotland.

On 31 May 1659 Newcastle's eldest son Charles, Viscount Mansfield, died unexpectedly at Bolsover. He left no son, and as soon as it could be proved that his wife was not pregnant the title and estates passed to his brother Henry. This event emphasised the frailty of Newcastle's posterity. Henry had as yet only daughters living – his two sons, both named for their grandfather, had died soon after birth.

Before Henry took up residence at Welbeck and Bolsover there were inventories to be made and inevitably recriminations over missing items. The young Viscountess Mansfield and her servants had apparently taken away some cases of crimson velvet – intended for the chairs in the parlour at Bolsover; some hangings were missing, and gold lace and embroidery from a purple velvet bed worth £300. In addition, some of the Cavendish collection of Van Dycks and Steenwjcks had been damaged and were in need of restoration. Eventually they were all reframed with the Cavendish crest to match the portraits which Newcastle commissioned in Antwerp from Diepenbeke.

Diepenbeke was also responsible for engraving the illustrations for Margaret's books, including a fascinating portrait of the whole Cavendish family sitting around a table together. Margaret and her husband sit at the head crowned with laurel wreaths, Charles and Henry on Margaret's left and Jane, Frances and Elizabeth on Newcastle's right. It was however, purely imaginary, for the whole family were never all together under the same roof. Newcastle, still with no thought of an imminent return, wrote to his son under a pseudonym, urging him and his wife to live at Welbeck and assuring Henry that he renounced his interests in the house contents completely and that Margaret was of the same mind, 'for she is as kind to you as she was to your brother, and so good a wife as that she is all for my family, which she expresses is only you'.

In England things were moving fast. Richard Cromwell's failure to control the army as well as Parliament resulted in his downfall in April 1659. He was never formally toppled – simply deprived of power and allowed to fade into the background. The tightrope act of balancing civil and military power was a feat that his father had performed with consummate skill. It required political expertise as well as intelligence, and although Richard certainly possessed the latter he had never held an important political post prior to 1658. Those responsible for his fall, Lambert and Fleetwood, found the task equally impossible. Only General Monck, with a large part of the army behind him, had the necessary authority to assume control.

By December 1659 England had sunk into a condition approaching anarchy. The Rump had reinstated itself, but found it impossible to raise enough money via taxes to carry on effective government. There were too many factions within Parliament for any one of them to get an Act passed or business approved. There was outright conflict between the army and Parliament. A Royalist rising in Cheshire was put down, but there were murmurings which it was feared presaged more widespread insurrection. In January 1660 Monck marched into London, and after a confrontation with Lambert, whose men refused to fight, took control of the city, undermined the power of the Rump and began secret communications with King Charles on the subject of his Restoration.

The last days of the Commonwealth were troubled and confused, although a kind of unity in adversity was once more emerging. 'We had all suffered so deeply under those oppressions that even the contrary party to the king did heartily wish an alteration from those pressures . . .,' wrote Alice Thornton in her memoirs. 'In this distraction, each man looked upon other strangely, none knowing whom to trust.' It was in the end Parliament and not the General who recalled the King – a successful piece of political engineering by Monck, the instigator and manipulator. He was something of a political chameleon, having been a Royalist prisoner of war before serving under Cromwell. With the Restoration he came full circle, demonstrating his ability to ride the tide of changing fortunes. Margaret found this turn-around difficult to accept. It was incomprehensible to her that a people who could have murdered their lawful King eleven years earlier should now agree almost unanimously to enthrone his son. 'What kind of Fate was it,' she asked Newcastle in her biography, that produced such 'a perfect contrariety between the fortunes' of Charles I and his son?

Chapter Twelve

Restoration
1660 – 3

2nd Gentleman: *A Woman write a Play! Out upon it, out upon it, for it cannot be good, besides you say she is a Lady, which is the likelier to make the Play worse; a Woman and a Lady to write a Play? Fie, fie.*
1st Gentleman: *But if a Woman hath Wit or can write a good Play, what will you say then?*
2nd Gentleman: *Why I will say nobody will believe it, for if it be good, they will think she did not write it, or at least say she did not, besides the very being a Woman condemns it, were it never so excellent and rare, for men will not allow Women to have Wit, or Women to have Reason, for if we allow them Wit, we shall lose our Pre-eminency.*

> Introduction contributed by William
> Cavendish to Margaret Cavendish,
> *Plays*

While in Antwerp, Margaret had turned to yet another genre in her search for a style and a medium in which to express herself: encouraged by Newcastle, she had begun to write plays. Much struck with Jaen Potage's travelling troupe, she wrote all her female parts for female players, though they were never intended to be performed on the stage. 'It would make me a little melancholy to hear my harmless and innocent plays go weeping from the stage,' she wrote in the Preface. They were meant only to be read. In any case the theatres of England were closed and performance seemed only a remote possibility. Despite Margaret's apologies for the poor quality of her plays, she sent them to England to be printed and was devastated when the ship carrying the manuscript sank in a Channel storm. They had to be copied out again, and it was 1662 before they were finally published.

The plays are disappointing. They tend to be episodic, with no attempt to create dramatic tension. Some of the Acts have as many as twenty-nine Scenes, and characters sometimes speak for pages at a time. But there are exceptions. The heroines are fascinating because most of them are modelled on Margaret herself. Lady Sanspareille, who dazzles with her intelligence and learning, appears as frequently as Mistress Bashful, the shy and apparently stupid girl who carries off a matrimonial prize despite the malicious machinations of those around her. *The Presence* and *The Bridals* give a rare and interesting glimpse of the life of a lady in waiting at court.

Some of the plays display the quick ear for dialogue that Margaret had shown in her Puritan satires in *The World's Olio* and *Sociable Letters*. This is particularly evident in a speech by Brigid Greasy from *The Matrimonial Trouble*, a play about a lord who has married his maid. The maid immediately begins to give herself airs and graces.

> She called for a candle and a candlestick, . . . and I for haste run up with the candle and forgot the candlestick, and had left it behind me; when I came, 'What' said she, 'do you bring a candle without a candlestick?' 'Alas' said I, 'I have forgot it, but hold you the candle' said I 'and I will run and fetch it straight.' And so I put the candle into her hand: with that she up with her hand, and gave me a box on the ear. 'What' said she, 'do you give me a greasy candle to hold? I will teach you more manners', said she 'against the next time.'

Margaret's plays are sometimes coarse and explicit in the manner of Restoration comedy, but no more so than those of Shadwell or Massinger. Both Margaret and Aphra Behn were criticised for obscenity in scenes that would not have raised an eyebrow if penned by one of their male contemporaries. Sexual activity was a prohibited subject for women; to write about it was immodest.

The plays reveal Margaret's developing attitude to the relationships between men and women, and an increasingly progressive approach to the position of women in society. When Lady Bashful declares her intention to have a private wedding she asks the world at large why she should 'celebrate entry into a lifetime of slavery'. Plays like *The Ladies' Academy* and *Bell in Campo* identify Margaret as one of the most radical feminists of her time. She agreed with Shadwell in hating a 'dull Romantick whining play, where poor frail Woman's made a Deity, with senseless amorous Idolatry'. Her heroines are never passive: they are lovers, soldiers, adventurers and scholars.

Bell in Campo is the most successful of the plays, and still well worth reading. The Kingdom of Reformation is preparing for war against the Kingdom of Faction. The wives, led by Lady Victoria, refuse to stay at home and insist on accompanying their husbands to war. Lady Victoria asks her troops of women to live like men in order to become strong, to bear arms at all times, to occupy their free time in wrestling and throwing the bar, and when they march to sing of the heroic actions performed by women in history. They were forbidden to have contact with men, 'lest their resolution should be corrupted'. Lady Victoria lectures them on one of Margaret's favourite themes – that women were weaker than men only from custom and lack of education and training.

> Had our education been answerable to theirs we might have proved as good soldiers and Privy Councillors, Rulers and Commanders as men are. Wherefore if we would accustom ourselves we may do such actions as may gain us such a reputation, as men might change their opinions, insomuch as to believe we are fit to be co-partners in their governments.

Lady Victoria rallies her troops at the scene of battle with the cry: 'Now or never is the time to prove the courage of our sex, to get liberty and freedom from female slavery, and to make ourselves equal with men.' Lady Victoria's husband is utterly routed by the army of Faction, but the day is saved by the army of women who put the enemy to flight. On their return to the capital they are feted and the King in gratitude decrees that 'all women shall hereafter . . . be mistresses in their own homes and families'. They shall keep the purse, order their servants, claim their own goods and order them as they will, wear whatever they like, and come and go without control 'or giving any account thereof'.

The germ of the idea for such an unusual play seems to have come partly from the story of Joan of Arc, partly from the antics of the Grande Mademoiselle during the Fronde, and partly an incident during the reign of Ferdinand of Spain. His victory against the King of Granada was apparently 'chiefly occasioned' by Queen Isabella and her army of damsels. The tales that Margaret had read in the newssheets of women like the Countess of Derby and Lady Brilliana Harley defending their homes and even whole towns against military attack must also have influenced her, and there is evidence from contemporary ballads that women in men's attire did follow the army – going into battle with the men during the Civil War.

Margaret was fully aware of the faults in her plays, comparing them to 'dead statues, which is the reason I send them forth to be printed, rather than keep them concealed in hopes to have them first acted'. This raises the question of why she published them at all. The answer lies in her complex personality. Because she was so shy she could communicate with people eloquently only on paper.

The medium of the printed page enabled her to transcend the limitations of her sex, dispute with learned philosophers and create an ideal world where women stood on an equal footing with men. She was very conscious of her role as the first woman writer. She gave her books to friends and acquaintances and learned institutions, and through their distribution and the controversy they provoked she was becoming well known. To achieve lasting fame she was prepared to accept adverse criticism. 'A horse of a noble spirit,' she wrote, 'slights the bawling of a petty cur.' But blanket criticism of whatever she did, largely because she was a woman, blunted her own critical faculties. She had to believe in herself and rely on her own judgement. Her conceptions were very precious: she could hardly bear to discard anything she had created herself, however dissatisfied she was with it. Over a dozen Scenes which had to be left out of *The Presence* were included at the end of the volume as 'a Part of a Play'. She published everything she wrote, hoping that one day her work would be valued and appreciated.

While Margaret put her plays and letters in order, Newcastle went to Holland to be near the King. By April 1660 people in England had begun openly to drink the King's health. Pepys recorded that boys were saying 'Kiss my Rump' instead of 'Kiss my arse', and it wasn't long before William Lilly could write that the citizens of London were deriding Parliament by procuring rumps of beef and publicly burning them in the streets.

On the advice of General Monck Charles had tactfully moved from the Spanish Netherlands (Spain and England were at war) to Holland. There, on 4 April, with considerable assistance from the Earl of Clarendon, Charles signed the famous Declaration of Breda. Its weasel words promised a free pardon to all other than those who may 'hereafter be excepted by Parliament'. Lucy Hutchinson, whose husband was one of those affected by it, recorded that it 'Promised or at least intimated, Liberty of Conscience, remission of all offences, enjoyment of liberties and estates'. Reassured by its contents, Parliament approved a Resolution on 1 May inviting Charles to assume the government of his kingdom, an invitation that the King immediately accepted. Those who went from England to Holland to negotiate with him were struck by the shabby state of his clothes. Pepys wrote that when he gave the King the money voted by Parliament for his relief Charles gazed and gazed at it as it lay in the trunk, admitting that he had never seen so much money in his life.

Newcastle was among those who went to The Hague to swear an oath of allegiance and jostle for office. The King dealt with him 'very graciously', but ignored the treatise of advice that he had written for him. Newcastle had been his father's man, and the King's trust rested entirely in Clarendon, who did not get on well with Newcastle. The position of master of the horse, on which he had set his heart, was given to General Monck.

Charles, while conscious of obligations to those who had fought for his father, and therefore indirectly for him, did not consider himself bound by them. Circumstances dictated the inclusion of new men in the King's council, and in order to appease his enemies a new web of loyalties would have to be woven by the exercise of patronage. Those who had placed Charles on his throne had the first claim on his generosity. It would have taxed anyone's ingenuity to find places or employment both for all those who had served him or his father and for the new generation. Even Sir Richard Fanshawe was passed over for the promised post of Secretary of State, which was given to one of Monck's men.

The Duke of York offered to transport Newcastle to England with the King's party, but he refused – perhaps partly out of pique, but possibly much more from the antipathy he felt for those who had hitherto been his enemies, and towards whom he must now dissemble. Newcastle was so anxious to return to England that he did not bother to return to Antwerp but informed Margaret of his intentions by letter. He went to Rotterdam to search for a ship, but the demand was so great that he could find only 'an old rotten frigate'. It was so obviously unseaworthy that some of his company refused to sail in it, and their pessimism was borne out by the fact that the ship foundered on the very next voyage. However, the eager Newcastle shrugged off their warnings and embarked with his intrepid friend Lord Widdrington. The weather was so good that they were becalmed for six days at sea, passing the time in celebration of the King's Restoration. This not only meant that they were not there to welcome the King at Dover (causing some offence), but that Newcastle's son, hearing that his father had embarked some days before the King in a leaky vessel, feared that he had drowned. Eventually he arrived at Greenwich to be reunited with his family. Newcastle described the sensation as being woken from a sixteen-year-long dream. His supper that night 'seemed more savoury to him than any meat he had hitherto tasted', and some 'scraping fiddlers' the best music he had ever heard.

The Restoration was everywhere an excuse for an outburst of the joy and high spirits which had been suppressed by the sobriety of the Commonwealth. In many parts of the country there were sporting activities, dancing and country fairs. Pepys recorded that from Rochester to Blackheath the highway was so crowded with people striving for a glimpse of the King on his way to London that it seemed like 'one continuous street wonderfully inhabited'. The King and his entourage had replaced their old clothes with cloth of silver, purple velvet and silver lace which, mingled with the red robes of the Aldermen, made a brilliant spectacle. Monck met the King at Blackheath with fifty thousand horse and foot, and all the gentry of the kingdom who could contrive to be there went either to Dover or to London to swear their fealty. 'Indeed,' wrote Lucy Hutchinson, 'it was a wonder in that day to see the mutability of some and the hypocrisy of others and the servile flattery of all.'

Before he left Rotterdam Newcastle wrote to Margaret 'commanding' her to remain in Antwerp in pawn for his debts. She was also instructed to discharge his obligations to the various dignitaries of the city, which in his haste to reach The Hague he had neglected to do. Margaret was not unduly perturbed by this situation; if anything she seemed proud that Newcastle had entrusted her with so much responsibility. She had absolute faith that he would ensure her speedy redemption and occupied herself in packing up their belongings.

But the position in England was difficult for those returning exiles who had been denied composition and whose estates had passed into the hands of others. At this time it was uncertain whether they would ever get them back. Newcastle found himself almost as penniless in London as he had been in Antwerp, and it was just as difficult to borrow money. Now he needed £5000 to maintain himself and his family until the future of his estates could be determined, as well as money to discharge the debts in Antwerp. Eventually he borrowed sufficient for the latter from an Antwerp merchant, but it was not enough to cover the debts that Margaret had run up in the meantime, or the cost of her transportation with all their domestic goods back to England. Margaret was forced to borrow £400 more from another merchant, a relative of the first. Margaret's expectations of the Restoration proved to be rather more realistic than her husband's. A little earlier she had written in one of her letters, published in *Sociable Letters*:

As for our husbands' going into their native country in a glorious condition as you were pleased to say in your last letter you were in hopes they should do, give me leave to tell you I hope well of our going into our native country, but I doubt of the Glory, for our noble husbands' losses will eclipse that splendour, for we shall only find ruins, meet opposers and have debts attend upon us.

The magistrates of Antwerp came to take their ceremonial leave, and Margaret's neighbour Senor Duartes offered his assistance as an interpreter. She was glad of his support. This was the kind of formal public occasion that Newcastle graced with courtesy and easy familiarity and Margaret dreaded, though she declared herself willing to 'show herself' on public occasions when her husband asked her to. Through Senor Duartes she accepted the civic dignitaries' expressions of civility and good wishes for a happy return to England. She expressed Newcastle's apologies for his hasty departure and their gratitude for the hospitality which had been extended to them, and in her biography of her husband declared how sorry she was not to be able 'to make an acknowledgement answerable to them'. Afterwards, according to custom, the magistrates sent round a gift of wine, which was gratefully received on behalf of the Marquis. Margaret rarely touched alcoholic liquor herself, preferring to risk the hazards of the drinking water.

She travelled to Flushing, where she was able to hire a cargo vessel to carry sixteen years' accumulation of household goods and baggage, but was unable to find an English man-of-war for herself and her household, and was too nervous a sea traveller to trust herself to anything smaller. However a Dutch ship lay at anchor nearby, taking on supplies for the conveyance of a company of merchants to England, and Margaret sent for the captain, who declared his readiness to transport her if she could obtain the Dutch government's permission. This was quickly granted and Margaret was able to embark for England, crossing the Channel for the last time.

Despite Margaret's pessimistic expectations expressed in Antwerp, the reality of the situation shocked her. Newcastle's lodgings were so small that some members of the household had had to stay elsewhere. It seemed like Paris all over again. Even worse was his position with regard to the court. She wrote tartly, with considerable understatement, that 'my lord's condition' was not 'such as I expected'. There was little of the glory or honour for which Newcastle had hoped. The elderly Cavalier had been shouldered aside by those anxious to prove new loyalties and by others more ambitious and less scrupulous. The establishment of a new regime provided the opportunity for the sort of pandering that Newcastle always detested. Margaret, like that other future Duchess, Sarah Churchill, had a much greater regard for place and position than did her husband. When she dressed for public occasions it was, she wrote in 'A True Relation', to honour Newcastle's position in the world,

> perceiving the world is given or apt to honour the outside more than the inside, worshipping show more than substance . . . I am so proud, or rather just to my Lord, as to abate nothing of the quality of his Wife, for if honour be the mark of Merit . . . it were a baseness for me to neglect the Ceremony thereof.

Newcastle, she averred in her biography, never regarded 'place except it be for ceremony; to the meanest person he'll put off his hat, and suffer everybody to speak to him'. She wrote uncomprehendingly that this aristocratic ease of manner only seemed to increase respect for him, while her own correct and distant demeanour, learnt from Elizabeth Lucas, occasioned ridicule.

New lodgings were now found in Dorset House, an elegant residence in a more fashionable part of town, although only a part of it was rented to them and Margaret was still dissatisfied on Newcastle's behalf. To have lost so much and endured sixteen years in penniless exile, and then to come back to such penury and neglect, seemed monstrous. Newcastle told Margaret gently, as she recorded in her life of him, that she should imitate an experienced sailor and either trim her sails to the wind or take them down 'so should I either comply with Time or abate my passion'. His sentiments towards his monarch never wavered. When Margaret taunted him with the fact that the King did not love him so well as he loved the King, he replied that he cared not, that his love was above wife, children and even his own life.

After the coronation Charles gradually established a court that bore little resemblance to that of his father. It was graced by the beautiful Barbara Palmer, Lady Castlemaine, the King's new mistress, and that liaison set the tone for those around him. Charles was burying the unhappy years of want in an avalanche of pleasure. It was cynically rumoured that a happily married man would be excluded from office; it was necessary to have at least one mistress in order to find favour. Virtuous ladies were suddenly in the minority. Anne, Countess of Pembroke, declared that she would not go to court unless she was allowed to wear blinkers.

The Newcastles attended the King's coronation, where every lady, according to an onlooker, was dressed like a queen. They were still in London when the news broke of James, Duke of York's secret marriage to Clarendon's daughter Anne Hyde. James was a close friend of Newcastle's, despite the age gap, and Margaret had known Anne in Antwerp. Judging from the private visits made between them, the Newcastles' support for the couple seems to have been unswerving through a particularly difficult time.

Newcastle was created Knight of the Garter and invested on 15 April 1661, when he was also formally admitted to the Privy Council, but it was a formality in both senses of the word. It did not take Newcastle long to assess the situation, and having been restored by Act of Parliament to those estates not already sold and in the possession of others, he told Margaret that they were to leave London for the country. She was initially piqued, because this had been her advice to Newcastle a year earlier and he had refused to take it. Margaret was rarely angry, but admitted that she could be severe when opposed. When she assured her husband that she was only ever cross with those whom she loved well, he begged her humorously not to love him best. However, Margaret much preferred the country to the town, and it was with real pleasure that she ordered her household once more to pack for the long journey north.

Newcastle requested leave to go from the King, and his feelings at the time were recorded by Margaret in her biography: 'I am not ignorant that many believe I am dissatisfied, and 'tis probable they'll say I retire through discontent; but I take God to witness that I am in no kind or ways displeased.' The very need to disclaim such sentiments argues their presence. However, disillusionment might have been a more appropriate word to describe the sixty-eight-year-old Marquis' feelings as he kissed the King's hand and received permission to quit the court. In 1644 he had fled after Marston Moor to avoid his enemies' pleasure in seeing him humiliated. Now once more he did the same, with hardly more money in his pocket than he had had before and no more honour. It was another three years before the Dukedom asked for and promised was finally granted. Those most honoured and rewarded at the Restoration were those who, like Monck, had previously been enemies, but Newcastle harboured no resentment against the King.

It was a dismal homecoming. Some of Newcastle's old estates were in the hands of the Duke of York, the King having given the estates of all the Commonwealth malefactors to his brother. These were graciously restored to the Marquis. For others he had to resort to process of law, not always successfully; Nottingham Castle had to be repurchased. The condition of most of the parks was poor: nothing was more characteristic of the Commonwealth than its destruction of the woods and parks of the rich and privileged. Large tracts of English woodland vanished overnight. In Clipstone Park, which had been Newcastle's favourite, not one tree had been left standing, and the rich reserves of deer and other game had either disappeared or been destroyed.

Newcastle, normally philosophical in the face of misfortune, was more upset by this than by anything else. Margaret sensitively recorded in her biography that she 'never perceived him sad or discontented for his own losses and misfortunes, yet when he beheld the ruins of the park, I observed him troubled, though he did little express it, only saying he had been in hopes it would not have been so much defaced as he found it'. He remarked to some labourers cutting up a tree blown down in a gale that he was like a tree himself for 'in like manner have I been cut down by Lady Fortune'. His estate amounted only to the chips left by the woodcutters, although it was still substantial.

Newcastle's principal estates occupied an area of Nottinghamshire and Derbyshire now known as the Dukeries – undulating, fertile country, still thickly wooded today. Welbeck and Bolsover, thanks to his brother Sir Charles Cavendish, were still in Newcastle's possession, though both houses had sustained a great deal of damage. Bolsover, at one stage bought by a speculator for building materials, had had all the roofing lead removed, and as a result the weather had reached the grand rooms built on by Newcastle before the war. Margaret described it in *Description of a Blazing New World* as a 'naked house'. The small castle with its pretty wainscoted rooms and painted ceilings was more or less intact, but the outer walls had been partly demolished by the Commonwealth government to render it useless as a fortified building and save the expense of a garrison. The graceful house adjoining the castle that had once been host to the King and Queen was a damp, hollow shell. Eighteenth-century prints show Bolsover roofed and externally sound, though the buildings were never completely restored. They are now in a state of total ruin, only prevented from collapse by scaffolding. Windows, door lintels and carvings have been worn away by rain and atmospheric pollution. The little castle built by Newcastle's father has fared better, and its romantic decor has been lovingly restored.

Welbeck had been stripped of most of its furnishings, hangings and pictures. But Sir Charles, and then Viscount Mansfield, had at least preserved the park and bought back some of the furniture. Contemporary paintings and engravings show a graceful house of modest proportions in the same soft stone as Bolsover, with tall Elizabethan chimneys and large lattice windows. It is now virtually unrecognisable. A Norman arch in a basement corridor hints at its monastic origins. A curved gable rising among a jumble of eighteenth- and nineteenth-century rebuilding, and a few carved fireplaces, are all that remain of the original house, though Newcastle's riding school stands virtually unaltered. The house is very secluded, set in a hollow on the fringes of Sherwood Forest overlooking a small lake, and concealed from the road by more than a mile of carriageway and thick clumps of trees.

Margaret loved it. She had always preferred the solitude of the country to the hurly-burly of town life, with its obligatory ceremonial and the fear of unexpected visitors to throw her out of countenance. When friends urged her to return to London, she refused. *Sociable Letters* reveals that she was

> so much pleased with a solitary country life that I cannot bring any argument to myself, which can induce or persuade me to a city life, which is but a gossiping and vain life . . . and if I lived there and did not speak idly and spend vainly as others do I should be out of fashion, and there is an old saying, 'better out of the world, than out of fashion'.

She was indeed morally out of step – one of those 'old formal creatures', as Shadwell described them in *The Virtuoso*, 'that were in fashion in the year 1640, and censure all ladies that have freedom in their carriage'. The new court morality did not find any favour with Margaret, who had been prudishly critical even of the more decorous court of Charles I and Henrietta Maria. Now she was disgusted. Lady Contemplation in the play of the same name observes that 'In this age mothers bring up their daughters to carry letters, and to receive messages, or are left to watch at the door lest their fathers should come unawares.'

Margaret and her husband lived a 'shepherd's life' as she put it in *Sociable Letters*. She had inherited more than she realised of her mother's shrewd head for business, and quickly became more adept at the 'management of sheep and the ordering of a grange' than pleased Newcastle's steward at Welbeck, Andrew Clayton. Dealing with people had never come easily to Margaret. She was distant and awkward with the servants as well as with others, and her shyness never had anything to do with the social status of those with whom she came into contact. 'Were I to enter amongst a company of Lazaruses I should be as much out of countenance as if they were all Caesars or Alexanders', she admitted in her autobiography. The old Cavendish retainers found her incomprehensible and instinctively distrusted her, and she was never able to form more than an uneasy truce with her stepchildren. But her time alone with her husband in Antwerp had forged strong links between them, and their relationship was well able to withstand problems that might otherwise have soured it. The anguish she had felt so keenly as a young, inexperienced girl coming into an established household was now tempered by the knowledge that she was secure in Newcastle's affections. He defended her resolutely against his family, assuring them often that Margaret had their best interests at heart, whatever they might think of her.

One of the areas of friction was her maid Elizabeth Chaplain. She had been a faithful companion and friend to Margaret in exile, willingly pawning her own goods when the Newcastles were in need. The merchant she had married in Antwerp, Francis Topp, had proved invaluable to the Marquis, extricating him from financial difficulties on several occasions. Newcastle had come to depend on his shrewd advice. It is possible that Francis Topp had done it with an eye to the future, but he well deserved the knighthood that he now received. Elizabeth, now Lady Topp, and her small daughter continued to live at Welbeck. The Topps were regarded as Margaret's creatures by Newcastle's old servants, who not only resented their influence but felt that they were enriching themselves at the Newcastles' expense.

Though the Newcastles remained in the country they were still closely in touch with events. The spirit of universal reconciliation had not lasted long, and the time had come for reprisals. Initially it was only those who had been responsible for the death of Charles I who had to be brought to justice. The Bill of Indemnity, passed in 1660, had excepted them so that 'they might be made sacrifices to appease God's wrath and satisfy divine justice'. The King ordered Cromwell's, Ireton's and Bradshaw's bodies to be exhumed and their rotting corpses hung at Tyburn, as a grisly symbol of his vengeance. This was only the beginning. Lucy Hutchinson wrote bitterly that 'the Presbyterians were now the white boys, and according to their nature fell a-thirsting, then hunting after blood, and urging that God's blessing would not be upon the land till justice had cleansed it from the late King's blood'. The far-sighted had foreseen that it could end in nothing else.

The army had been disbanded and gangs of men roamed the countryside, living by theft. There were plots, both real and imagined, against the King's life. In Nottingham and Leicester Papists with scarlet ribbons in their hats burned hay barns. Francis Topp wrote to Newcastle in August 1662 from the west country that 'every day there is preaching and rumour of rebellion, and until that be over, which I hope will be soon . . . then men will buy land, which they will not do now'. As late as October 1663 a Colonel Frecheville wrote that a party of rebels were to rendezvous at Skipton in Yorkshire, and requested Newcastle's assistance for 'these parts are all in arms'. The French ambassador watched events carefully and thought it not unlikely that the English might be tempted to try to establish a Commonwealth again.

Colonel Hutchinson and his wife Lucy, the Newcastles' neighbours, had supported the other side in the Civil War. The bookish and clever Lucy had much in common with Margaret. Her memoirs of Colonel Hutchinson and her short autobiography were modelled on Margaret's biographical works, although she was able to go into more detail and be very frank because she never intended them for publication. They were for the eyes of her family only, and she did not have to worry about libel or the reactions of a hostile public.

The Colonel had been as honourable and obstinate on the side of the Commonwealth as Newcastle had been on that of the King. He had great courage and despised dissembling, and refused now to make the necessary retraction of his political views to Parliament in order to save his life. In the end it was Lucy who wrote a letter to the House in his name, forging his signature on the bottom. Hutchinson was discharged from office and Parliament as a punishment for his part in the Civil War. Unfortunately his enemies in Whitehall did not allow it to rest there. In October 1663 he was arrested and brought before Newcastle as Chief Justice in Eyre. Newcastle was characteristically fair, and showed Hutchinson letters from the Duke of Buckingham ordering his arrest on suspicion of plotting against the King. Newcastle refused to imprison him and sent him home on bail, only to be overruled by Buckingham. Hutchinson was taken to London and locked in the same tower room as Richard III's little princes. It was impossible to ascertain where the charges against him originated. The Colonel bore it all with fortitude and, whatever he knew of the various plots against the King, refused to give any information in order to save himself. Others were not so loyal – a man called Waters gave information that put his wife in prison, smeared the reputation of his brother-in-law and hanged his closest friend. But all Newcastle's attempts to do justice, and the intercession of Lucy's Royalist connections, were useless, and the Colonel died after months in custody without being formally charged. Lucy herself had been asked to give information as the price of her husband's 'pardon' but, with a fortitude Margaret would have admired, always refused, safety being in her words 'not worth the price of honour and conscience'.

Margaret's life of seclusion at Welbeck did not prevent rumour from embellishing her reputation. With the publication of her *Plays*, in 1662, she was once more in the public eye. People were avid for news of her. Sir Charles Lyttleton, accompanying the Duke and Duchess of York on a journey north, met the Newcastles' carriage on the road to York. In a letter he wrote that the Duchess' behaviour 'was rather to be seen than told. She was dressed in a vest, and, instead of courtesies made legs and bows to the ground with her hand and head'. Male attire was much in vogue at the time, and even Charles II's bride, Queen Catherine of Braganza, appeared in breeches. Whatever Margaret wore now was likely to be the subject of gossip. On 2 February 1664 the King held a ball at court, and the Chevalier de Grammont described how he had been accosted outside by 'the devil of a phantom in masquerade'. He told the King that 'it is worth while to see her dress, for she must have at least 60 ells of gauze and silver tissue about her, not to mention a sort of pyramid upon her head, adorned with a hundred thousand baubles'. 'I bet,' replied the King, 'that it is the Marchioness of Newcastle.' It was in fact the Countess of Muskerry intent upon embarrassing her husband, but the incident shows how Margaret was regarded.

Chapter Thirteen

The Virtuosi
1663 – 5

Philosophers should be men of years, with grave and austere looks . . . 'tis a prodigious thing, a girl to read Philosophy. O Divine Plato, how thy soul will now be troubled, Diogenes repents his tub, and Seneca will burn his books in Anger. And Old Aristotle wish he had never been the master of all schools, now to be taught and by a girl.

Scene contributed by William
Cavendish to Margaret Cavendish,
Youth's Glory and Death's Banquet,
from *Plays*

When she went to live in the country Margaret had resolved to occupy herself industriously with the restoration of the house and other womanly concerns, but she was forced to confess to Newcastle, as she noted in *Philosophical and Physical Opinions*, that 'I cannot for my life be so good a housewife as to quit writing.' She had been toying with the idea of a book of orations, apparently suggested by a friend, but was at first discouraged by her own ignorance. 'How should I write orations who know no rules in rhetoric nor never went to school, but only learned to read and write at home?' she wrote in a letter subsequently included in *Sociable Letters*.

But fortunately the idea took root in her mind and flourished. Casual, short pieces directly addressed to the reader in a conversational manner, like the letters and the little anecdotes in *The World's Olio*, suited Margaret ideally. The orations are more formal in style, but they allowed Margaret to range over a vast variety of subjects and required no sustained effort of concentration. She could write what she was unable to speak.

> Though I love Justice best and trust to Valour most, yet I admire Eloquence and would choose Wit for my pastime. Indeed natural orators that can speak on a sudden and extempore upon any subject are nature's musicians, moving the passions to harmony making concords out of discords, playing on the soul with delight.

Among male orators whom she sought to emulate she admired Julius Caesar most:

because he was a man that had all these excellencies, as Courage, Prudence, Wit and Eloquence in great perfection, insomuch as when I read of Julius Caesar, I cannot but wish that Nature and Fate had made me such a one as he was; and sometimes I have that courage, as to think I should not be afraid of his destiny, so I might have so great a Fame.

The short orations allowed Margaret to put forward her own individual opinions on such diverse subjects as war, politics, freedom of conscience and the position of women in society. She returned once more to the argument that if women were to imitate men, their bodies and minds would become more masculine. Women were unaware of their own capabilities, falsely believing themselves to be incompetent. 'How should we know ourselves, when we never made a trial of ourselves?' she pleaded, 'Or how should men know us, when they never put us to the proof?' She took pains to argue the case from both sides, but the only time her pen catches fire is when she defends her sex:

> It is not only uncivil and ignoble, but unnatural for men to speak against women and their liberties . . . Men are happy and we women are miserable, for they possess all the ease, rest, pleasure, wealth, power and fame, whereas women are restless with labour, easeless with pain, melancholy for want of pleasure, helpless for want of power and die in oblivion for want of fame; nevertheless men are so unconscionable and cruel against us as they endeavour to bar us of all sorts of kinds of liberty, as not to suffer us freely to associate amongst our own sex, but would fain bury us in their houses or beds as in a grave; the truth is we live like bats or owls, labour like beasts, and die like worms.

Passages like this cause the reader to think very deeply about Margaret's own relationship with her husband. She professed herself happily married to a good and loyal man, yet everywhere she equates marriage with slavery and the negation of the female personality. Her stories, letters and anecdotes are crammed with tales of male tyranny and infidelity. Her view of marriage can only be assessed as cynical. It was formed by what she saw in society around her, but does not appear to be qualified by her own personal experience. In the letter she wrote to her unmarried sister Anne, later published in *Sociable Letters*, she stressed the invidious position of the wife, equating it to that of a servant even in a good marriage. She ended by advising Anne to be mistress only of herself 'which in a single life you are'.

Even the publication of Margaret's books required the permission of her husband, who, she wrote in *Philosophical and Physical Opinions*, fortunately was 'pleased to peruse my works and approve them so well, as to give me leave to publish them, which is a favour few husbands would grant their wives'. This was a situation for which Margaret had no remedy and she was extremely pessimistic about the future.

> Alas men, that are not only our tyrants but our devils, keep us in the hell of subjection, from whence I cannot perceive any redemption or getting out . . . we may complain and bewail our condition, yet that will not free us . . . our words to men are as empty sounds . . . our tears as fruitless showers, and our power is so inconsiderable as men laugh at our weaknesses.

The Commonwealth had done little in a practical way to advance the cause of women. They were as uneducated as before, and though Milton had written pamphlets advocating divorce for mere incompatibility, and for a time civil marriage and divorce had been possible, the situation was now as it had been before. Milton in fact was one of the most misogynistic of the Puritan writers, portraying Eve as a seductive little woman who preferred to have the instructions of God relayed to her via her husband.

However, the Civil War and the Commonwealth had provided opportunities for women to occupy roles normally reserved for men. The questioning of the relationships between Church, King and State had led to a reassessment of other relationships, particularly that of husband and wife. The Puritan sects, especially the Levellers, believed that all men and women were born free and equal. It was no coincidence that Margaret's years of greatest literary production were those of enormous social upheaval and the emergence of new modes of thought. Women had played a large part in the conduct of the Civil War and in the organisation and daily worship of the Sects, and as a result a larger part in everyday life. The restoration of the monarchy restored the patriarchy of the Anglican Church and the more traditional views of women's role in society, though it was impossible to restore the status quo completely. A handful of women, like Margaret, had glimpsed the possibilities. 'There was on the part of women,' wrote Myra Reynolds in *The Learned Lady in England*, 'a blind and unfocused, but persistent and stimulating sense that larger and more varied opportunities were awaiting them.

Latent powers had been stirred into self-consciousness and could not be lulled into the old quiescence.' The figure of Rebellion in the King's coronation procession was a woman, dressed in crimson, wielding a bloody sword and surrounded by writhing snakes.

The change in attitude towards women is revealed by the way women are portrayed in Restoration drama. There are no more Violas, no more Portias. The audience is no longer invited to laugh with the heroine or sympathise with her position. Women are the butts of humour, victims and pawns in a cynical sexual game. The King's open flouting of his marriage bond and the multiplicity of his mistresses and bastards sanctioned the double standards that Margaret so bitterly opposed. The high-class courtesans of the court and their titled offspring drew too much attention to those aspects of womanhood most deplored by Margaret and by Bathsua Makin, and the King's lifestyle appealed to most male egos.

Margaret ignored all pleas to return to town and court, preferring the solitary life to that of a 'metropolitan city spread broad with vanity'. She would, she wrote in a letter printed in *Sociable Letters*, 'weep myself into water if I could have no other fame than rich coaches, lackies and what State and Ceremony could produce, for my ambition flies higher – I would be known to the world by my wit, not by my folly'.

She occupied the hours at Welbeck reading widely in philosophy, as she wrote in *Philosophical and Physical Opinions*, to 'learn those names and words of Art that are used in schools'. Her struggle to educate herself was made more difficult by the obscure language used in some of the texts and the frequent presence of words borrowed from Latin and Greek.

Had they not been explained to me, and had I not found out some of them by the context and connection of the sense, I should have been far enough to seek, for these hard words did more obstruct than instruct me. The truth is, if anyone intends to write philosophy either in English, or any other language, he ought to consider the property of the language as much as the subject he writes of, or else to what purpose would it be to write . . . What are words but marks of things? And what are philosophical terms, but to express the conceptions of one's mind in that science? . . . wherefore those that fill their writings with hard words put the horses behind the coach and instead of making hard things easy, make easy things hard.

Margaret went out of her way to avoid 'inkhorn' terms and 'scholastical expressions' in her work. At Welbeck she expanded and corrected her original *Philosophical Fancies* and in 1663 brought out the third edition, entitled, like the second, *Philosophical and Physical Opinions*. *Sociable Letters* and a companion volume of *Philosophical Letters* appeared in 1664, and in 1666 she published *Observations on Experimental Philosophy*, the most thoughtful and polished of her scientific works.

Her beliefs are sometimes captivating, as in her description of an intelligent universe, in the 1663 edition of *Philosophical and Physical Opinions*:

> I conceived that it was not probable that the universe and all the creatures therein could be created and disposed by the dancing, and wandering and dusty motions of Atoms, the reason why I think so is as follows; it is not probable that the substance of Infinite Matter is only infinite, small senseless fibres moving and composing all creatures by Chance, and that Chance should produce all things in such order and method . . . such distinctions of several kinds.

There must be 'sense and reason, life and knowledge', not only beyond and above, but also within each atom itself. But she was unable to imagine how this could be, or how one atom could agree to join with another without quarrelling.

She distrusted the microscope. Magnification, she claimed in *Observations on Experimental Philosophy*, falsified, making a louse appear like a lobster. 'If the edge of a knife or point of a needle were naturally and really so as the microscope presents them, they would never be so useful as they are.' She preferred the evidence of her own eyes, observing assiduously the different motions of leather, water, stone and wood when thrown on the fire. She watched how water spread upon the ground when the maids threw it out, 'in a half circle in a Convex figure, and the end of the flow is narrow like . . . a pear', she recorded in *Philosophical and Physical Opinions*. Her knowledge of anatomy was gleaned from observing the butchers ripping up dead beasts as her coach passed the shambles.

Some of her comments in this work are strikingly modern. She discusses music as a cure for madness, and those who fall ill by 'conceit of imagination'. Certain theories, like the association of light and colour, were beyond her comprehension. She argued that 'Grass is green as much in the night as in the day, whether the eye sees it or not.' She asks impossible, but intelligent, questions such as 'Why . . . have birds their shapes, and beasts their shapes and men and fish and trees their shapes . . . and not other kinds of shapes?' And everywhere she vigorously defends her assertion that everything has 'sense and knowledge'. Man may have a 'different knowledge from beasts, birds, fish, worms and the like and yet be no wiser or knowing than they; for different ways in knowledge make not knowledge more or less, no more than different paths enlarge one compass of ground.' Among the stranger anecdotes she relates is that a 'little mouse will run up and through the trunk or snout of a great elephant and eat out his brain and kill him'.

It was Margaret's great desire that her books should be accepted by the universities and given a valued place among the established works of philosophy, but she knew that this was unlikely, and suspected that her books would lie buried in the dust of the university libraries. She placed all her trust in posterity, hoping for a 'glorious Resurrection, . . . since Time brings Strange and Unusual things to pass'. She sent copies of her books to the Universities of Oxford and Cambridge, and to the great European centres of learning. Her motives were clearly stated in the Preface to *Philosophical and Physical Opinions*:

> I here present to you this Philosophical Work, not that I can hope wise schoolmen and industrious, laborious students should value it for any worth, but to receive it without scorn, for the good encouragement of our sex, lest in time we should grow irrational as idiots by the dejectedness of our spirits, through the careless neglect and despisements of the masculine sex to the female, thinking it impossible we should have either learning, understanding, wit or judgement . . . and we out of a custom of dejectedness think so too.

Officially the universities sent further obsequious letters of praise. They embraced her epistles and poems 'with the same mind with which we do all sublime and excellent things'. Her philosophy has 'lightsome and piercing acuteness'. She owes nothing to Nature, 'for how much soever she hath graced you with an incomparable lustre in your Feature, or pregnancy of Wit, your Grace hath returned all of it in these elegancies of Philosophy'. When Horace Walpole came to write his *Royal and Noble Authors* he commented that these 'inflated eulogies . . . must have been enough to turn any brain, previously diseased with cacoethes scribendi'. Some of the universities hoped for a handsome endowment. St John's College, Cambridge wrote to Margaret, addressing her as 'Most Illustrious

Princess' and explaining that 'we are so unhappily engaged in Building, that we can neither leave off nor go on, without the help and assistance of others; yet we would be content to change our design and wholly leave what we have in hand to erect a statue to your Grace's Name and Memory'.

Walpole was not the only person to consider Margaret's gift a disease. She defended herself vigorously in *Grounds of Natural Philosophy*. 'To be infected with the same disease which the devoutest, wisest, wittiest, subtlest, most learned and eloquent men have been troubled withall is no disgrace – but the greatest honour that can happen to the most ambitious person in the world.' The Prefaces to her books were becoming increasingly defensive, in the face of adverse criticism. In *Sociable Letters* she pleaded with her readers to be tolerant:

> I hope you will not make the mistake of a word a crime in my *Wit*, as some former readers have done, for in my *Poems* they found fault that the Number was not just, nor every line matched with a perfect rhyme . . . As for my work the *World's Olio*, they may say some words are not exactly placed, which I confess to be very likely. Concerning my *Philosophical Opinions* some did say they were too obscure and not plain enough for their understanding . . . I am not nature to give them wit and understanding; as for my book of *Plays* some find fault they are not made up exactly, nor the scenes placed justly.

She added, with a complete disregard for truth, 'I matter not their censure, for it would be an endless trouble to me to answer everyone's foolish exception.'

Margaret concentrated more and more on natural philosophy. In 1662 the Royal Society had been founded, receiving King Charles' approval the same year. The variety of subject matter was as wide as the interests of its members, and membership was fashionable rather than springing from a genuine passion for scientific discovery. The members formed a coterie to exchange information and argue theories, something that Margaret desperately needed but could achieve only vicariously through her books and correspondence with other members, and through her husband's involvement with the Society – which was minimal due to his age and the distance of Welbeck from London. The 150-mile journey took two or three days even when the weather was good and the roads clear.

Both Margaret and her husband were Virtuosi, the talented amateurs brilliantly satirised by Shadwell in a play dedicated to

Newcastle after Margaret's death. Shadwell, Dryden and Richard Flecknoe owed a considerable debt to the Duke's patronage, and although they sailed close to the wind none published anything that might be construed as a direct satire of the Duchess. Shadwell's *Sullen Lovers*, published in 1669, has a Lady Vaire who is a Virtuosa and is learned in physick. Dryden's *Mock Astrologer* of 1668 has a similar character called Donna Aurelia, but both ladies use the learned terms which Margaret specifically avoided and owe more to the salons of Paris than to Welbeck Abbey. After Margaret's death it was a different matter. The woman writer and the woman scientist were two of the most frequent comic figures on the Restoration stage and it is possible to detect traces of Margaret's legend in many of them. The most recognisable portrait was that of the eccentric Phoebe Clinket, created by Alexander Pope and his friend John Gay in 1717. During Margaret's lifetime the opinions of contemporary writers were tempered by the position which she and her husband occupied as patrons of literature.

Dryden, by far the most gifted of the Duke's three literary protégés, had been recommended to Newcastle by Davenant, who was now managing the Duke of York's Theatre. The disillusioned poet made his living from a succession of successful stage plays and was capable of the kind of literary acrobatics that enabled him to produce within the space of a year sorrowful verses on the death of Cromwell and a celebration ode on Charles II's coronation. He had a gift for satire, portraying Shadwell first as Og the seditious poetaster in *Absalom and Achitophel*, and then as the Prince of Dullness in *MacFlecknoe*, which jeered at both Shadwell and Flecknoe. He defended his venomous attack by claiming that 'he who writes Honestly is no more an enemy of the Offender, than the physician to the Patient when he prescribes harsh Remedies to an inveterate Disease'.

Shadwell, a corpulent opium-taker, was an odd protégé and easily the most sycophantic of the three. Flecknoe was probably the most interesting. Described by Marvell as 'black habited, camel tall', so thin 'as if he only fed had been with consecrated wafers', he had a reputation for rudeness and lived on patronage. It was said that he was a man who would never eat at home if he could dine from someone else's table. He liked to tell heavily embroidered tales of his travels, and when he published some of them as *Ten Years' Travels in Europe* the Duke wrote a Preface in verse. Though he wrote both poetry and plays he had little success with either.

This odd triumvirate showed Newcastle their plays, discussed them and wrote fervent dedications to their patron, occasionally mentioning his wife. Shadwell wrote to the Duchess in execrable verse:

> Whilst others study books, I study you
> And can b' experience this affirm for true
> Of all your sex you have the greatest worth
> As ever yet these later times brought forth,
>
> There being nothing so sublime and High
> But you can read in all Philosophy
> Nor so profound and deep again but you
> With ease, can dive; and penetrate into.

Sometimes Newcastle produced some of his own work for their approval; it was rewritten by them, but graciously produced on stage under the Duke's name. After the Duke's death both Dryden and Shadwell discreetly re-registered plays in their own names. Newcastle had a talent for a witty turn of phrase and a piece of lyric verse, and an ear for tavern conversation. Some of the best scenes in Margaret's plays, from a dramatic point of view, are those contributed by her husband. But he was an amateur, content to dabble and leave the real work to those whose livelihood it was.

Newcastle's eldest daughter Elizabeth, Countess of Bridgwater, died in childbirth in 1663. She was a lady of strict piety who left behind a book of *Meditation, Prayers and Devout Contemplations* which was published after her death. The Earl of Bridgwater was devastated by his loss and never remarried.

Money worries continued to cause problems for the family. In 1663 Viscount Mansfield admitted himself in debt to the tune of £8000, £500 of which he had spent on linen for himself and his wife and £700 on two coaches and eight Flemish mares. Newcastle himself was selling off land in order to repurchase Nottingham Castle which, despite the fact that he was now over seventy, he intended to rebuild – the position of the site, with its spectacular view, was irresistible. But there was never enough money for the task. A letter from Francis Topp to Newcastle's steward lists £4000 worth of debts paid for Newcastle by a man called George Shaw in 1660, including £1200 for the hire of Rubens' house, £1000 to a mercer and £1152 to various brewers and wine merchants, of which some principal and interest were still owing in 1669. Viscount Mansfield's debts must have put an added strain on a relationship that was far from close.

In 1664 Newcastle asked Viscount Mansfield to approach the King for further recognition of his services to the crown. Though promised, the reward was not spontaneously forthcoming and Newcastle had to prompt the King with a formal request. In June the King wrote acknowledging receipt of a letter, and inviting Newcastle to 'send me therefore word, what titles you desire to have'. The Dukedom was eventually granted, Margaret recorded in her biography, for 'eminent actions, which he hath faithfully and valiantly performed to Us, Our Father, and Our Kingdom'. New-castle's son was created Earl of Ogle, but there was no monetary compensation to the family for losses incurred.

At the end of September 1665 Anne Hyde, now Duchess of York, paid a visit to Welbeck. The Duke had intended to accompany her but sent Newcastle his regrets at the last moment, having been commanded to meet the King at Oxford. It was a low-key affair. Welbeck's hospitality was muted now that there was no money for the extravagant masques and entertainments that Newcastle had once lavished upon his royal guests. He had also become disillusioned with the results of such pandering. In any case Margaret had little taste for entertaining.

Newcastle spent his days with his horses, or working quietly in a room set aside for his literary activities. He produced further editions of his book on horsemanship, and judicial and other estate duties occupied much of his time, though many of the latter had now been taken over by Margaret. Upstairs in her own apartments she was already formulating another book. In an epistle to her husband which she included in *Sociable Letters*, she wrote humorously 'Perchance some may say that if my understanding be most of Sheep and a Grange it is a beastly understanding. My answer is I wish Men were as Harmless as most Beasts are, then surely the World would be more quiet and happy than it is.' The world's view of the Duke and Duchess was recorded by Horace Walpole a century later in *Royal and Noble Authors*: 'What a picture of foolish nobility was this stately poetic couple, retired to their own little domain, and intoxicating one another with circumstantial flattery on what was of consequence to no mortal but themselves!'

Chapter Fourteen

Mad Madge
1665 – 8

An attendant on the Court announced suddenly to their Majesties that a lady, who would only announce herself as a Peeress of England, desired to be admitted into the presence.

'I could be sworn,' said a nobleman in attendance, 'that it is some whim of the Duchess of Newcastle.'

'In the name of madness then,' said the King, 'Let us admit her. Her Grace is an entire raree-show in her own person – a universal masquerade – indeed a sort of private Bedlam-hospital, her whole ideas being like so many patients crazed upon the subjects of love and literature, who act nothing in their vagaries, save Minerva, Venus, and the nine Muses.'

Sir Walter Scott, *The Peveril of the Peak*

The idea of writing a biography of her husband had been in Margaret's mind for a long time. While still in Antwerp she had written a letter to a friend announcing her intention, but it was not until the Newcastles were settled in Welbeck that the project began to take shape. Some time in 1666 Margaret completed the dedicatory Preface:

> It hath always been my hearty prayer to God, since I have been your wife, that first I might prove an honest and good wife, whereof your Grace must be the only Judge. Next, that God would be pleased to enable me to set forth and declare to after ages, the truth of your loyal actions and endeavours, for the service of your King and Country.

The book was in part Margaret's answer to Newcastle's critics, who were now openly sarcastic about his part in the Civil War. The Duke refused to defend himself and exasperated Margaret, who accused him of being too generous to his enemies. She had already furiously relieved some of her own feelings in *Divers Orations*, inveighing 'Against those that lay aspersions upon the Retirement of Noble Men', thinking that they have retired through 'Pride, Ambition and Revenge, being discontented that they are not the Chief Ministers of State, Rulers in Government, or Counsellors for

Advices'. She suggested that dissatisfaction was the cause, and the audience was invited to imagine that a hypothetical country had been in a civil war, that certain noble men had ventured and lost all in the service of their King, endured great misery in banishment, and upon the restoration of the King had their loyalty rewarded by neglect and affront.

Margaret began the biography with the admirable intention of describing his life and actions 'with as much brevity, perspicacity and truth as is required of an Impartial Historian'. She is however, far from impartial. Margaret writes that his courage, humility, virtue, 'Noble Bounty and Generosity is so manifest to all the World, that I should light a Candle to the Sun, if I should strive to illustrate it'. In the course of the Civil War, 'whatsoever was lost or succeeded ill, happened in his absence, and was caused either by Treachery, or Negligence, and Carelessness of his Officers.' The only fault she allowed him was a love of women, which in a man was hardly esteemed a fault at all. It is a hagiography, much as Evelyn's life of Margaret Godolphin was, except that it is pithier and less saccharine than Evelyn's. Margaret intrudes herself less into the account, and the Duke emerges as a real man – Evelyn's Lady Godolphin is an angel. Margaret's loyalty to her husband, and the naïvety that enables her to call him 'the best lyric and dramatic poet of this age' and believe it, invests the whole book. She dwells much on his many enemies, knowing that 'this unjust and partial Age is apt to suppress the worth of meritorious persons', and, determined that the Duke's 'noble actions' should not be obscured by 'unjust aspersions', she declares her intention 'to represent these obstructions which conspired to render his good intentions and endeavours ineffectual, and at last did work his ruin and destruction'.

Like most biographers of living subjects, she was unable to tell the whole truth, and Newcastle placed additional constraints on her. 'One thing I find hath much darkened it,' she wrote, 'which is that your Grace commanded me not to mention anything or passage to the prejudice or disgrace of any Family or particular Person, although they might be of great Truth and would illustrate much the actions of your life.' Her omissions are therefore of great significance. General King, whom Newcastle blamed for the defeat at Marston Moor, is hardly mentioned at all. Nor does Clarendon feature often on its pages, though he had been a near neighbour in Antwerp.

The book begins with a dedication to the King, whom Margaret declares her husband loves enough to sacrifice 'life and posterity' for, and this is followed by a moving letter to Newcastle which pays tribute to his loyalty and devotion and dwells heavily on injustice:

> My Lord, you have had as many enemies and as many friends as ever one particular person had; and I pray God to forgive the one and prosper the other; nor do I much wonder at it, since I a Woman, cannot be exempt from the malice and aspersions of spiteful tongues, which they cast upon my poor writings. Since I have been your lordship's wife, I have lived for the most part a strict and retired life . . . therefore my Censurers cannot know much of me, since they have little or no acquaintance with me . . . Indeed, my Lord, I matter not the censures of this age, but am rather proud of them; for it shows that my actions are more than ordinary, and according to the old Proverb, 'It is better to be Envied than Pitied'; for I know well that it is merely out of spite and malice, whereof this present age is so full, that none can escape them, and they'll make no doubt to stain even your Lordship's loyal, noble and heroic actions as well as they do mine, though yours have been of war and fighting, mine of contemplating and writing, yours were performed publicly in the field, mine privately in my closet, yours had many thousands of eyewitnesses, mine none but my waiting maids. But the great God that hath hitherto blessed both your Grace and me, will I question not, preserve both our Fames to after ages.

The style and form which the biography should take presented Margaret with a few problems. She observed that there were three categories of history: general history, national history and particular history – under the last of which headings she placed Caesar's *Commentaries* and Plutarch's *Lives*. She concluded that her own book must also fall under the third heading, being written by a 'spectator of those affairs and actions' described in it. She had for her pattern only the great classical lives available in translation and which, she complained, set a high value on 'feigned orations, mystical designs and fancied policies'. In others there were 'in the relation of Wars and of Military Actions such tedious descriptions that the Reader, tired with them will imagine that there was more time spent in Assaulting, Defending and taking of a fort or petty garrison than Alexander did employ in conquering the greatest part of the world'. Nevertheless she was nervous about undertaking such a difficult task herself, and asked Newcastle for some 'learned Historian' to assist her. But he wisely refused. When Margaret pressed him, afraid that 'the history would be defective', he replied that 'Truth could not be Defective. I said again that Rhetorick did adorn Truth, and he answered that Rhetorick was fitter for Falsehoods than Truths. Thus I was forced by his Grace's commands to write this History in my own plain Style.' The result was a milestone in the development of biography.

It is divided into four books, the first covers his early life and conduct during the Civil War up to the time of Marston Moor. She relied for this on her husband's recollections and on his secretary, John Rolleston. The second book describes his life in exile, of which Margaret had first-hand knowledge. It ends with a detailed breakdown of Newcastle's financial position before the war and the losses he suffered. The third book deals with 'his own person, his natural humour, disposition, qualities, virtues, his pedigree, habit, diet, exercises etc', and some 'Remarks and Particulars'. This section provides information about the garrisons in Northumberland, Yorkshire, Cumberland, Nottinghamshire, Derbyshire and Lincolnshire. She lists the officers in Newcastle's army, as well as giving a detailed account of his 'misfortunes and obstructions' in the conduct of the war. Margaret cites lack of adequate financial support; the fact that Newcastle sent his best troops to escort Queen Henrietta Maria to Oxford and the King neglected to return them, leaving him seriously weakened; and the fact that he was prevented from marching south at a critical point – an action that might have routed Cromwell's forces – but was importuned by the commander in chief to return to Yorkshire, a command he obeyed and discovered to have been entirely unnecessary. Margaret also alleges 'juggling, treachery and falsehood' in his own army, although in obedience to her husband she names no names. She also states that if Newcastle's counsel had been followed at Marston Moor and the battle deferred by three or four days the Royalists would not have been defeated.

What she does reveal is considerable confusion in the Royalist ranks; conflicting commands, the problems of communication and supply, and the lack of decisive planning and control that ultimately lost the day for the King. Margaret also asserts that loyalty could not have been 'overpowered by Rebellion, had not Treachery had better Fortune than Prudence'. Apparently, one of the messengers sent by the King to Newcastle had told him in private that some of the nobility at court 'desired him to side with them against his Majesty', an offer which Newcastle scornfully rejected, but without disclosing the existence of the plot to the King. Margaret dwells much on Newcastle's loyalty and courage, making no attempt to conceal the fact that he had gone voluntarily into exile – one of the most damaging criticisms, and an action which even his supporters condemned.

A comprehensive list of Newcastle's titles is given and copies of the preambles to the patents for his honours. His prudence in political affairs is illustrated by a list of persons who had come seeking his advice. Margaret even claims that he had warned the King of approaching civil war. She lists his blessings, including among them his first wife, 'a very kind, loving and virtuous lady'.

Newcastle's education is described, as are his conversations with Hobbes and Van Helmont, to illustrate his 'wit and understanding'. His disposition, she says, is gentle, and she admits him to be a kind husband; his discourse she described as 'free and witty'. He dresses according to fashion so long as it is 'not troublesome and uneasy for men of Heroic Exercises and Actions'. He changes his clothes once a day, and always after exercise, spending some time in dressing, though 'not as long as many effeminate persons are'. He has a glass of sack and bread for breakfast, an egg and small beer for supper, as well as one good meal a day with two glasses of small beer and a glass of sack. Contemporary portraits show a gentle, rather amiable countenance, greying fair hair, neatly trimmed, and a slim figure.

Margaret notes that after observing how quick he was to take cold after exercise, she has prevailed upon him to give up 'frequent use of the Mannege'. Otherwise he spends his time practising swordplay, and supervising the training of his horses and the organisation of a racecourse. This last was an innovation at Welbeck and very popular. Newcastle drew up detailed rules for the event and held a race meeting once a month.

The fourth book contains 'several essays and Discourses gathered from the Mouth of my Noble Lord and Husband. (With some few notes of my own).' This includes such gems as 'I have heard my Lord say . . . that there should be more praying and less preaching, for more preaching breeds faction; but much praying causes devotion'; 'That many laws do rather entrap, than help the subject'; and 'That it is a great Error in a State to have all affairs put into Gazettes (for it overheats the people's brains and makes them neglect their private affairs, by over busying themselves with state business).' The Duke is reported to have made some cynical observations on fortune, having observed 'that ill-fortune makes wise and honest men seem Fools and Knaves, but good Fortune makes Fools and Knaves seem wise and honest men'.

Among the 'Few Notes of the Authoress' at the end Margaret quotes an old proverb: 'It is better to be at the latter end of a Feast than at the beginning of a Fray; for most commonly those that are in the beginning of a Fray get but little of the Feast; and those that have undergone the greatest dangers, have least of the spoils.' The message was clear.

The biography is one of the best-ordered and well thought out of all her works. The writing is controlled and she also exercises discipline with regard to prefaces and editorial comment, keeping herself in the background for much of the book. The major innovation is the inclusion of personal detail – what he ate, what kind of carriage he rode in, how often he changed his shirts and how much he spent. This was a delightful novelty, a glimpse of the intimate lives of the rich and famous, much desired by a society which queued to get a view of the King and Queen eating their supper and enjoyed a vicarious thrill from seeing Lady Castlemaine's underwear drying in the shrubbery.

The biography was, like Margaret's other books, privately printed at Newcastle's expense, and copies liberally distributed among their friends and acquaintances. The book was also sold by the printer, and although no details are available, judging by the number of copies which were in circulation it may well have been a profitable venture. Pepys described it as 'ridiculous', but sat up all night to read it; others devoured it avidly for the old scandals they could read between the lines; some laughed at Margaret's attempt to defend her husband, but the general reception was good.

Margaret's neighbour, Lucy Hutchinson, was inspired by her example to write a biography to vindicate the reputation of her own husband, who had died in prison under unsubstantiated charges. One of Margaret's old companions at the court in Oxford, Anne Fanshawe, also wrote a similar account of her husband's life and of her own 'birth and breeding'. These were, however, private documents and written without the constraints of publication, and this has to be taken into account when they are compared with Margaret's.

Dryden was one of those who approved Margaret's endeavours, though he assigns the credit to Newcastle. He dedicated his play *The Mock Astrologers* to the Duke, referring to the Duchess as 'a Lady whom our Age may justly equal with Sappho of the Greeks or the Sulpitia of the Romans, who by being taken into your bosom, seems to be inspired with your genius. And by writing the history of your life in so masculine a style, has already placed you in the Number of the Heroes.' A letter from the Vice Chancellor and Senate of Cambridge University is more genuine, and contains less hyperbole and bombast than most of their communications. They admire 'the loftiness of the argument, and elegancy and spruceness of the style and composition' and 'retain a singular affection' for the work.

Early in 1667 the Duke and Duchess paid a visit to London. Their house at Clerkenwell had been bought back and was far enough out of the city to have escaped the ravages of the Great Fire which had destroyed large areas of London the previous year. King Charles was one of the first to pay them a visit.

London society was eager for a glimpse of Mad Madge, as she was now nicknamed (though the source is impossible to trace). Her appearance and the publication of her books were the subject of much gossip and stimulated people's curiosity. Much of what was said was untrue – where insufficient information about her antics existed it was quickly invented. Pepys recorded that 'all the town talk is nowadays of her extravagances' and he had 'heard her often described'. He queued with many others in Whitehall when it was rumoured that she was coming to court. 'The whole story of this lady is a romance,' he enthused, 'and all she doth is romantic.'

The newsletters reported every detail of her visit. On 22 April she went to court in a coach drawn by six horses. It was preceded by a coach containing her four gentlemen and followed by another containing her ladies in waiting. She was taken to the King accompanied by one young woman dressed in white satin who held up her ermine-lined train. An apocryphal tale was told of her presentation, and repeated by Sir Walter Scott, that her train was so long that much of it and the maid carrying it were still in the ante-room when she made her curtsey to the King – but this was quite untrue. After she had paid her respects to the King the Lord Chamberlain was requested to conduct her to Queen Catherine. The following day she visited Anne Hyde in the same equipage. On May Day she was mobbed in her coach on a tour of Hyde Park, and on another occasion Pepys saw her carriage leaving Whitehall pursued by a hundred boys and girls running alongside straining to see inside. Margaret had captured the public imagination.

One of the reasons for their visit to London was a performance of the Duke's play *The Humorous Lovers* at the Duke of York's Playhouse. Some people were under the impression that it was Margaret's play, and her conduct at the theatre did nothing to contradict it. Pepys wrote that the play was 'the most ridiculous thing that ever was wrote, but yet she and her Lord mightily pleased with it, and she at the end made her respects to the players from her box and did give them thanks'. Whether Margaret did have a hand in her husband's play is impossible to tell. Newcastle contributed Scenes to her own plays, and it is possible that she may have collaborated with him on this occasion.

Margaret took pains to live up to public expectations of her, though the total effect was stylish rather than eccentric. She appeared in public in velvet 'antick' dresses and velvet caps, her hair curled about her ears, and with a black velvet jacket. She had adopted the French fashion for placing patches on her face, declaring that a patch 'judiciously applied' was like 'the punctuation in a sentence', adding meaning to the countenance. Pepys attributed them unkindly to pimples. His lustful eyes also noted the lowness of her neckline. But the really striking thing about her public appearances was that her carriage and her footmen were decked out in black and white velvet and trimmed with silver to match her clothes.

Evelyn was one of those whose curiosity was gratified by a personal meeting with the Duchess. He paid a number of visits to the house, accompanied on at least two of them by his wife. His first impression was good. He declared himself 'much pleased with the extraordinary fanciful habit and garb and discourse of the Duchess'. Ten days later, on 27 April, however, she received him in 'a kind of transport, suitable to her extravagant humour and dress, which was very singular'. One can only imagine that Margaret had been overcome by one of her attacks of shyness, causing her conversation to become stilted and her demeanour forced and awkward.

Her attempts to be friendly and welcoming to Mrs Evelyn went similarly awry, and Mrs Evelyn was less restrained than her husband when describing, in a letter to Ralph Bohun, Margaret's conduct.

> I was surprised to find so much extravagance and vanity in any person not confined within four walls . . . her mien surpasses the imagination of poets and the descriptions of a romance heroine's greatness – her gracious bows, seasonable nods, courteous stretching out of her hands, twinkling of her eyes, and various gestures of approbation show what may be expected of her discourse, which is as airy, empty, whimsical and rambling as her books.

Mrs Evelyn's comments may well have been inspired by envy, when she observed Margaret's attempts to preserve her fading beauty. 'Her habit, particular, fantastical, not unbecoming a good shape, which she may truly boast of. Her face discovers the facility of the sex, in being yet persuaded it deserves the esteem years forbid, by the infinite care she takes to place her curls and patches'. At forty-four Margaret was, not unnaturally, concerned to appear at her best advantage.

On 30 May Margaret visited the Royal Society, who were now meeting at Arundel House in the Strand, having lost their previous premises in the Great Fire a year before. The visit to this exclusive club from which women were barred was a historic occasion. The previous week Lord Berkeley, a family friend, had expressed Margaret's great desire to visit the Society and watch some experiments. There had been considerable opposition from some of the members: the amount of attention that the Duchess was attracting in London made them afraid that some of the ridicule directed against her might rub off on them. The Society had only recently been established and its opposers were quick to poke fun at its proceedings: Pepys recorded that members feared the town would be 'full of ballads'. But in the end another friend of Margaret's, Walter Charleton, persuaded them, and the invitation was extended. Robert Boyle, whose sister, Viscountess Ranelagh, was herself a noted scholar, was asked to arrange the demonstration of a vacuum, an experiment involving colour, and the dissolving of a piece of flesh in acid.

The weather was appalling on the day of the visit and Margaret was late. The room was crowded with members more eager to see the Duchess than the experiments. After a long delay Lord Brounker, the President, a friend of the Newcastles and groom of the bedchamber to the Duke of York, began the proceedings without her. When Margaret finally arrived Lord Brounker, preceded by the ceremonial mace, went to the door to receive her. She admired the workmanship of the mace, and according to the sceptical Pepys kept repeating that she was 'full of admiration' for everything. She was accompanied by her usual retinue of gentlemen and ladies in waiting, and the latter caused some disturbance. One of the ladies had brought with her a small boy who ran up and down the room laughing loudly. Another of Margaret's ladies, nicknamed La Ferrabosco, was the focus of current gossip because of her beauty, and Pepys recorded that she was the object of much gallantry among the members. As for the Duchess, Pepys was forced to admit that, although she was a comely woman, her dress was so strange and her deportment 'so unordinary' that he decided he did not like her at all, though tantalisingly he refuses to go into detail.

The Duchess sat at the President's right hand and he removed his hat in her honour; it was normally his privilege to keep it on. Robert Boyle weighed a quantity of air, then exhausted it and weighed the vessel now containing the vacuum. Margaret had always been confused about vacuums. Now she was amazed that air, which was nothing, should actually weigh something. Boyle was an expert on colour, having published in 1664 a book called *Experiments and Considerations Touching Colours.* He now proceeded to turn a glass of red wine green by adding a few drops of steel solution. He then dissolved a piece of mutton in sulphuric acid. The microscope which Margaret distrusted was demonstrated, and finally the lodestone, whose magnetic properties had called forth her most fantastic speculations. A huge lodestone, weighing many pounds, was held at the other end of the room and made to move a compass needle to and fro. These experiments were a spectacular kind of entertainment, designed to titillate the Virtuosi rather than satisfy scientific curiosity. Margaret was finally shown the library – a gift from the previous owner of Arundel House – and then, still professing her admiration for everything, she was escorted to her coach by John Evelyn. Her visit was the subject of scurrilous verses attributed to him.

> But Jo! her head gear was so pretty
> I ne'er saw anything so witty
> Though I was half afeared
> God bless us! When I first did see her
> She looked so like a Cavalier
> But that she had no beard!

Less reductive was a pamphlet printed by Sarah Griffin in London in 1667, attributed to 'H.J. of Grays Inn', which also celebrates Margaret's visit to London.

> What cunning Aristotle darkly writ
> As with intent to Vizard mask his wit,
> Your Grace has drawn the Curtain, and we see
> Into each crevice of his subtlety . . .
> The residue of the Sciences would
> Wait on your Grace did you not think them bold;
> For without leave it may be thought no less
> Than an intrusion on their Patroness.

The proliferation of ballads feared by the Royal Society did not materialise.

In August the Duke had another play produced at the Duke of York's Playhouse. This was *Sir Martin Mar-All*, an adaptation by Newcastle of one of Molière's plays, *L'Etourdi*. The finished work owed a great deal to the polish of Dryden and was universally known to be 'made by my Lord Newcastle, but as everybody says corrected by Dryden'. Pepys laughed until his head ached and was still laughing when he went to bed, but this time the Duke was not there to watch its triumph.

The Newcastles did not remain long in London. The situation at court was disturbing, and Newcastle probably thanked fortune that he had not been given office. Clarendon, who until now had enjoyed the King's esteem, had grown old and out of step with the new court and was banished in 1667. Everyone was 'talking of the badness of the government, where nothing but wickedness, and wicked men and women command the King'. The problem was, Pepys wrote, that the King would not 'gainsay anything that relates to his pleasures'. That 'Whore My Lady Byron', reputed to be his seventeenth mistress, had exacted plate worth £4000 as a parting present, and the others were equally voracious.

Margaret's brother John Lucas incurred gross displeasure when he put popular feeling into words in the presence of the King in the House of Lords. The speech, quoted by Horace Walpole in *Royal and Noble Authors*, is a complaint against the King that the high hopes of the Restoration have been disappointed. There has been no relief from 'those heavy burthens under which we have lain so long apprest'. High taxes, now so difficult to meet, are not being employed for 'king and kingdom' but find their way into the 'purses of private men'.

> While in the mean time, those that have faithfully served the King are exposed to penury and want and scarce sufficient left to buy them bread. And is this, my Lords, the reward of our services? Have we for this, borne the heat of the day, been imprisoned, sequestered, ventured our lives and families, our estates and our fortunes?

Foreign affairs were also troubled. England was at war with Holland, and in June the Dutch sent a raid up the River Medway and Aphra Behn was sent to Antwerp to spy for the government. It is interesting to speculate whether she and the Duchess ever met. In *The Passionate Shepherdess* Maureen Duffy suggests that Aphra may have been in the Duke and Duchess of York's party at York and that the Duchess could have met her on that occasion. But there is no evidence from either woman that a meeting ever took place. Margaret must have known of Aphra. She was patronised by the Duke of York – her plays were put on in his theatre – and she was intimate with Thomas Killigrew, into whose family Margaret's sister Mary had married. But Aphra was too far down the social scale to have met Margaret in a social context, and her plays appeared after Margaret's visit to London.

Chapter Fifteen

Welbeck's Illustrious Whore
1668 – 73

Lady Innocence: *To what purpose should I speak? For what can I say to those that make it their delight to accuse, condemn and execute? Or what justice can I expect to have, where there is no equity? wherefore, to plead were a folly, when all hopes are cut off.*

Margaret Cavendish, *Youth's Glory
and Death's Banquet,* from *Plays*

Throughout 1667 and 1668 Margaret carried on writing; she found it impossible to stop, she admitted in *Grounds of Natural Philosophy*.

> It is also a great delight and pleasure to me, as being the only pastime which employs my idle hours insomuch that, were I sure nobody did read my works, yet I would not quit my pastime for all that, for although they should not delight others, yet they delight me, and if all women that have no employment in worldly affairs should but spend their time as I do, they could not commit such faults as many are accused of.

In 1668 she published another volume of plays, though admitting that they were rather 'Dialogues upon Several Subjects, ordered into Acts and Scenes'. They contain two vivid sketches of court life, *The Presence* and *The Bridals*; her own experiences of Queen Henrietta Maria's court and her latest visit to that of Charles II provided the material. In the former there is a spirited indictment of the court pander, and the ladies are criticised for hanging upon men's breasts, being embraced by them, jumping up to sit on the tables, lying wantonly on the carpets, running about in a wild manner, 'pinching one, shoving another, pulling a third, embracing a fourth, dancing a piece of a dance with a fifth', winking and making mouths at the men.

Another volume of philosophy discussed the relationship of madness in the brain to its physical manifestations. She pointed out that fear makes the body tremble, the heartbeat irregular and the stomach sick, so why should sickness of the mind not also affect the body. She asserted that miscarriages were caused by 'irregularities' in either mother or child, and discusses the possibilities of telepathy. However, a great deal of *Grounds of Natural Philosophy* was taken up with an idea that probably had the Royal Society choking on their wine: she attributed the rejuvenation of all things in spring to 'Restoring beds or Wombs' in the earth.

Her last book was the most fantastic of all: a crazy journey into the world of fantasy, where Margaret imagines herself as empress of a world of her own creation. Gone are the disguises of Mistress Bashful and Lady Sanspareille; the Duchess of Newcastle herself is the heroine of *Description of a Blazing New World*. The book, a unique blend of fiction, philosophy and wish fulfilment, has the quality of a dream. It begins with an abduction – 'A merchant travelling in a foreign country fell extremely in love with a young lady.' He carries her off, but their boat is struck by a tempest and eventually blown out of this world and into another. By some strange chance the men on the ship are all dead and the girl lacks the strength to throw their putrefying bodies overboard. Soon the boat is running between 'two plains of ice'. Strange creatures shaped like bears catch hold of it with their paws and carry out the lady, who faints with fear. The bears take her to their own caves and treat her kindly, but she is afflicted by the cold and unable to eat their food. So they carry her into a neighbouring land inhabited by foxes. The animal-men all agree to make her a present to their Emperor. They travel through country inhabited by giants and spider-men until they come to a crystal river. Satyrs and green-faced men and others like wild geese live on its islands, and there are cities of marble, alabaster, agate, amber and coral. Travelling on ships of gold driven by an ingenious wind engine they reach the Emperor's city, which is made of gold adorned with precious gems. The floor of the receiving room is paved with green diamond, while the Emperor's bed chamber has walls of jet, a floor of black marble and a roof of mother of pearl, 'where the moon and blazing stars were represented by white diamonds'. The Emperor soon makes the lady his wife, and the new Empress becomes a great patroness of arts and sciences. There are few laws in the kingdom, for 'many laws make many divisions'. They have a ruler rather than a Commonwealth, for the latter is 'like a monster with many heads'. There is one universal religion, but the women are not allowed in church.

At this point the book changes direction, leaving the story behind. In contrast to the novelty of the descriptive passages, many pages are devoted to tedious reports from the scientific societies that the Empress has created, and she herself advances all Margaret's favourite theories on the deception of optical glasses and colour. The Empress forms a congregation of women, discusses Ben Jonson's *Alchemist* and discourses with spirits on matter and the immateriality of rational souls. Eventually the Empress asks the spirits for the soul of one of the 'most famous modern writers', to keep her company. They suggest the Duchess of Newcastle 'for the principle of her writings is Sense and Reason'.

In a scene which is pure farce the Duchess and the Empress meet and embrace. The Empress tells her that she was 'recommended to me by an honest and ingenious Spirit'. 'Surely,' replies the Duchess, 'the spirit is ignorant of my hand writing.' Margaret confesses to the Empress that she is melancholy because of her ambition to be an empress herself. They consult the spirits, who suggest that the Duchess should create for herself a celestial world from her own fancy. She examines the theories of Thales, Pythagoras, Plato, Epicurus, Aristotle, Descartes and Hobbes, but dismisses them all in favour of her own opinions. Although the Duchess' soul lives in the new world, her body remains in the real one, 'governed by her sensitive and rational corporeal motion'. Their souls can also travel freely, and the Duchess takes the Empress on a visit to Welbeck in vehicles made of air. She declares that Nottinghamshire is a fine place to travel in, 'a dry, plain, woody place', not dirty or dusty. The Duchess complains that Fortune has crossed her Lord 'ever since he could remember'. The Empress taxes Fortune with this and there is a mock trial, with Margaret putting the case for the prosecution. Honesty speaks for the Duke, chiding the Duchess for 'desiring so much Fortune's favours' and telling her that she should not 'mistrust God's blessings'. The Duke's ill fortune comes from the fact that he puts Honesty and Prudence before Fortune.

The book ends with an attack on the Blazing New World, and in the ensuing war the Empress follows the advice of the Duchess. There is a tremendous victory accompanied by great celebrations and 'swimming dances'. Margaret describes herself in the epilogue as Honest Margaret Newcastle, Empress of the Philosophical World.

American scholars have seen in the book the origins of modern science fiction and source material for Coleridge's 'Rhyme of the Ancient Mariner'. Contemporaries used it as evidence of insanity. The story is certainly fantastic, but there is such naïvety in it, such transparent vanity and longing for personal recognition and respect, and such a display of wasted talent and cankered genius, that it is impossible to ascribe it to the wanderings of an unbalanced mind. If she had removed the philosophy and kept herself out of the narrative the story would have won acclaim as a brilliant piece of fiction. As it was, people remembered her poem 'Foolish Ambition' from *Poems and Fancies* and took it as a personal manifesto.

> Give me a fame that with the world may last
> Let all tongues tell of my great actions past,
> Let every child that learns to speak, my name
> Repeat, to keep the memory of my fame.
> And then great fortune, give to me thy power
> To ruin man and raise him in an hour,
> Let me command the fates, and spin their thread
> And death to stay his sith when I forbid.
> And Destiny give me your chains to tie
> Effects from causes to produce thereby
> And let me like the Gods be High, Alone,
> That nothing may but by my will be done.

The book did nothing to decrease public fascination with the Duchess. Speculation about her personality and state of mind continued, even within Newcastle's own family.

Margaret's relations with her step-grandchildren were generally rather better than with their parents. She was less shy with young children than with adults, and they were entranced, rather than repelled, by her extravagant clothes. Newcastle's daughter Frances, Lady Bolinbroke, was childless, but Henry had four daughters (one called Margaret) and a rather delicate son, born in 1663 and named for his father. Newcastle's grandchildren were often at Welbeck, and he wrote to his son that young Harry 'loves my wife better than anybody and she him'.

The Duke was now seventy-five, a very respectable age for the times, and still physically fit. He did nothing to excess: a little exercise carefully supervised by Margaret, a moderate diet and an active intellectual life all combined to keep him as active and healthy as many men half his age. But it seemed unlikely that he would live for many more years. He worried about Margaret's future after his death. His dear Peg, as he called her in private, still only in her forties, had nothing of her own and no children to defend her interests. Newcastle began to settle land on her, to ensure her future security. He gave her his favourite properties, Bolsover and Clipstone, plus land in Sherwood Forest and the town house in London.

His family, who had grown more and more estranged from their stepmother, were at first troubled and then outraged by what they saw as misappropriation of their family property. They suspected the undue influence of a young and strong-willed wife over their elderly father, and the persuasion of her 'minion' Sir Francis Topp. Newcastle's son Henry, Earl of Ogle, wrote to a friend, 'I am however, melancholy, finding my father more persuaded by his wife than I could think it possible.' He also refers to 'unkindness' at Welbeck. This may not entirely be due to Margaret. Letters between Newcastle and his son reveal strain, and show that Henry held his father in awe. After Margaret's death a timid, obsequious letter from Henry and his wife begging Newcastle to allow them to live with him in order that he may be well looked after ends with the admission that they write what they dare not ask in person.

They were all quite wrong about Margaret's ambitions. She would never refuse financial security, remembering the hard years at Antwerp, but she had little interest in acquiring property, writing in 'A True Relation' that 'my ambition is . . . not for beauty, wealth, titles, but as they are steps to Fame's Tower, to live by remembrance in after ages'.

Francis Topp was also much resented by Newcastle's family on his own account, and not just because he was Margaret's 'minion'. The Topps had managed most of Newcastle's business after his return to England, and Sir Francis was not known for his tact. He knew all the details of the Earl of Ogle's debts and distributed the allowances that Newcastle made to his daughters. Jane wrote to her sister-in-law that she had met Topp in his coach in Hyde Park where he had been very condescending about her money when she asked for an advance. 'I am of the opinion, he intends none of my Lord's children any good and am very sorry he should so waste the estate as you mention; methinks there might be some means contrived to hinder him; I would assist in anything I could.' Newcastle's steward, Andrew Clayton, felt similar animosity towards him. Whether any active representations were made to Newcastle about Sir Francis is not recorded, but some time in 1669 he and his wife left Welbeck and did not return. Unfortunately this was not the end of the matter.

Newcastle's daughter Jane died in October 1669, and so can have had little to do with the hideous libel of 1670. Of Newcastle's numerous progeny only Henry and Frances survived, and apart from their feelings towards Margaret there is no evidence that either of them was involved in the conspiracy organised by Clayton.

On 14 July 1671 one John Booth confessed before James Chadwick, JP, that 'he had written a libel against the Duchess' for the purpose of making dissension between the Duke and Duchess. The libel was of the crudest and most unlikely sort – alleging adultery between the Duchess and Francis Topp. Physical passion had never been part of Margaret's character, and no one who knew her could have believed such an unlikely tale. But her public image was highly eccentric, her books dubbed 'obscene', and she was a relatively young woman married to an old man. The situation seems to have originated from Andrew Clayton's jealousy, possibly encouraged by the attitude of her stepchildren. Clayton was not entirely trust-worthy, and Margaret's keen eye had caught him out several times. Since the departure of the Topps it had been Margaret who went over the estate accounts. Clayton admitted that he had 'ever under-hand contradicted her Grace's designs the which she more and more discovered and hated him perfectly for it'. Newcastle, however, refused to let such a long-serving family servant go.

In 1668 Frances Liddell, the Duke's tenant, had given Clayton horses to the value of over £100 as a bribe to have his rent reduced and a bond of £500 paid off by the Duke. This promise was not kept because, Clayton said, the Duchess examined the estate returns too narrowly. On 29 October 1670 Clayton said that the Duchess was gradually procuring the estates for herself as her jointure, with a view to a second husband, and that there would be little left for the family if she were not prevented. He spoke of being involved in 'sharp and passionate quarrels between their Graces'.

On 30 October Clayton had the idea of giving her Grace a 'dead blow' and at the same time taking Newcastle's affections away from her. Clayton induced John Booth, a receiver for Newcastle's Northumberland estates, to join them by claiming that Margaret intended to ruin him. An anonymous letter was written to the Duke on the 31st, telling him in what honour he had been held before the Rebellion and how that honour had decreased because of the Duchess. It was Clayton's idea to include the name of Francis Topp and the alleged adultery. Then the conspirators knelt down with their right hands over the letter and swore an oath of secrecy before posting the letter at Grantham. The original draft was concealed in Liddell's stocking and burnt while Newcastle and Margaret were hosting a reception for the 'Gentlemen' of Nottingham.

Fearing that their faces might give them away, the conspirators arranged to be out of the house when the letter was delivered. It arrived at Welbeck on 3 November. As soon as it was put into his hand the Duke sent for Clayton and asked if he recognised the handwriting. He did not let him read the letter, but told him that it 'abused Peg abominably'. To conceal his knowledge Clayton asked if it was in verse, and told Newcastle that he did not know who it could be from.

When Newcastle showed the letter to Margaret she immediately suspected Andrew Clayton. Newcastle somewhat obscurely suspected the parson of Mansfield, and tried to convince Margaret that Clayton was innocent. He questioned various postmasters, and Margaret sent one of her ladies in waiting in a coach to make enquiries about the origin of the letter, but no further information came to light. There was nothing else to do but to let the matter rest. It was a miserable winter.

However, when John Booth visited Welbeck the following summer he wrote to Clayton and the contents of his letter somehow became known. At this point he resolved to tell the truth. Clayton tried to prevent Booth from implicating him, but on 1 July 1671 Booth made a full confession in writing, which he swore before a justice of the peace a fortnight later. Liddell also signed it. Clayton's chamber was searched and various incriminating papers found there were sent to the Duke. Clayton left the Duke's service discreetly, and although there were no public proceedings the ugly incident caused much pain and laid a stain on Margaret's reputation that all the denials could not totally remove. A man called John Stainsby, a friend of Elias Ashmole the astrologer, called Margaret 'Welbeck's Illustrious Whore'.

In 1671, on top of the Clayton scandal, Margaret's eldest brother John died, aged sixty-six. The wide age gap between them meant that they had never been particularly close, but she had admired his scholarship and he had given her valuable support in her fight for subsistence from Newcastle's estates. Like her other brother, Charles, he seems to have been a difficult character, and he had been expelled from the Royal Society in 1666. He died without male issue, and the barony, granted by Charles I for services to the crown, passed with the estates to the eldest son of their illegitimate brother Thomas.

If Margaret's personal life was marred by malice and bereavement, matters were improving on the literary front. Her position as a woman writer was now no longer so isolated. Katherine Philips, described in Thomas Phillips' *Theatarum Poetarum* of 1674 as 'the most applauded, at this time, Poetess of our Nation, either of the Present or former Ages, and not without Reason', published her *Collected Poems* in 1667. In 1670 Aphra Behn's first play, *The Forced Marriage*, opened at Lincoln's Inn Fields with Thomas Betterton in the leading role, and *The Amorous Prince* followed in 1671. At the same time she was writing poetry and prose, including stories like *Oroonoko* which remained in print for over two hundred years. The year 1673 saw the publication of Bathsua Makin's famous *Essay to Revive the Ancient Education of Gentlewomen*, in which she asked only for women's education and not equality. In fact she affirmed women's domestic role, declaring that

> to ask too much is the way to be denied all. God hath made Man the Head, if you be educated and instructed as I propose, I am sure you will acknowledge it and be satisfied that you are helps, that your Husband do consult and advise with you, which if you be wise they will be glad of, and that your Husbands have the Casting-Voice in whose determinations you will acquiesce.

She paid tribute to Margaret, who 'by her own genius, rather than any timely instruction, over-tops many grave Gown-Men'.

That same year Poulain de la Barre published *De l'Egalité des Deux Sexes*, in which he addressed questions raised by anti-feminists and covered various issues that had been treated by Marie de Gournay and Anna van Schurman. In his views he was closer than any other writer of the period to Margaret. He proclaimed that it was only custom, tradition and lack of education that made women inferior to men, and that there was no justification, either scriptural or historical, for their subjection. His book was quickly translated into English and ran into several editions.

After 1668 Margaret published nothing further, though letters and manuscripts show that she was still working on her scientific theories. Dr Benoist wrote from London in August 1672 to acknowledge receipt of 'the filings of the Lodestone, which I intend to show to several Persons, to have their opinions whether it be right or no'. In another letter he referred to books and Dutch quills sent to Margaret, also 'lozenges' from a Dr Willis.

Margaret's health seems to have been giving cause for concern. Earlier letters from a Dr Boucheret refer to prescriptions of sarsaparilla, lignum vitae and sassafras. She had apparently been suffering from disorders of the stomach since 1666, and though only middle-aged she had ruined her health by subjecting herself to a rigorous diet and frequent purges. The King's physician had once warned her that 'too much scouring wears the pot into holes', but she took little heed. She drank water and ate a little bread and chicken, and sometimes an egg. But the most damaging thing was her lack of exercise: she took only 'two or three turns about her room' and was occasionally persuaded to go out in her coach. She was torn between a desire to indulge her contemplations undisturbed and fear that, with lack of external stimulation, they would dry up altogether. The Duke was concerned, but neither his persuasions nor the efforts of friends could make her change her ways.

> I give you many thanks for your counsel and advice concerning my health, for certainly an overstudious mind doth waste the body . . . I am sometimes in dispute with myself whether it is better to live a long and idle, than a short but profitable life. Tis true, death is terrible to think of, but in death no terror remains, so as it is life that is painful to the body and mind, and not death.

Nor did she trouble herself about the disposition of her body after death, having observed in *Sociable Letters* 'that in this last war the urns of the dead were digged up, their dust dispersed and their bones thrown about . . . wherefore it is but a folly to be troubled and concerned where they shall be buried or for their graves . . . since not only time, but wars will ruin them.'

On 15 December 1673 Margaret, still only fifty, died suddenly at Welbeck. No cause of death was recorded. Her body was embalmed and carried to London – an unenviable journey in the biting midwinter cold – where she lay in state at Newcastle House. Friends, relatives, royalty and the curious came to pay their last respects. On the evening of 7 January, under a black velvet pall, her coffin was carried to Westminster Abbey by torchlight procession and interred in the tomb reserved for herself and her husband. Her two surviving sisters attended the funeral as well as Newcastle's daughter Frances. Henry and his wife were there, and Elizabeth's widowed husband Lord Bridgwater. Newcastle himself had been judged too frail to make the long journey south and he mourned alone at Welbeck, perhaps taking comfort from the doleful verses 'On the Death of the Incomparable Princess Margaret' which his protégés were churning out. Shadwell's were particularly dubious. The Duchess

> from our sight is hurled
> And gloriously shines in the true Blazing World

Nor was his next remark particularly tactful in view of the fact that Newcastle now had only one son living and one frail grandson to carry on his line:

> She was not as most of her frail sex are
> Who are fruitful Wombs but Barren Brains.

Newcastle was devastated by Margaret's death. He had always believed that she would outlive him and had made elaborate financial provisions for that eventuality. Now over eighty and very frail, without Margaret to protect him he was prey to the malicious attentions of those around him. When his son Henry wrote begging to be allowed to live with him he referred to 'some young women, who being presumptuously and extravagantly ambitious, do with their foolish thoughts fill town and country, doing what they can to dishonour your Grace'.

Alone at Welbeck, Newcastle wrote melancholy love poems in a faint, trembling hand, only legible in a secretary's copy. One refers to a dream in which the 'she' of the poem is present in the room with him, although he knows that she is dead. Margaret's magnificent tomb in the north transept of Westminster Abbey bears an inscription composed by Newcastle himself, a reminder to posterity of his wife's accomplishments:

> This Duchess was a wise, witty and learned Lady, which her many Books do well testify; she was a most Virtuous and a Loving and careful Wife, and was with her Lord all the time of his banishment and miseries, and when he came home never parted from him in his Solitary Retirements.

But her most fitting epitaph is a passage from her autobiography in *Nature's Pictures*, in which she declares,

> I repine not at the gifts that Nature or Fortune bestows on others, yet I think it no crime to wish myself the exactest of Nature's works, my thread of Life the longest, my Chain of Destiny the strongest, my mind the peaceablest, my Life the pleasantest, my Death the easiest, and the greatest Saint in Heaven. Also to do my endeavour, so far as Honour and Honesty doth allow of, to be the Highest of Fortune's Wheel and to hold the Wheel from turning if I can.

Chapter Sixteen

The Wheel of Fortune

Laughed out of Reason, Jested out of Sense.

Lady Chudleigh *The Ladies' Defence*

Posterity has not accorded Margaret the fame and honour she coveted for herself. The paradoxes apparent in Margaret's work and in her personality are partly responsible for this neglect. In *Reason's Disciples* Hilda L. Smith writes that

> No work of a seventeenth-century feminist poses so many interpretive problems as the writings of the first of their number, the Duchess of Newcastle. Her views were at once the most radical and far reaching and the most contradictory. She appears to have understood better than any of her sisters, the multi-faceted nature of women's oppression.

Margaret's stories and plays often depict an ideal world in which women astound men by their intellect and wisdom, fight battles for the equality of their sex and are universally respected. But at the same time she displays a keen awareness of the reality of their position – particularly with regard to the double sexual standard – and the necessity of living with the status quo. For every passage which laments women's lack of opportunity there is another which castigates women for their conduct. She may have been one of the most ardent advocates of women's equality, but she was also one of the most severe critics of her own sex. The dichotomy between the ideal and the reality was the source of many of Margaret's apparent inconsistencies. Whatever its interpretive problems, Margaret's work was the most radical and detailed assessment of the situation of women in society until Mary Wollstonecraft.

Another drawback for the reader has been the sheer bulk of Margaret's work and the unevenness of its quality. In his *History of Welbeck Abbey and Its Owners* A. S. Turberville made a serious appraisal of her writing. His conclusions were that

> The unfortunate effect of her ponderous plays and philosophic dissertations has been to create such a reputation for her that

readers have been kept away not only from those arid tracks which they could not have endured, but also from charming pathways which they might have trod with pleasure.

Of her feminism he asked: 'Has the women's movement of the nineteenth and twentieth centuries produced anything wiser and more penetrating than the writings of Margaret Cavendish on women's powers and women's rights?'

Margaret's great importance lies not just in the picture which she drew for posterity of how women thought and felt, but in the example which she set for others. Her torrent of printed works broke a long silence, and though her eccentric figure may well have frightened many women away from education (Virginia Woolf claimed that she became a bogey with which to frighten clever girls) her achievements could not be ignored and they created a precedent for others. After Margaret, women could write specifically for publication without coyly repudiating the act, although it was a long time before they could be accepted without first hiding behind a pseudonym. In order to understand why Mary Ann Evans became George Eliot, and the Brontë sisters wrote as Currer, Acton and Ellis Bell, it is necessary to know something of the ridicule to which Margaret and her contemporaries were subjected.

One of these women was Anne Winchelsea, who was a maid of honour at the court of Mary of Modena. Banished from court with the fall of Mary's husband, James II, and childless like Margaret, she filled her solitary hours writing poetry that is sometimes sublime. Her first selection of verses appeared in 1713 under the pseudonym Ardelia; later editions carried her own name. Some of her most moving poetry concerns the problems of the woman writer whose hand:

> delights to trace unusual things
> And deviates from the known and common way,
> Nor will in fading silks compose
> Faintly the inimitable rose.

Her contemporary, Mary Astell, put forward *A Serious Proposal* (for the education of women) and *Reflections on Marriage*, both of which echoed Margaret's themes. Eliza Haywood became the Barbara Cartland of the eighteenth century and edited the first women's magazine, the *Female Spectator*. Mary Manley, who died in 1724, edited a satirical political journal called the *Female Tatler* and succeeded Swift as editor of the *Examiner*. With the exception of Anne Winchelsea they all lived independent lives outside the boundaries of matrimony, and had to endure continual accusations of immorality.

By the beginning of the eighteenth century there were many others, too numerous to mention, who owed their freedom to write to their predecessors – Katherine Philips, Anne Bradstreet, Bathsua Makin and Margaret Cavendish. Because of her prominent position in society, and the quantity and breadth of her published work, Margaret is the most important of them all. Her scope, encompassing science, letters, fiction and drama, has rarely been equalled. The nineteenth-century critic Sir Egerton Bridges reprinted her autobiography in 1814 and asked:

> Who now reads Mrs Katherine Philips, better known by her poetical name of Orinda? And Mrs Behn, who lived somewhat later is more remarkable for her licentiousness than for any better quality. Even of Mrs Killigrew, the encomium bestowed by Dr Johnson is generally thought to be undeserved. The Countess of Pembroke, Lady Carew, Lady Wrothe and a few others succeeded; but their productions are now unnoticed.

Too often Margaret's work has been eclipsed by the legend which grew up around her name. Recognisable portraits of the Duchess on the Restoration stage proliferated after her death. Wright's *The Female Virtuosos* of 1693 featured Lord and Lady Meanwell, a married couple not unlike the Newcastles, and Lady Meanwell made a 'high boast of her Philosophy'. Charles Johnson's *The Generous Husband* featured a Philosophress much addicted to contemplation, who prefers a Good Book to a Bad Husband. In Colley Cibber's *The Ladies' Philosophy* of 1735 the heroine, Sophronia, is afflicted by prudery and madness. Cibber is one of those responsible for perpetuating the myths surrounding Margaret: he acted in a play by Pope, Arbuthnot and Gay called *Three Hours After the Marriage*, published in 1717 and one of the most remarkable attacks on the literate woman ever published.

The half-crazed figure of Phoebe Clinket in this play owes something to Anne Winchelsea and Lady Mary Wortley Montagu, two of the most learned and accomplished eighteenth-century women writers, but much more to the myth which had grown up around Margaret Cavendish in the forty years since her death. The play is a fascinating and horrifying glimpse of the ridicule to be braved by any woman with pretensions to learning or authorship. Phoebe Clinket is a lady of quality, but 'instead of puddings she makes

Pastorals; or when she should be raising Paste is raising some Ghost in a new Tragedy'. The stage direction reads: 'Enter Phoebe Clinket and her maid bearing a writing desk on her back. Clinket writing, her headdress stained with ink, and pens stuck in her hair.'

Maid: I had as good carry a Raree Show about the street. Oh! how my back aches!
Clinket: What are the labours of the back to those of the brain? Thou scandal to the Muses. I have now lost a thought worth a Folio by thy impertinence.

There follows a brilliant satire on what Pope called 'the maudlin poetess' at work.

Clinket: Read me the last lines I writ upon the Deluge, and take care to pronounce them as I taught you.
Maid: [Reads with affected tone] 'Swelled with a Dropsy, sickly Nature dies/And melting in a Diabetes, dies.'
Clinket: Still without cadence!
Maid: 'Swelled with a Dropsy –
Clinket: Hold, I conceive! 'The roaring seas o'er the tall woods have broke/And Whales now perch upon the sturdy Oak.' Roaring? Stay. Rumbling, roaring, rustling. No. Raging seas. [Writing] 'The raging seas o'er the tall woods have broke/Now perch thou Whale, upon the sturdy Oak.' Sturdy Oak? No. Steady, strong, strapping, stiff. Stiff? No, stiff is too short.

The references to the 'raree show' and the fantasy of the maid and the desk, even the words 'I conceive', are all part of the legend which surrounded Margaret.

Women's writing is not just marginalised in the play – it is quite literally incinerated. One of the characters, Fossile, flings Phoebe's works into the fire. The ensuing dialogue is an interesting example of the difference between what men thought should be important for a woman, and what the female author thinks.

Clinket: Ah! I am an undone woman.
Plotwell: Has he burnt any Bank-bills or a new Mechlen head-dress?
Clinket: My works! My works!
1st Player: Has he destroyed the writings of an estate or your billet-doux?
Clinket: A Pindaric Ode! Five similes! and half an Epilogue!
2nd Player: Has he thrown a new Fan, or your Pearl Necklace into the flames?

A Glorious Fame

Clinket: Worse, worse! The tag of the acts of a new Comedy! A prologue sent by a Person of Quality! Three copies of recommendatory verses! And two Greek Mottos!

Lady Mary Wortley Montagu, whose lack of cleanliness contributed to the portrait, begged her own daughter to conceal her learning 'with as much solicitude as she would hide crookedness or lameness'.

Not everyone was unkind. In 1674 Thomas Phillips described Margaret in his *Theatarum Poetarum* as 'a very obliging lady to the World'. Joseph Glanville admired her 'candour and goodness'. Charles Lamb retained a special affection for her; she was, he wrote in the *Essays of Elia*, 'somewhat fantastical, original-brained and generous'. His favourite books were her *Sociable Letters* and her life of the Duke, for which he claimed 'no casket is rich enough, no casing sufficiently durable to honour and keep safe such a jewel'. Lady Mary Wortley Montagu took Margaret's books with her when she went into exile. In the preface to his edition of her life Egerton Bridges was also enthusiastic:

> That the Duchess was deficient in a cultivated judgement; that her knowledge was more multifarious than exact; and that her powers of fancy and sentiment were more active than her powers of reasoning, I will admit; but that her productions, mingled as they are with great absurdities, are wanting either in talent or in virtue, or even in genius, I cannot concede.

Only one of her books has been reprinted for sale to the general public since her death, though one or two private editions have appeared. In 1766 *A Treasure of Knowledge*, by Alexander Nicol, Schoolmaster, contained some extracts from *Nature's Pictures* 'wherein is delineated the experienced traveller'. An account of her life was given by Cibber and Ballard in their *Lives of the Poets* and *Memoirs of Several Ladies* in 1752. Margaret's most fervent advocate in the twentieth century was Virginia Woolf, one of the first to realise the importance of early women writers not only for her own generation, but for an understanding of the world of George Eliot, the Brontës and Jane Austen. Of Margaret she wrote in *The Common Reader*, 'Though her philosophies are futile and her plays intolerable and her verses mainly dull, the vast bulk of the Duchess is leavened by a vein of authentic fire. One cannot help following the lure of her erratic and lovable personality as it meanders and twinkles through page after page.'

The Wheel of Fortune

It is only in the last two decades that the importance of women like Margaret has been fully recognised and their work reassessed. They are important – the bad as well as the good – because, as Elaine Showalter explains in *A Literature of Their Own*, these minor writers are the 'links in the chain' that bind one generation to the next and provide 'a very clear understanding of the continuities in women's writing'. Those who were not 'great' have been left out of 'anthologies, histories, text books and theories', giving the impression that Jane Austen and her contemporaries sprung into being out of nowhere, like Athene fully armed from the head of Zeus. To omit the women novelists of the eighteenth century, and the first fumbling attempts at fiction in the seventeenth, is to omit a whole chapter in the development of the novel. Neither is it possible to ignore the first stumbling steps of feminist awareness which grew eventually into the political sensibility that produced Mary Wollstonecraft.

Margaret's reputation for eccentricity still overwhelms her achievements as a writer. Her latest accolade is a mention in *The Book of Heroic Failures*, as the most ridiculous poet. It is perhaps not surprising that Margaret has continued to be known for her failures rather than her successes. Louise Bernikow, in her Introduction to *The World Split Open*, writes that the rebellious woman poet was a subversive element in society, and for this reason has been ignored by literary tradition and edited out of literary history. Women writers were an aberration, labelled mad and eccentric, an image which persists into the twentieth century with the legends of Edith Sitwell, Stevie Smith and Sylvia Plath.

Virginia Woolf argued that the women of the seventeenth and eighteenth centuries had been ignored because their work was distorted by anger and resentment, and no one expressed better than Margaret the bitterness generated in women by their condition. In the end Katherine Philips has been remembered as the ideal woman poet, the chaste wife, the loving friend and modest author who dissociated herself from the publication of her works and wrote as if she wore white gloves. But oh, how dull her poetry is! Margaret, energetic, fiery, outrageous, pushing her talent far beyond its boundaries, always taking risks and not always succeeding, produced some superlative passages in which her own distinctive voice can clearly be heard.

Margaret Cavendish is one of the most important links between the fully fledged women writers of the twentieth century and what Shakespeare in *Twelfth Night* called:

A Glorious Fame

> The spinsters and the knitters in the sun
> And the free maids that weave their thread with bones

who chanted their poetry as they worked. She deserves to be remembered for her achievements, and given the fame and honour she coveted so much.

Chronology

1612   Bathsua Makin born.

1613   *The Tragedy of Mariam*, Lady Elizabeth Falkland.

1620   Lucy Hutchinson born.

1621   *Urania*, Mary Wrothe.

1622   *Egalité des Hommes et des Femmes* (Paris), Marie de Gournay.

c. 1623   Margaret Cavendish (née Lucas) born.

1625   Anne Fanshawe born.

1631   Katherine Philips born.

1637   *Fame's Roule*, Mary Fage.

1640   Aphra Behn born.

1641   *The Learned Maid* (Leyden), Anna van Schurman.

1642   Outbreak of Civil War.

1644   Queen Henrietta Maria escapes to France attended by Margaret. Battle of Marston Moor – Marquis of Newcastle in exile.

1645   Margaret marries Marquis of Newcastle in Paris.

1646   Commonwealth established.

1648   Newcastles move to Antwerp.

1649   Execution of King Charles I. *Artemène ou le Grand Cyrus* (Paris), Madeleine de Scudéry.

1651   *The Tenth Muse*, Anne Bradstreet.

1652   Margaret Cavendish visits London.

1653   *Poems and Fancies* and *Philosophical Fancies*, Margaret Cavendish. Margaret returns to Antwerp.

1655   *The World's Olio* and *Philosophical and Physical Opinions*, Margaret Cavendish.

1656   *Nature's Pictures*, Margaret Cavendish.

1660   Restoration of King Charles II – Newcastles return to England. Anne Killigrew, poet and painter, born.

1661   Lady Anne Winchelsea born.

1662   *Divers Orations* and *Plays*, Margaret Cavendish. Unauthorised edition of Katherine Philips' poems appears.

1663   Revised edition of *Philosophical and Physical Opinions*, Margaret Cavendish. Mary de la Riviere Manley born.

1664   *Sociable Letters* and *Philosophical Letters*, Margaret Cavendish.

1666 *Observations on Experimental Philosophy*, Margaret Cavendish.

1667 *Life of William Cavendish, Duke of Newcastle*, Margaret Cavendish.
Margaret visits the Royal Society.
Collected Poems, Katherine Philips.

1668 *Description of a Blazing New World; Plays Never Before Printed;* and *Grounds of Natural Philosophy*, Margaret Cavendish.

1669 Katherine Philips dies.

1670 Aphra Behn's first play produced.

1673 *An Essay to Revive the Ancient Education of Gentlewomen*, Bathsua Makin.
De l'Egalité des Deux Sexes, Poulain de la Barre.
Margaret Cavendish dies.

1674 Bathsua Makin dies.

1678 *Princesse de Clèves* (Paris), Madame de La Fayette.

1680 Anne Fanshawe dies.

1685 Anne Killigrew dies.

1686 *Poems*, Anne Killigrew.

1689 Aphra Behn dies.

1693 Eliza Haywood born.

1694 *A Serious Proposal*, Mary Astell.

1696 *The Lost Lover*, Mary Manley (first play).

1709 *The New Atlantis*, Mary Manley.

1711 *Poems*, Lady Anne Winchelsea.
Mary Manley succeeds Swift as editor of the *Examiner*.

1719 Eliza Haywood's first novel.

1744 Eliza Haywood edits *Female Spectator*.

Bibliography

Place of publication is London unless stated otherwise.

Agrippa, Cornelius (trans. H. Care), *Female Pre-eminence or the Dignity and Excellence of That Sex Above the Male*, 1670.
Anon, *Haec Vir*, 1620.
Anon, *Hic Mulier*, 1620.
Ashley, Maurice, *Life in Stuart England*, 1964.
Ashley, Maurice, *The English Civil War*, 1974.
Ashmole, Elias, and William Lilly, *The Lives of Elias Ashmole and William Lilly by Themselves*, 1774.
Astell, Mary, *A Serious Proposal*, 1694.
Aubrey, John, *Brief Lives*, 1898.
Ballard, G., *Memoirs of Several Ladies*, 1752.
Bastwick, John, *The Litany of John Bastwick*, 1637.
Behn, Aphra (ed. Summers), *Complete Works*, 1915.
Bence-Jones, Mark, *The Cavaliers*, 1976.
Berry, Mary, *Comparative View of Social Life in England and France*, 1844.
Berry, Mary, *Home Life of English Ladies in the Seventeenth Century*, 1860.
Birch, Thomas, *History of the Royal Society*, 1756.
Calendar of State Papers Clarendon.
Calendar of State Papers Domestic.
Calendar of State Papers Venetian.
Carter, Matthew, *A Most True and Exact Relation of that as Honourable as Unfortunate Expedition of Kent, Essex and Colchester*, 1650.
Cavendish, Margaret, *Philosophical Fancies*, 1653.
Cavendish, Margaret, *Poems and Fancies*, 1653.
Cavendish, Margaret, *The World's Olio*, 1655.
Cavendish, Margaret, *Philosophical and Physical Opinions*, 1655 and 1663.
Cavendish, Margaret, *Nature's Pictures Drawn by Fancies Pencil to the Life*, 1656.
Cavendish, Margaret, *Divers Orations*, 1662.
Cavendish, Margaret, *Plays*, 1662.
Cavendish, Margaret, *Philosophical Letters*, 1664.
Cavendish, Margaret, *Sociable Letters*, 1664.
Cavendish, Margaret, *Observations on Experimental Philosophy*, 1666.

Cavendish, Margaret, *Life of William Cavendish*, 1667.
Cavendish, Margaret, *Description of a Blazing New World*, 1668.
Cavendish, Margaret, *Grounds of Natural Philosophy*, 1668.
Cavendish, Margaret, *Plays Never Before Printed*, 1668.
Cavendish, Margaret, *The Duchess of Newcastle's Philosophy*, 1668.
Cavendish, Margaret (ed. Sir Egerton Bridges), 'A True Relation of the Birth, Breeding and Life, of Margaret Cavendish, Duchess of Newcastle, Written by Herself', Lee Priory Press, 1814. (See also Cavendish, Margaret, *Nature's Pictures*)
Chudleigh, Lady, *The Ladies' Defence*, 1699.
Cibber, Colley, *An Account of the Lives of the Poets*, 1753.
Clarendon, Earl of (ed. Macray), *The History of the Rebellion and Civil Wars in England*, Oxford, 1888.
Clark, Alice, *The Working Lives of Women in the Seventeenth Century*, 1919.
Clarke, Samuel, *The Lives of Sundry Eminent Persons*, 1683.
Constable, John, *Letters*, in *Calendar of State Papers Domestic* (1644).
de Gamache, Father Cyprien, *The Court and Times of Charles I*, 1848.
de la Barre, Poulain, *De l'Egalité des Deux Sexes*, Paris, 1673.
de Montpensier, Anne Marie, *Memoirs*, 1828.
Duffy, Maureen, *The Passionate Shepherdess*, 1977.
Du Verger, *Humble Reflections on Some Passages of the Marchioness of Newcastle's Olio*, 1657.
Dyce, Alexander, *British Poetesses*, 1827.
Ellis, Sir Henry, *Original Letters*, 1825 and 1827.
Evelyn, John, *I'll Tell Thee Dick*, Public Record Office SP29/450.
Evelyn, John, *Diary*, 1850 and 1907 (Everyman) edns.
Everett Green, M. A. (ed.), *Letters of Queen Henrietta Maria*, 1857.
Fanshawe, Lady Anne, *Memoirs of Lady Fanshawe*, 1829.
Fiennes, Celia, *Through England on a Side Saddle in the Time of William and Mary*, 1888.
Fontenelle, *Discovery of New Worlds*, translated by Aphra Behn, 1688 and Joseph Glanville, 1701.
Fraser, Antonia, *Cromwell: Our Chief of Men*, 1973.
Fraser, Antonia, *Charles II*, 1979.
Fraser, Antonia, *The Weaker Vessel*, 1984.
Furnivall, F. J., *Child Marriage and Divorces in the Diocese of Chester*, 1897.

Bibliography

Gay, John, *Three Hours After Marriage*, 1717, in *Works*, 5 vols, 1772.

Gisborne, Thomas, *Duties of Women*, 1796.

Godfrey, Elizabeth, *Home Life under the Stuarts*, 1903.

Goulding, R. W., *Letters of Margaret Lucas to Her Future Husband*, 1909.

Goulding, R. W., *Margaret Lucas*, 1925.

Grammont, Count, *Memoirs of Count Grammont*, 1906.

Grant, Douglas (ed.), *The Phanseyes of William Cavendish, Marquis of Newcastle, Addressed to Margaret Lucas and Her Letters in Reply*, 1956.

Grant, Douglas (ed.), *Margaret the First*, 1957.

Guigot de Witt, Madame, *Lady of Lathom*, 1869.

Halifax, Lord, *Advice to a Daughter*, 1688.

Hatton correspondence, Camden Society, 1878.

Hieron, Samuel, *A Helpe unto Devotion*, 1613.

Hill, Bridget, *The First English Feminist: Reflections on Marriage and Other Writings by Mary Astell*, 1986.

Hill, Christopher, *The World Turned Upside Down*, 1972.

Historical Manuscripts Commission, 12th Report, Portland Mss, Vol. II.

Howell, James, *Familiar Letters*, 1634.

Hutchinson, Lucy (ed. Firth), *Memoirs of the Life of Col. Hutchinson*, 1885.

Jenkins, Edward (ed.), *The Cavalier and His Lady*, 1872.

Johnson, Samuel, *Lives of the Poets*, 1781.

Killigrew, Anne, *Poems*, 1686.

Lamb, Charles, *Essays of Elia*, 1901.

le Moyne, *Gallerie des Femmes Fortes*, 1647.

Letters in Honour of the Incomparable Princess Margaret, 1676.

'The Loyal Sacrifice', pamphlet, 1648.

MacLean, Ian, *Woman Triumphant*, Oxford, 1977.

McLeod, Enid, *The Order of the Rose: the Life and Ideas of Christine de Pisan*, 1976.

Mahl, M. R., and H. Koon, *The Female Spectator*, Indiana University Press, 1977.

Makin, Bathsua, *An Essay to Revive the Ancient Education of Gentlewomen*, 1673.

Maland, David, *Culture and Society in Seventeenth-century France*, 1970.

Manning, Brian, *The English People and the English Revolution*, 1976.

Mercurius Aulicus (contemporary newssheets).

Mercurius Pragmaticus (contemporary newssheets).

Mercurius Rusticus (contemporary newssheets).

Mintz, Samuel L., 'The Visit of the Duchess of Newcastle to the Royal Society', in *Journal of English and Germanic Philology*, 1952.

Morgan, Fidelis, *The Female Wits*, 1981.

Oman, Carola, *Queen Henrietta Maria*, 1936.

Osborne, Dorothy, *Letters*, New York, 1888.

Philips, Katherine, *Poems*, 1673.

Philips, Katherine, *Letters from Orinda to Poliarchus*, 1705.

Phillips, Thomas, *Theatarum Poetarum*, 1674.

Pile, Stephen (ed.), *The Book of Heroic Failures*, 1979.

Reynolds, Myra, *The Learned Lady in England*, New York, 1920.

Richards, S. A., *Feminist Writers of the Seventeenth Century*, 1914.

Rogers, K. M., *Feminism in Eighteenth-century England*, 1982.

Round, J. H., 'The Case of Lucas and Lisle', in *Transactions of the Royal Historical Society*, 1894.

Ryan, Dr M., *A Manual of Midwifery*, 1841.

Scott, Eva, *The Wanderings of Charles II*, 1904.

Scott, Eva, *The Travels of the King*, 1907.

Scott-Thompson, G., *Life in a Noble Household 1641–1700*, 1936.

Shadwell, Thomas, *The Virtuoso*, 1676.

Showalter, Elaine, *A Literature of Their Own*, 1978.

Smith, Hilda L., *Reason's Disciples*, University of Illinois Press, 1982.

Sowernam, Esther, 'Esther hath Hang'd Haman or an answer to the Lewd Pamphlet entitled the Arraignment of Women by J. Swetnam', 1617.

Spencer, Herbert, *The Principles of Ethics*, 1904.

Stanley, Thomas, *History of Philosophy*, 1655, 1701.

Stoye, J. W., *English Travellers Abroad 1604–1667*, 1952.

Swetnam, John, *Arraignment of lewd, idle, froward and unconstant women*, 1615.

Ten Eyck Perry, Henry, *The First Duchess of Newcastle and Her Husband as Figures in Literary History*, 1918.

Thomas, K. (ed.), 'Women and the Civil War Sects', in *Past and Present*, 1958.

Thomas, Moy (ed.), *Letters of Lady Mary Wortley Montagu*, 1892.

Thompson, Roger, *Women in Stuart England and America*, 1974.

Thornton, Alice, *Memoirs*, 1873.

Bibliography

Trease, Geoffrey, *Portrait of a Cavalier*, 1979.

Turberville, A. S., *History of Welbeck Abbey and Its Owners*, 1938.

van Schurman, Anna (trans. Clement Barksdale), *The Learned Maid*, 1659. Published in Paris as *Question Célèbre*, 1646.

Walpole, Horace, *Royal and Noble Authors*, 1759.

Walpole, Horace, *Bess of Hardwick*, in *Works*, 1798–1823.

Warwick, Sir Philip, *Memoirs*, 1813.

Whitelocke, Bulstrode, *Memorials*, 1682.

Winchelsea, Lady Anne, *Poems*, 1713.

Winstanley, Gerard, *The True Leveller's Standard Advanced*, 1649.

Woolf, Virginia, *A Room of One's Own*, 1929.

Woolf, Virginia, *The Common Reader*, 1938.

Young, P., *Marston Moor*, 1970.

The unpublished letters and poems of William Cavendish, Margaret Lucas and Elizabeth Lucas are in the Portland Mss, housed in the British Library and Nottingham University.

Index

Index